NEWMAN AND TRUTH

Louvain Theological and Pastoral Monographs is a publishing venture whose purpose is to provide those involved in pastoral ministry throughout the world with studies inspired by Louvain's long tradition of theological excellence within the Roman Catholic tradition. The volumes selected for publication in the series are expected to express some of today's finest reflection on current theology and pastoral practice.

LOUVAIN THEOLOGICAL & PASTORAL MONOGRAPHS
39

NEWMAN AND TRUTH

edited by

Terrence Merrigan & Ian Ker

PEETERS
LEUVEN – PARIS – WALPOLE, MA

WILLIAM B. EERDMANS PUBLISHING COMPANY
GRAND RAPIDS, MICHIGAN/CAMBRIDGE, U.K.

2008

Published jointly 2008
in Belgium by
Peeters Publishers
Bondgenotenlaan 153
3000 Leuven
and in the United States of America by
Wm. B. Eerdmans Publishing Company
2140 Oak Industrial Dr. N.E., Grand Rapids, Michigan 49505 /
P.O. Box 163 Cambridge CB3 9PU U.K.
www.eerdmans.com

Manufactured in Belgium

12 11 10 09 08 5 4 3 2 1

A catalogue record for this book is available from the Library of Congress

Eerdmans ISBN 978-0-8028-6477-2
Peeters ISBN 978-90-429-2140-5
D. 2008/0602/127

TABLE OF CONTENTS

PREFACE

The fourth Oxford International Newman Conference was held at Somerville College, Oxford from 14-18 August 2004. The theme of the conference was 'Newman and truth'. Like its predecessors, this conference set itself a twofold task. The first was to examine Newman's own thought on the matter under consideration, in this case, the nature of religious truth. The second was to investigate whether Newman's thought has any relevance to contemporary debates about this matter and, more importantly, any contribution to make to these debates. As was the case with previous conferences, we once again opted for a multidisciplinary approach, out of the conviction that only such an approach does justice to the breadth and depth of Newman's thought. This volume comprises a selection of the principal papers delivered during the conference.

Terrence Merrigan examines Newman's understanding of human subjectivity as rooted in conscience, and compares and contrasts it with postmodern perspectives. John Milbank asks whether Newman's turn inwards did not betray him into a thoroughly modern apologetic that divorces the religious sensibility from society and communal wisdom. Michael J. Buckley argues that it was precisely Newman's profound awareness of the turn to atheism in nineteenth-century society which inspired his appeal to conscience. Keith Hanley portrays Newman's journey towards the truth as a series of homecomings, each of which needs to be transcended (or perhaps even transgressed) if justice is to be done to a reality that draws us inexorably onwards while it continually eludes us. Brian Daley explains that Newman's devotion to the Alexandrian Fathers was inspired by their account of the way in which that same truth nevertheless sustains and permeates our fractured human existence, thereby transforming history and materiality into occasions for encounter with the divine. Paul Griffiths argues that Newman's own theological perspective could not account for the obligation to always speak the truth, a deficiency which he attributes to Newman's imperfect grasp of the axioms of Christian orthodoxy. Colin Barr claims that Newman's liberal approach to university education is only comprehensible in light of his conviction that truth can never threaten Catholic faith. Ian Ker attributes Newman's willingness to contemplate new manifestations of the life of faith to his confidence in the charismatic dimension of the Church, understood as the communion of those who have received the Holy Spirit in baptism.

The fourth Oxford International Newman Conference was made possible by the generous support of the Flemish Fund for Scientific Research (FWO-Vlaanderen), and the Research Council of the Katholieke Universiteit Leuven, Belgium, and in cooperation with the members of the research group, "Orthodoxy: Process and Product," of the Faculty of Theology of the same university. The conveners would like to thank all those who sponsored or took part in the conference and to thank David Pratt for his help with the editorial work for this volume.

"MYSELF AND MY CREATOR"
NEWMAN AND THE (POST-)MODERN SUBJECT

Terrence MERRIGAN

Introduction

Like other prominent thinkers, Newman has served as a source for a number of memorable phrases. These include, "… To live is to change, and to be perfect is to have changed often,"[1] "Life is for action,"[2] and "Growth is the only evidence of life" (a borrowing from Thomas Scott).[3] Perhaps, however, his most frequently-cited remark is his observation in the *Apologia* that his adolescent conversion experience had led him to rest in "the thought of two and two only luminously self-evident beings, myself and my Creator." This remark is often invoked as evidence of Newman's so-called Platonism or of his tendency to introversion.[4] In other words, it is

[1] John Henry Newman, *An Essay on the Development of Christian Doctrine* (Notre Dame, IN: University of Notre Dame Press, 1989) 40. The full quotation is as follows: "In a higher world it is otherwise, but here below to live is to change and to be perfect is to have changed often."

[2] John Henry Newman, *An Essay in Aid of a Grammar of Assent*, ed. Ian Ker (Oxford: Clarendon, 1985) 67.

[3] John Henry Newman, *Apologia Pro Vita Sua* (London: Longmans, Green & Co., 1902) 5.

[4] Terrence Merrigan, "'Numquam minus solus, quam cum solus': Newman's First Conversion and Its Significance for his Life and Thought," *Downside Review* 103 (1985) 99-116. Regarding the application of the term 'platonic' to Newman, see Terrence Merrigan, *Clear Heads and Holy Hearts: The Religious and Theological Ideal of John Henry Newman*, Louvain Theological and Pastoral Monographs, 7 (Leuven: Peeters; Grand Rapids, MI: W. B. Eerdmans, 1991) 23-29; Louis Dupré, "Newman and the Neoplatonic Tradition in England," *Newman and*

usually taken to illustrate that Newman's most significant religious experience was profoundly personal, even idiosyncratic. As such, it serves to highlight the distance between Newman and those of us who cannot lay claim to such intimate experiences of God. Viewed in this light, Newman becomes something of a spiritual master of the type described by William James (or, more recently, by John Hick), that is to say, those spiritual giants whose religious experience the rest of us can only approximate and then, at best, only sporadically and with varying degrees of intensity.[5]

In what follows, I would like to challenge this view of Newman's religious experience. More importantly, however, I would like to suggest that Newman's way to God provides valuable lessons for the understanding of that troubled entity known as the modern and/or postmodern subject. I will attempt to do this in four steps. In the first place, I shall briefly introduce the theme of 'subjectivity'. Then I shall attempt to clarify the notion of the subject as it functions within modern (section two) and postmodern (section three) discourse. In a fourth step, I shall reflect on Newman's understanding of the subject especially as this comes to light in his reflections on conscience. Finally, I shall attempt to relate Newman's thought to some of the themes that emerge from the contemporary discussion of the subject

the Word, ed. Terrence Merrigan & Ian T. Ker, Louvain Theological and Pastoral Monographs, 27 (Leuven: Peeters; Grand Rapids, MI: W. B. Eerdmans, 2000) 137-154.

[5] For a discussion of James' view of the religious genius, see Nicholas Lash, *Easter in Ordinary: Reflections on Human Experience and the Knowledge of God* (London: SCM, 1988) 55-60. For a discussion of Hick's approach to religious experience, see Terrence Merrigan, "The Historical Jesus and the Pluralist Theology of Religions," *The Myriad Christ: Plurality and the Quest for Unity in Contemporary Christology*, ed. Terrence Merrigan & Jacques Haers, Bibliotheca Ephemeridum Theologicarum Lovaniensium, 152 (Leuven: University Press & Peeters, 2000) 61-82.

I shall begin with a brief reflection on the theme of the subject in modern and postmodern discourse.

1. The Notion of the Subject in Modern and Postmodern Discourse

In a recent study of theories of subjectivity from the time of Sigmund Freud (1865-1939) up to the present day, Nick Mansfield, explains that the word 'subject' is "the term used to describe interior life or *self*hood [author's emphasis], especially as it is theorized in terms of its relationship to gender, power, language, culture and politics, etc."[6] From our point of view, Mansfield's definition is useful for two reasons. In the first place, it equates subjectivity with selfhood, something which Newman himself does in the formulation we are considering in this paper.[7] Secondly, it highlights the fact that the discussion of subjectivity is essentially a discussion of the subject's relationship with other realities,

[6] Nick Mansfield, *Subjectivity: Theories of the Self from Freud to Haraway* (New York: New York University Press, 2000) 185. Mansfield is a lecturer in Cultural Studies at Macquarie University in Australia. See p. 3: "'Subjectivity' refers, therefore, to an abstract or general principle that defies our separation into distinct selves and that encourages us to imagine that, or simply helps us to understand why, our interior lives inevitably seem to involve other people, either as objects of need, desire and interest or as necessary sharers of common experience. In this way, the subject is always linked to something outside of it — an idea or principle or the society of other subjects. It is this linkage that the word 'subject' insists upon. Etymologically, to be subject means to be 'placed' (or even thrown) under'. One is always subject *to* or *of* something. The word subject, therefore, proposes that the self is not a separate and isolated entity, but one that operates at the intersection of general truths and shared principles."

[7] This equation is by no means self-evident. See Eric Rosseel, *Het onschatbare subject: Aspecten van het postmoderne Zelf* (Brussels: VUB Press, 2001) 65-90 where Rosseel discusses the many terms that enter the discussion about selfhood. These include: subject, consciousness, ego (I), person, identity, and personality.

something which, as I have suggested, is not quite so obvious where Newman is concerned.

Writing in 1991, Jacques Derrida maintained that the "question of the subject and the living 'who' is at the heart of the most pressing concerns of modern societies."[8] More recently, it has been argued that the way in which human subjectivity is understood constitutes the fault line, so to speak, between modernity and postmodernity.[9]

While so-called modern thinkers, represented, for example, by Sigmund Freud and Jacques Lacan, regarded subjectivity as the legitimate object of a (lifelong) personal quest, i.e., as an ideal to be 'constructed',[10] postmodern thinkers like Friedrich Nietzsche and Michel Foucault portrayed it as an illusion fostered by 'those'[11] intent on manipulating us. While the moderns seek to analyze and harness the dynamic process that — if properly managed — will issue in a "self-sustaining individual,"[12] the postmoderns seek to expose the lie contained in the idea that a more or less stable 'center' of subjectivity can exist at all.

What unites both approaches is the recognition that 'subjectivity' is never simply 'given',[13] that it is, at best, so to speak, a work in

[8] Mansfield, *Subjectivity*, 1 quoting Jacques Derrida, "'Eating Well', or the Calculation of the Subject: An Interview with Jacques Derrida," in Eduardo Cadava, et al., *Who Comes After the Subject?* (New York: Routledge, 1991) 96-119, at 115.

[9] Mansfield, *Subjectivity*, 36, 51.

[10] *Ibid.*, 8, 9, 37; see also pp. 1, 11.

[11] In fact, the 'those' referred to here are not so much particular individuals as the will to power that is manifest in social organization. See *ibid.*, 55.

[12] *Ibid.*, 36: "To Freud, the subject has a knowable content, and an analyzable structure. In other words, the subject is full to the brim of identifications, emotions and values, separating it from the subjects around it, even though the processes from which this subjectivity is derived are seen to be as good as universal experiences." See also p. 9.

[13] *Ibid.*, 51-52: "... Both the Lacanian and Foucauldian points of view dispute the model of the subject as a free and autonomous individual. They also see the

progress. Indeed, it is precisely this conviction that distinguishes contemporary theories of the subject from those of early modernity, as exemplified in the work of Jean-Jacques Rousseau (1712-1778) and in Romantic poetry. There the subject is portrayed "as autonomous and free, as authentic and naturally occurring," as, in short, "the 'individual'," the "thinking, feeling, agent making its way through the world, giving expression to its emotions and fulfillment to its talents and energies."[14] This is, in Mansfield's words, "the image of the self as compromised by the world, yet recoverable beneath the detritus and inauthenticity of day-to-day life," and it continues to exert a "powerful attraction."[15]

As I hope to indicate, this early-modern understanding of the subject is far removed from Newman's vision of authentic selfhood. In this regard, at least, Newman would appear to be most at home with the late-modern and postmodern recognition that the subject cannot, as it were, be simply presupposed. But are there any other points of contact between Newman and contemporary theorists? To answer that question, we must delve more deeply into the understanding that has emerged in the past one hundred years. It hardly needs to be said that our discussion in this regard

subject as a *construct* [author's emphasis]. For both, the subject does not come into the world with all its nature and scope encapsulated within itself in embryonic form. Subjectivity is made by the relationships that form the human context. To psychoanalysis, dominant amongst these are family relationships defined in terms of gender and sexuality. For Foucault, they are the broad relationships of power and subordination that are present everywhere in all societies." See also pp. 8, 11, 64.

14 *Ibid.*, 51.

15 *Ibid.*: "From the counter-cultural call to act purely according to spontaneous desire, to the pop psychological truism that you should 'be yourself', the modern era has been saturated by the dream that social life is a place of compromise and debasement, that — somewhere — your true self remains hidden, free and available, if only you can find the right social group, language or personal style."

is necessarily limited and constructed with a view to those themes that are most relevant to our discussion of Newman.

2. The Late-Modern Subject

In his study of theories of subjectivity, Mansfield portrays Freud as the most important representative of what we might call the late-modern view. According to the Freudian view, the subject is, as it were, a "thing," by which Mansfield means that it is a "quantifiable and knowable" 'object of analysis', possessed of a "fixed structure, [and] operating in knowable and predictable patterns."[16] While "the subject is full to the brim of identifications, emotions and values," distinguishing it from other subjects, "the processes from which this subjectivity is derived are seen to be as good as universal experiences."[17] The aim of psychoanalysis is to gain insight into those processes and thereby to assist the subject in overcoming its alienation from its true self. Freud's preferred term for the 'true self' was the German personal pronoun, *ich* (or the noun form, *das Ich*) which is the equivalent of the English word, I. His English translators, however, opted to employ the Latin equivalent, *ego*. Freud's very deliberate choice for the ordinary, indeed the most ordinary term, which people use to refer to themselves was not without significance. For Freud — as indeed for us — the word 'I' means quite simply "my entire self, my total personality,"[18] the person I *really* am. The 'I', in other words, is my *true* self, my rational, conscious self. Of course, Freud was well aware that we are not always faithful to our true selves, that indeed we are engaged in a life-long battle with the irrational and

[16] *Ibid.*, 9. See also p. 36.

[17] *Ibid.*, 36.

[18] Bruno Bettelheim, *Freud and Man's Soul* (New York: Random House, 1982) 55.

unconscious aspects of our personality. His preferred term for these aspects was the German neuter pronoun, *es* or 'it' (and its noun form, *das Es*), for which his English translators once again employed a Latin equivalent, *id*. Here, too, the translation obscures the original meaning of the word. In German, 'es' or it, is used to refer to a child in the early stages of their development, that is to say, before they have developed a personal identity, before, as it were, they have learned to order their passions and their impulses. To describe the controlling mechanism that develops as the fruit of the subject's struggle to order its complex and chaotic persona, Freud coined the phrase, the *Über-Ich* which was translated by the Latin 'superego', but which might just as easily (and more appropriately) have been translated as the 'above-I'. In the original German, the emphasis falls on "the second part of [Freud's] compound noun," that is to say, the 'I'. This is significant, since it highlights the fact that what is at stake here is "an integral part of the person."[19] The above-I is "created by the person himself." It is "the result of his own experiences, desires, needs and anxieties, as they have been interpreted [and internalized] by him." The above-I comprises what traditionally fell under the word, 'conscience', that is to say, those controlling aspects of our personality of which we are conscious, but also those darker aspects that psychoanalysis is designed to expose, namely, the "unconscious, unreasonable, compulsive, punitive and persecutory aspects" of our personality.[20]

It has been observed that the translation of these everyday words into their Latin equivalents "turned them into cold technical terms, which arouse no personal associations," while in the original German, "the pronouns are invested with deep emotional significance." What is intended by these terms is in fact "the *least* [author's emphasis] theoretical aspects of our mind —... that in us which is

[19] Mansfield, *Subjectivity*, 57.

[20] Bettelheim, *Freud*, 58-59.

most primitive, most irrational, and can be expressed, if at all, only in the most ordinary, least complicated language."[21]

The object of Freud's investigations was nothing less than the 'soul' of the human person (though his translators preferred to speak of the 'mind'),[22] and he recognized that the components of that soul were "inextricably and permanently related to one another," and could only be separated from each other in theory."[23] Therefore, the purpose of psychoanalysis was not to eradicate either the so-called id or the superego, but "to 'strengthen the I,'' to enable it to acquire ever-greater independence from the superego (above-I) and ever-greater insight into the id (or 'it').[24]

We shall return to the notion of the superego when we examine Newman's understanding of conscience (or perhaps, equally accurately, consciousness). For the moment, it is sufficient to draw two conclusions regarding the subject as it emerges from Freud's (late modern) analysis.

The first is that all human subjects are, so to speak, caught up in the same dynamic process of becoming, that there is some shared

[21] *Ibid.*, 53, 56.

[22] *Ibid.*, 72-74.

[23] *Ibid.*, 58.

[24] *Ibid.*, 106, quoting from Freud's *New Introductory Lectures on Psychoanalysis*. The translation from which we quote is Bettelheim's own. The text reads as follows: "The purpose of psychoanalysis is 'to strengthen the I, to make it more independent of the above-I, to widen its field of perception and to extend its organization so that it can appropriate to itself new portions of the it'..." See also pp. 62-63, where Bettelheim notes that, in the thirty-first of these lectures, Freud "updated his thoughts on the structure of the human psyche... At its conclusion, he summed up the purpose of psychoanalysis as theory and as therapy with the statement 'Where it was, there should become I'. By this he did not mean that the I should eliminate the it or take over the it's place in our psyche, since according to his theoretical constructs the it is the source of our vital energy, without which life itself would not continue. ('The it cannot be controlled beyond certain limits', Freud wrote in *Civilization and its Discontents*. 'If more is demanded of a man, a revolt will be produced in him or a neurosis, or he will be made unhappy'.)"

(or 'universal') experience that shapes the development of each and every self. The second is that, in the final analysis, each and every subject is, in a very real sense, personally responsible for its self-development. These two themes, the presumption of a universal experience, and the insistence on personal responsibility will figure largely in Newman's understanding of subjectivity.

3. The Postmodern Subject

The precise nature of postmodernity — and by implication its relationship to modernity — is itself one of the topics preoccupying contemporary theorists in very nearly all the human sciences. As one author has observed, the term, postmodernism, "like other categorical terms — say poststructuralism, or modernism, or romanticism, for that matter —... suffers from a certain *semantic* [author's emphasis] instability: that is, no clear consensus about its meaning exists among scholars."[25]

One prominent theorist, the sociologist Zygmunt Bauman, distinguishes the terms, postmodernity and postmodernism. According to him, postmodernism refers to "the collection of works of art or intellectual products created under the conditions, or within the period, of postmodernity." Postmodernity is the term used to describe a complex historical process that has been characterized, above all, by a radical clash of paradigms in "philosophy and the philosophically informed social sciences." This clash is manifest especially in the determination to challenge nearly all of the accepted verities of modernity, particularly those which "went unnoticed" because they were simply taken for granted. Central among these are the convictions that underpinned "modernity's self-confidence," especially "its conviction of its own superiority

[25] Ihab Hassan, "Toward a Concept of Postmodernism," *Postmodernism: A Reader*, ed. Thomas Docherty (New York: Harvester Wheatsheaf, 1993) 146-156 at 149.

over alternative forms of life, [which were] seen as historically or logically 'primitive'; and its belief that its pragmatic advantage over pre-modern societies and cultures, far from being a historical coincidence, can be shown to have objective, absolute foundations and universal validity." More concretely, postmodernity no longer endorses the "hierarchy of values imposed upon the world" by the Eurocentric tradition of thought and practice. Every element in this worldview is now open to challenge.[26]

It is not surprising, therefore, that one commentator has described postmodernity as characterized by "a vast will to unmaking," a tendency reflected in the preponderance of terms in postmodern discourse that denote "indeterminacy" (words such as 'ambiguity', 'decenterment', 'difference', and so forth). Such words are "signs" of a movement toward the deconstruction of every notion of a subject that is simply unmediated or self-grounding,[27] whether that subject be the body politic or the individual psyche.[28]

[26] Zygmunt Bauman, "The Fall of the Legislator," *Postmodernism: A Reader*, ed. Thomas Docherty (New York: Columbia University Press, 1993) 128-140 at 135-136, writes that, during the modern period, "it was evident to everybody except the blind and the ignorant that the West was superior to the East, white to black, civilized to crude, cultured to uneducated, sane to insane, healthy to sick, man to woman, normal to criminal, more to less, riches to austerity, high productivity to low productivity, high culture to low culture. All these 'evidences' are now gone. Not a single one remains unchallenged."

[27] See David Tracy, *Plurality and Ambiguity: Hermeneutics, Religion, Hope* (San Francisco, CA: Harper & Row, 1989) 59 observes that Derrida's goal is "to produce a rhetoric of radical destabilization to expose any pretensions to full self-presence, any self-congratulatory Western resting in an untroubled, alinguistic, self-present, grounding ego." Charles E. Winquist, "Analogy, Apology, and the Imaginative Pluralism of David Tracy," *Journal of the American Academy of Religion* 56 (1987) 307-319 at 314 refers to this passage, but incorrectly identifies the source as Tracy's *The Analogical Imagination: Christian Theology and the Culture of Pluralism* (New York: Crossroad, 1981) 59.

[28] Hassan, "Toward a Concept of Postmodernism," 153. See David Tracy, "The Post-Modern Re-Naming of God as Incomprehensible and Hidden," *Cross*

In light of this evolution, Bauman is able to say that "the postmodern debate is about the *self*-consciousness [our emphasis] of Western society, and the grounds (or the absence of grounds) for such consciousness."[29] Whereas modernity was, above all, the "era of certainty," especially regarding "the objective superiority" of Western rationality and culture, the "most poignant of the postmodern experiences is the *lack* [author's emphasis] of self-confidence."[30]

What is even more striking about postmodernity, however, is its abandonment of the quest for certainty, its willingness to live "life under conditions of permanent and incurable uncertainty." The postmodern has resigned herself to an existence lived "in the presence of an unlimited quantity of competing forms of life," none of which can "prove their claims to be grounded in anything more solid and binding than their own historically shaped conventions."[31] The most appropriate word to describe such a situation is perhaps not 'pluralism', but rather 'polycentrism'. As the American theologian, David Tracy, has pointed out, "there is no longer a Western cultural center with margins. There are many centers now, of which the West is merely one."[32]

What divides the late-modern from the postmodern understanding of the subject, then, would seem to be, above all, the question of whether the quest for subjectivity is worthy of pursuit. Indeed,

Currents 50 (2000) 240-247 at 240: "A great deal of post-modern thought is directed towards exposing two illusions of modernity: the unreality of modernity's belief in self-presence in modernity's self-understanding as *the* [author's emphasis] present: and the unreality of the modern understanding of the autonomous, self-grounding self."

29 Bauman, "The Fall of the Legislator," 134.

30 *Ibid.*, 135. See also pp. 137, 138, 140.

31 *Ibid.*, 135.

32 David Tracy, "Fragments: The Spiritual Situation of Our Times," *God, the Gift and Postmodernism*, ed. John D. Caputo & Michael J. Scanlon (Bloomington, IN: Indiana University Press, 1999) 170-184, at 170.

for some postmoderns like Foucault, this quest is actually nefarious, a symptom of society's essential defect, namely, its tendency to totalitarianism, its urge to impose 'sameness' on what is irreducibly different and unquantifiable.[33] Accordingly, Foucault's position has been described as 'anti-subjective'.[34] For him, the subject as such does not exist. The subject is the product of "haphazard, historical development." It is "always everywhere a fiction, and has no intrinsic reality or structure." The only identity that the (transient) subject can ever possess is the one that it 'contrives' as an "alternative, albeit fanciful or ephemeral" to the identity which society seeks to impose on it.[35]

Ironically, then, the late-modern subject has been undone (or 'deconstructed) by the relentless scrutiny of its basic structure undertaken during modernity. "The linguistic, psychoanalytic, ethical, and political critiques of the centered autonomous subject"[36]

[33] Mansfield, *Subjectivity*, 54-55

[34] *Ibid.*, 36, 64, 10.

[35] *Ibid.*, 63-64; see also p. 179. See Hassan, "Toward a Concept of Postmodernism," 153. Hassan describes the "two central, constitutive tendencies in postmodernism" as 'indeterminancy' and 'immanence'." He explains that he uses the latter term "without religious echo to designate the capacity of the mind to generalize itself in symbols, intervene more and more into nature, act upon itself through its own abstractions and so become, increasingly, im-mediately [sic], its own environment. This noetic tendency may be evoked further by such sundry concepts as diffusion, dissemination, pulsion, interplay, communication, interdependence, which all derive from the emergence of human beings as language animals, *Homo pictor* or *Homo significans*, gnostic creatures constituting themselves and determinedly their universe, by symbols of their own making. Is 'this not the sign that the whole of this configuration is about to topple, and that man is in the process of perishing as the being of language continues to shine ever brighter upon our horizon?' Foucault famously asks." The reference to Foucault is to his *The Order of Things* (New York, 1970) 386.

[36] Richard J. Bernstein, "Radical Plurality, Fearful Ambiguity, and Engaged Hope," Review of David Tracy, *Plurality and Ambiguity: Hermeneutics, Religion, Hope* (San Francisco, CA: Harper & Row, 1987), in *The Journal of Religion* 69 (1989) 85-91, at 89.

have exposed it as at best an illusion and at worst (as in the case of Foucault) a fraud perpetrated by vested interests.

While Foucault's anti-subjectivist stance[37] is, admittedly, an extremist position, it is useful as a means to highlight what is, from our point of view, the most alarming implication of all postmodern discourse, namely, the apparent death of ethics. Tracy has pointed to this dimension of the postmodern project. "With some notable exceptions," he observes, "too many post-modern thinkers feel free to deconstruct the history of past and present without actualizing any concrete ethical-political hope. They wish to deconstruct the *status quo* in favor of the *fluxus quo*."[38] If the subject — the self — is no more than "an obscure and shifting impersonal matrix of relationships, politics and bodies,"[39] then it is meaningless to speak of *personal* responsibility or of obligation. After all, *who* is there to be responsible, to *feel* obligation?[40] With regard to the

[37] See Mansfield, *Subjectivity*, 64: "To those who work with Foucault's ideas, subjectivity is always everywhere a fiction, and has no intrinsic reality or structure, neither one given to us at our birth or as a result of the relationships and experiences of our early lives. This fiction may be exploded, or remodeled as a subversion of the demands power places on us." Bernstein, "Radical Plurality, Fearful Ambiguity, and Engaged Hope," rightly challenges the meaningfulness of this sort of discourse and Tracy's apparent endorsement of it. The philosophical notion of the subject (as distinct from the concrete and embodied human person) is also criticized by Vincent Descombes, "Apropos of the 'Critique of the Subject' and of the Critique of this Critique," in Eduardo Cadava, et al., *Who Comes After the Subject?* (New York: Routledge, 1991) 128. For a qualification of the view that Foucault (or at least, the later Foucault) 'effaced' the subject, see Derrida, "'Eating Well', or the Calculation of the Subject," 97.

[38] Tracy, "The Post-Modern Re-Naming of God as Incomprehensible and Hidden," 244.

[39] Mansfield, *Subjectivity*, 174.

[40] See, in this regard, Descombes, "Apropos of the 'Critique of the Subject' and of the Critique of this Critique," 130: "... The 'critique of the subject' [conducted by those who wish to regard it merely as a 'postulate' in order to ground practical philosophy] appears in fact paradoxical, since it ends by saying that we

theme of feeling, it is important to note that the postmodern deconstruction of the ethical subject is, at the same time, the deconstruction of the feeling subject. As Fredric Jameson observes, "... The liberation, in contemporary society, from the older *anomie* of the centered subject [i.e., the Freudian subject engaged in the quest to overcome its alienation from its true self] may also mean, not merely a liberation from anxiety, but a liberation from every other kind of feeling as well, since there is no longer a self present to do the feeling." Jameson explains that this 'waning of affect', as he calls it, does not mean that the postmodern condition is devoid of feeling but it does mean that what feelings there are will be "free-floating and impersonal."[41]

In the light of the disappearance, so to speak, of any identifiable subject, Jameson comments that the shift from (what I have called) the 'late-modern', to the postmodern is essentially "one in which the *alienation* of the subject is displaced by the *fragmentation* of the subject"[42] [our emphasis]. Of course, as Foucault's thoroughgoing anti-subjectivism illustrates, there is good reason to think that even the 'fragmented' postmodern subject will fare no better than the much lamented Humpty Dumpty, namely, that after we have watched him fall, we will be incapable of putting him together again. The question, then, is whether his fall is inevitable.

shouldn't really attribute to someone his acts and gestures, unless by way of a kind of conventional fiction. But if we can never point to a subject when it is a matter of answering the question *Who?*, it is, philosophically speaking, no longer possible to take practical questions seriously."

[41] Frederic Jameson, "Postmodernism, or The Cultural Logic of Late Capitalism," *Postmodernism: A Reader*, 62-92, at 72. Jameson continues by observing the following: "This is not to say that the cultural products of the postmodern era are utterly devoid of feeling, but rather that such feelings — which it may be better and more accurate to call 'intensities' — are now free-floating and impersonal, and tend to be dominated by a peculiar kind of euphoria..." See also Mansfield, *Subjectivity*, 165.

[42] Jameson, "Postmodernism, or The Cultural Logic of Late Capitalism," 71.

Is there another view of the subject possible, one that does justice to what is valuable in postmodern discourse without, however, issuing in postmodern disintegration? That will be the concern of the following discussion. Before we begin that discussion, however, it will be useful to indicate two elements of postmodern thought which deserve particular attention. The first of these is its sensitivity to the historical or, more accurately, the contextual character of human subjectivity. The second is its awareness of the provisional character of that same subjectivity, that is to say, its open-ended character.

In what follows, I hope to demonstrate that these themes find an echo in Newman's discussion of the nature of the self. At the same time, I also hope to indicate that Newman's reflections might serve as a corrective to the excesses of both the late-modern and the postmodern analysis of subjectivity.

4. Newman and Selfhood

In his *Philosophical Notebook* (a collection of reflections and jottings which was only published in 1970), Newman comments that, "... Being is not known directly, but indirectly through its states... Certain faculties then, or rather their operations, are a part of the initial idea of existence."[43] A little later, he writes as follows: "Though it is not easy to give a list of those primary conditions of the mind which are involved in the fact of existence, yet it is obvious to name some of them. I include among them, not only memory, sensation, reasoning, but also conscience."[44] So Newman

[43] John Henry Newman, *The Philosophical Notebook of John Henry Newman*, ed. Edward Sillem, 2 vols. (Louvain: Nauwelaerts, 1969-1970). See 2:43. See also 2:33-34.

[44] Newman, *Philosophical Notebook*, 2:43.

can write that it is as legitimate to say 'Sentio ergo sum', or 'Conscientiam habeo, ergo sum', as it is to say 'Cogito ergo sum'. In all these formulations, however, the linking 'ergo' is the product of a 'post-factum' analysis of what is originally "one complex act of intuition," in which 'apprehension' and 'judgment' are simultaneous.[45]

Among these 'mental operations', conscience, for Newman, occupies a unique place since, there, the subject apprehends not only itself, but itself as subject in relation to God. According to Newman, conscience is characterized by two indivisible, but not indistinguishable, dimensions which he described as a 'moral sense' and a 'sense of duty'. As a 'moral sense', conscience is manifest in the awareness that "there is a right and a wrong," which is not, of course, the same as knowing, in a particular instance, what is right or wrong. As a 'sense of duty', conscience is manifest as a "keen sense of obligation and responsibility," namely, to do good and avoid evil.[46] Newman speaks of these two dimensions, respectively, as "a rule of right conduct," and "a sanction of right conduct."[47] It is peculiar to conscience that it "has an intimate bearing on our affections and emotions." Indeed, in Newman's view, conscience "is always emotional." Hence, he sometimes speaks quite simply of "the feeling of conscience" to describe its operation. Newman describes this feeling as "a certain keen sensibility, pleasant or painful — self-approval and hope, or compunction and fear" which follows upon the performance of certain actions. For Newman, the feelings generated by conscience — or, more accurately, by our behavior — are possessed of profound theological significance. As he expresses it:

[45] *Ibid.*, 2:71; see also 2:33, 43, 45, 63, 83.

[46] Newman, *Grammar of Assent*, 74; see also 105. See also Newman's *Philosophical Notebook*, 2:49.

[47] Newman, *Grammar of Assent*, 74.

> ... These feelings in us are such as require for their exciting cause an intelligent being... If the cause of these emotions does not belong to this visible world, the Object to which [our] perception is directed must be Supernatural and Divine; and thus the phenomena of Conscience, as a dictate, avail *to impress the imagination* with the picture of a Supreme Governor, a Judge, holy, just, powerful, all-seeing, retributive...[48]

It is precisely in view of its role in generating an 'image' of God in the minds of men and women that Newman describes conscience as the "creative principle of religion." However, it is clear that religion or religious consciousness, in this context, is a profoundly ethical affair. It is born out of the inevitable requirement — the necessity — to act. One might say, then, that the soul's encounter with God in conscience is as much a question of volition as of sentiment — i.e., the emotions attendant on the performance of particular deeds — though it is, of course, the presence of these emotions which implies "a living object, towards which [conscience] is directed."[49]

The quality of the soul's response to the voice of conscience determines, in no small measure, the evolution of the nascent relationship between itself and the Divinity. Through its submission to, or alternately, its willful refusal of, the divine command (which, admittedly is not always 'clear and distinct') the soul itself sketches, as it were, its own likeness of the Divinity. As Newman expresses it:

> ... Whether [the image of the Divine within us] grows brighter and stronger, or, on the other hand, is dimmed, distorted, or obliterated,

[48] *Ibid.*, 76 (emphasis ours). For an extensive discussion of the nature and function of the imagination in Newman's work, see Merrigan, *Clear Heads and Holy Hearts*, 48-81, 177-178, 186-192; "The Image of the Word: John Henry Newman and John Hick on the Place of Christ in Christianity," *Newman and the Word*, 1-47.

[49] Newman, *Grammar of Assent*, 109.

> depends on each of us individually, and on his circumstances... Men transgress their sense of duty, and gradually lose their sentiments of shame and fear, the natural supplements of transgression, which... are the witnesses of the Unseen Judge.[50]

Hence, Walgrave could write that, while the apprehension of God by conscience is "spontaneous," it remains a free act which "supposes" a serious moral commitment, a willingness to obey the moral imperative, and a fundamental choice for generosity.[51] The relationship between the soul and God which attention to conscience makes possible is not therefore merely a matter of present religious experience — it is, above all, (to use another of Walgrave's formulations) an "absolute religious goal."[52] And for Newman, this goal is only realizable in and through a sustained moral commitment made incarnate in the mundane routine of every day.[53]

Newman's discussion of 'natural religion' mixes historical and what we would now call phenomenological analysis. As history, Newman's presentation is clearly not up to contemporary standards. The heart of his reflections, however, is not the history of religions, but the growth of religious consciousness. And on this point, Newman displays a remarkable sensitivity to the insights of modern psychology. He is, for example, well aware that the development of an 'image' of God is heavily dependent on all sorts of 'external' factors and circumstances

[50] *Ibid.*, 79-80.

[51] J. H. Walgrave, "La preuve de l'existence de Dieu par la conscience morale en l'expérience de valeurs," *L'existence de Dieu*, Cahiers de l'actualité religieuse, 16 (Paris: Casterman, 1961) 117.

[52] J. H. Walgrave, *Newman vandaag*, Periodieke uitgave van het Geert Groote Genootschap, 698 (Marienburg/'s Hertogenbosch, 1957) 25.

[53] Newman, *Grammar of Assent*, 116. See also John Henry Newman, *Fifteen Sermons Preached Before the University of Oxford Between A.D. 1826 and 1843* (Notre Dame, IN: University of Notre Dame Press, 1997) 80-81.

> How far this initial religious knowledge comes from without, and how far from within, how much is natural, how much implies a special divine aid which is above nature, we have no means of determining… Whether its elements, latent in the mind, would ever be elicited without extrinsic help is very doubtful.[54]

Newman insists that the "image" of God must be expanded, deepened and completed "by means of education, social intercourse, experience, and literature."[55] At least initially, and this remains the case if one's education and religious practice do not contribute to a "filling out" of one's emergent image of God, the individual experiences Him primarily as "Lawgiver" and "Judge."

However, while conscience reveals God primarily as a lawgiver, it also reveals Him as One who wills our happiness and has ordered creation accordingly. From the outset then, the individual looks to the divine lawgiver as to a benevolent ruler, who has one's best interests at heart.[56] This tensile experience issues in two major characteristics of 'natural religion', namely, prayer and hope, with the former serving as the vehicle par excellence for the expression of the latter.[57] The hope of which Newman speaks is perhaps best described as an irrepressible existential longing or perhaps even anticipation that the One who calls us to perfection will come to our aid. So Newman can write that,

[54] Newman, *Grammar of Assent*, 79.

[55] *Ibid.*, 80.

[56] *Ibid.*, 78. See also Terrence Merrigan, "'One Momentous Doctrine which Enters into my Reasoning': The Unitive Function of Newman's Doctrine of Providence," *Downside Review* 108 (1990) 254-281. Note that on p. 59 of the *Grammar of Assent*, Newman places the "thought" of "Divine Goodness" before the thought of "future reward," or "eternal life" as objects of real assent. See our discussion of this point in Merrigan, "'Numquam minus solus quam cum solus': Newman's First Conversion and Its Significance for His Life and Thought," 106-107.

[57] Newman, *Grammar of Assent*, 258-260.

> One of the most important effects of Natural Religion on the mind, in preparation for Revealed, is the anticipation which it creates, that a Revelation will be given... This presentiment is founded on our sense, on the one hand, of the infinite goodness of God, and, on the other, of our own extreme misery and need — two doctrines which are the primary constituents of Natural Religion.[58]

So it is that the expectation of a revelation, that is to say, of some initiative on the part of the divine, emerges, for Newman, as an 'integral part of Natural Religion'.[59] Newman was convinced that only the Jewish-Christian tradition could satisfy the religious hunger engendered by the experience of conscience.[60] Indeed, he insisted that the 'image' of God provided by natural religion is but "twilight" in comparison to "the fullness and exactness" of "our

[58] *Ibid.*, 272. See also his *Discourses to Mixed Congregations* (London: Burns, Oates & Co., 1886) 277-279.

[59] Newman, *Grammar of Assent*, 260-261.

[60] On a number of occasions throughout his life, Newman reflected on the inability of 'natural religion' to relieve the 'disquiet', as it were, generated in the hearts of its adherents. These included conscience's lack of a sanction, beyond itself, for its elevated claims about the Moral Governor and Judge. These are therefore prey to societal pressures and to the individual's own inclination to abandon the moral ideal as impracticable. In an early University sermon, (and it would seem, again in the *Grammar of Assent*), Newman maintains that it is, above all, the obscurity of the object of one's religious instincts and aspirations, that is, the dearth of information about God's 'personality', which saps one's moral resolve and raises the specter of the futility of the moral and religious enterprise. Elsewhere, it is the sense of one's culpability and one's inadequacy to the moral task which exposes natural religion's inherent insufficiency. In all three cases, Newman proposes that the only adequate complement to the essentially incomplete natural religion of man is 'revealed' religion, which is to say, the doctrine taught in the Mosaic and Christian dispensation, and contained in the Holy Scriptures," which does not supplant, but builds on, nature's authentic teaching. (See *Grammar of Assent*, 313; for a complete discussion of Newman's analysis of the deficiencies of natural religion, including the sources in his work where each position is elaborated, see Merrigan, "One Momentous Doctrine," 265-266.

mental image of the Divine Personality and Attributes" furnished by "the light of Christianity."[61]

This is not to suggest that there is any essential discontinuity between natural and revealed religion. "In Christians themselves," Newman writes, natural religion "cannot really be separated from their Christianity." Indeed, Newman describes the "true Christian" simply as one who "enthrones the Son of God in his conscience" and "who has faith in him, [so] as to live in the thought that He is present with him... in his innermost heart, or in his conscience." In both cases, the subject "reaches forward to something beyond itself," and precisely in this movement discovers its true self. In other words, in the case of Newman, religious introspectiveness is the gateway to the acknowledgement of the transcendent God, an "external being who reads [the subject's] mind, to whom he is responsible, who praises and blames, who promises and threatens."[62]

It was precisely this movement from interiority to exteriority, from the self to God, that led Erich Przywara to describe Newman's whole theological-philosophical program as the subjective 'counterpart' of the objective metaphysical system developed in classical Catholic thought. For Przywara, Newman's work describes the concrete realization, in the historical subject, of the religious 'reality' that is systematized and categorized in traditional Catholic philosophy and theology. With this in mind, Przywara, in 1923, made the striking claim that, in the contemporary setting, what was required for a comprehensive Catholic intellectual life was a synthesis of the historical and metaphysical

[61] Newman, *Grammar of Assent*, 81 (emphasis ours). Newman actually speaks of an "addition" to our image of God, and maintains that it is "one main purpose" of revealed religion to "give us a clear and sufficient object for our faith."

[62] *Ibid.*, 47.

approaches, epitomized respectively by Newman and St. Thomas.[63]

Does Przywara's conviction that Newman has something to teach a new age still hold true? More particularly, do his reflections on the subject resonate with any of the themes that characterize the post(modern) discussion? That will be the subject of our final section.

5. Newman and the (Post)Modern Subject

Our comparison between Newman's understanding of the subject and the contemporary debate will be undertaken with a view to highlighting those features which characterize Newman's position vis-à-vis modern and postmodern proposals. The upshot of the comparison will be a view of Newman as a thinker who would not have been especially ill at ease in our modern and postmodern epoch but who also represents a challenge to some of its tendencies. I have opted to group these concluding reflections under three headings that summarize Newman's views on the subject.

1. *The Humanized Subject*

Newman's reflections make it clear that his 'subject' is not the Cartesian *res cogitans*, that is to say, the self-grounding metaphysical subject of early modernity.[64] So Newman can write that,

[63] Erich Przywara, *Gottgeheimnis der Welt: Drei Vortrage über die geistige Krisis der Gegenwart* (Munich: Theatiner, 1923) 173: "... Das ist der Entschluß dieser Stunde, wo wir am Höhepunkt der geistigen Krise unserer Zeit stehen: nicht Thomas oder Newman, sondern, getreu dem Geist Katholischer Polarität — Thomas und Newman."

[64] Descombes, "Apropos of the 'Critique of the Subject' and of the Critique of this Critique," 126: "The classical philosophers of the subject, taking the word *subject* in a sense where it only applies to *that which thinks* [author's emphasis]

"Consciousness indeed is not of simple being, but of action or passion…"[65] Newman's subject is a fully 'humanized' *res extensa*,[66] a person of flesh and blood, the thinking, willing, feeling, imagining subject whose complex nature and convoluted quest for meaning he so masterfully describes in his writings. Sensitive as he was to the 'fleshly' character of our being, Newman had no difficulty whatsoever in acknowledging that the subject's religious consciousness — its knowledge of God — is the fruit of its human development, including the whole process of socialization. Long before Karl Rahner employed the expression, 'mediated immediacy', to describe the way in which God discloses Himself to us in and through the created order, Newman testified to the principle in

in Descartes, say that it is spirit, or consciousness, that acts as the thinking subject in Descartes. As for the critics of the philosophical subject, they find that the word *subject* is dangerous: this word, because of its familiar nonphilosophical [sic] use, appears to authorize the transfer of certain attributes of the person to *that which thinks* in the person" [author's emphasis].

65 Newman, *Philosophical Notebook*, 2:33. In Newman's original manuscript, the word 'exercising' was added between the lines.

66 I have borrowed the notion of a humanized subject from Descombes, "Apropos of the 'Critique of the Subject' and of the Critique of this Critique," 129: "In appearance, the 'critics of the subject' are opposed to the use of this concept whenever we speak of human affairs, whereas the 'defenders of the subject' wish to restore this concept to a central role. In fact, the quarrel concerns something entirely different. Nobody asks: Is there a subject (*ego* or *id*) distinct from the person by virtue of the subject to whom we attribute human operations? Nobody asks this because this point is already accepted by everyone. But the quarrel [between 'critics' and 'defenders' of the subject] concerns the point of knowing whether it is appropriate to humanize or dehumanize this philosophical subject. The 'critics of the subject' are instead then critics of the *human subject* [author's emphasis]. They in no way refuse to differentiate between the human person (the 'physical' or 'empirical' entity, that which we can name, locate, etc.) and the true subject of human operations (such as thinking, willing, desiring, etc.). What they refuse is the possibility that the human being can identify himself as the source of operations that he believes, insofar as he is naïve (or mystified by the ideologies of subjectivity), to be his."

his description of conscience as the 'echo' of God's voice in us.[67] The God disclosed in conscience is the God whose presence is always mediated, whose voice is never heard directly but only as it is 're-flected' in the chasms of our hearts and minds.

Newman's profound appreciation for the ordinariness, so to speak, of the growth to religious consciousness is especially evident, in his description, in the *Grammar of Assent*, of the development of conscience in the young child. In our discussion of Freud, we noted that he deliberately chose the language of everyday to describe the essential structure of the human soul. The same might be said of Newman's description, in the *Grammar*, of the remorseful child, pleading with the presence disclosed in conscience to set things right. In those passages, which are usually described as autobiographical,[68] Newman maintains that while it is impossible to assign a precise date to the time at which a child begins to perceive, in the dictate of conscience, the voice of a "living, personal and sovereign" Master (and this "without previous experiences or analogical reasoning"), the process appears to be well under way by the onset of the age of reason, which he places at about five or six years of age.[69]

Here, of course, we touch on one of the most sensitive topics in Newman's discussion of conscience, namely, its susceptibility to

[67] Newman, *Grammar of Assent*, 74-78.

[68] Anne Mozley (ed.), *Letters and Correspondence of John Henry Newman during his Life in the English Church*, 2 vols. (London: Longman, Green & Co., 1891) 1:13-15.

[69] Newman, *Grammar of Assent*, 77. The 'child' is described as one "safe from influences destructive of his religious instincts." An entry in one of Newman's diaries (dated April 8, 1843) confirms that this was his own experience: "The thoughts that struck me most [during a meditation] were, — that God put it into my heart, when 5 or 6 years old, to ask 'what' and 'why' I was, yet now I am forty-two, and have never answered it in 'my conduct'." See Henry Tristram (ed.), *John Henry Newman: Autobiographical Writings* (London: Sheed & Ward, 1956) 223.

Freudian critique. While a number of commentators have made the claim that Newman's position is vulnerable,[70] few have explored the charge at any length.[71] From our point of view, one thing in particular is especially worth noting, namely, that Newman, unlike Freud does not reduce the experience of conscience to that of 'bad conscience'.[72] As one commentator sympathetic to Freud has pointed out, the latter "insistently emphasizes [that] it is only out of the guilt feeling — the feeling of *moral* lapse [author's emphasis], or sin — that the terrible figure that is to become the omnipotent Father, and later the God or the Leader, emerges."[73] This stands in striking contrast to Newman who understands conscience as a dialectical relationship between 'good' and 'bad'. While the former discloses God's providential goodness, thereby securing us from that despair which would impede our quest for the good, the latter, through its disclosure of God's just judgments, shatters our Arcadian innocence and inspires us to the pursuit of moral perfection.[74]

From Newman's point of view, too, the description of the origins of the idea of God would not of itself invalidate the idea.

[70] See, for example, S.A. Grave, *Conscience in Newman's Thought* (Oxford: Clarendon, 1989) 79-81. Grave writes as follows: "Also worth noticing when Freud's views are brought into juxtaposition with Newman's, is the severity of conscience in their characterization of it." Grave fails to note Newman's discussion of the benevolence of the One disclosed in conscience.

[71] The only two authors known to me who have addressed the claim in a critical fashion are J. H. Walgrave, "Newman's leer over het geweten," in his *Selected Writings – Thematische Geschriften*, ed. G. De Schrijver and J. J. Kelly (Leuven: Peeters, 1982) 193-201, at 201-202, and John F. Crosby, *Personalist Papers* (Washington, DC: The Catholic University of America Press, 2004). See especially chapter 4 of *Personalist Papers*, entitled "Conscience and Superego," pp. 93-112. Crosby (pp. 101-112) devotes particular attention to the thought of Freud's disciple, Erich Fromm, since the latter distinguishes conscience and superego more clearly than Freud does.

[72] J. H. Walgrave, "Newman's leer over het geweten," 195.

That is precisely the point of his understanding of what I am calling the 'humanized' subject. Indeed, Freud appears to have been far more disturbed by the thoroughly human character of the evolution of conscience than Newman. The father of psychoanalysis noted, with deliberate irony, that our so-called 'God-given' conscience is "'an uneven and careless piece of work' since most people have only a modest amount of it or none at all."[75] Newman would not, I think, have been fazed by Freud's cynicism. His response would probably have been akin to that provided by George Bernard Shaw's Saint Joan, in his play of the same name, to one of her interrogators. The latter chides Joan that the voices she claims to hear, come not from God, but from her imagination. Unabashed, Joan replies, "Of course. That is how the messages of God come to us."[76]

Newman in fact elevates faithfulness to our essential humanity to one of the grounding principles of his whole theology. Walgrave speaks in this regard of the principle of the 'nature of things'. Simply put, this means that we must take things as we find them, and submit ourselves to the natural order as to a divine law. By the 'natural order of things', Newman means things as they are *in fact*, things as they show themselves to be *historically*. As Walgrave explains, for Newman, the 'nature' of a thing is not its "metaphysical essence," but what it discloses itself to be in

[73] Mikkel Borch-Jacobsen, "The Freudian Subject," in Eduardo Cadava, et al., *Who Comes After the Subject?* (New York: Routledge, 1991) 61-78, at 73.

[74] Walgrave, "Newman's leer over het geweten," 195.

[75] Ronald Ledek, *The Nature of Conscience and Its Religious Significance with Special Reference to John Henry Newman* (San Francisco, CA: International Scholars Publications, 1996) 67. Ledek is quoting from Sigmund Freud, *New Introductory Lectures*, trans. and ed. by James Strachey (New York: Norton, 1965) 61, 62.

[76] George Bernard Shaw, *St. Joan: A Chronicle Play in Six Scenes and an Epilogue*, Penguin Books (Harmondsworth: Penguin Books, 1979) 59.

experience.[77] This principle is at the root of Newman's defense of certitude in the *Grammar*. There he argues that if we wish to know how the mind attains to certitude, we must consider it in its actual operations — since it is most surely possessed of certitudes — and not dictate how it ought to proceed on the basis of some pre-conceived epistemological model. In short, to Newman's mind, confidence in, or more accurately, submission to, the factuality of our nature is the only reasonable ("philosophical") course open to humanity. "We are as little able to accept or reject our mental constitution, as our being,"[78] he argued.

2. *The Responsible Subject*

I have already pointed out that one of the major challenges facing postmodern thinkers is the quest for a foundation for ethics. For Newman, that foundation is located in the essence of the subject itself, namely, in the self-consciousness that is the fruit of the experience of conscience.

Newman acknowledged that his claim on behalf of conscience, namely, that "it has a legitimate place among our mental acts," or

[77] J. H. Walgrave, *J. H. Newman: His Personality, His Principles, His Fundamental Doctrines: Course Delivered by Professor J. H. Walgrave, Katholieke Universiteit Leuven 1975 – 1976 – 1977* (Louvain: By the Author, K.U.L., 1981) 74 (hereafter cited as *Lectures.*) It is to the work of Walgrave, in particular, that we must look for an analysis of the operation of this principle in Newman's thought. See Jan H. Walgrave, *Newman the Theologian*, trans. A. V. Littledale (London: Geoffrey Chapman, 1960) 221-223, 228; *Lectures*, 63-73, 148. The final arbiter in questions of judgment and action is the empirical order, i.e., "things as they are, not as you could wish them." See John Henry Newman, *The Idea of a University* (London: Longmans, Green & Co., 1921) 232.

[78] Newman does not think it proper to speak of having 'confidence' in, or 'trusting' our faculties though he does allow such speech once it is understood that it is merely figurative. See his *Grammar of Assent*, 46; *Philosophical Notebook*, 2:33-39. See also *The Letters and Diaries of John Henry Newman*, 19:247, 18:334-335.

"that we have by nature a conscience," constituted an unproved "assumption," a "first principle," the rejection of which made further discussion meaningless.[79] He makes no apology for this. In his *Lectures on the Present Position of Catholics in England* (1851) he declared that to think at all one must be possessed of at least some "opinions which are held without proof," and these are rightly called "first principles."[80]

However, for Newman the 'inevitability' of "first principles" does not divest the individual of responsibility in regard to them. It is basic to Newman's philosophical outlook that the human subject is "emphatically self-made," and charged with the task of "completing his inchoate and rudimental nature, and of developing his own perfection out of the living elements with which his mind began to be."[81] Here, too, the principle of the 'nature of things' is clearly operative. Where conscience is concerned, the implications of this principle are staggering. Not only is it one's "sacred duty" to acknowledge conscience's legitimate place among those "living elements" with which the mind begins (in accordance with "the law of our being"), the failure to do this prejudices, if it does not entirely pervert, the elaboration of a whole body of derivative principles. M. H. Abrams, speaking of S. T. Coleridge's view of the origins of metaphysical systems, observes that, "In Coleridge's opinion, a man is ultimately responsible for the kind of world he sees."[82] Abrams might just as easily have been speaking of

[79] Newman, *Grammar of Assent*, 73, 45-46.

[80] John Henry Newman, *The Present Position of Catholics in England* (London: Longmans, Green & Co., 1903) 279.

[81] Newman, *Grammar of Assent*, 225.

[82] M. H. Abrams, "Coleridge and the Romantic Vision of the World," *Coleridge's Variety: Bicentenary Studies*, ed. J. Beer (London: Macmillan, 1974) 126. See *Letters and Diaries*, 25:280, where Newman says of his *Grammar of Assent* that, "My book is to show that a right moral state of mind germinates or even generates good intellectual principles."

Newman, and the declaration could, indeed, be taken as a summary of his entire apologetic, since that apologetic is, in the final analysis, nothing other than a vindication of the religious interpretation of reality by an appeal to man's ethical nature, which, for Newman, is synonymous with conscience.

For Newman then, the task of thinking soundly is, from the outset, a moral, as well as a practical imperative, one to be fulfilled most 'conscientiously' in fidelity to our being.[83] The theme of fidelity to our essential being permeates Newman's consideration of conscience. Indeed, for him, 'Conscientiam habeo, ergo sum' is also — and more or less simultaneously — 'Conscientiam habeo, ergo Deus est'.[84] This is the real meaning of Newman's claim that, for him, there were "two and two only absolute and luminously self-evident beings, myself and my Creator."[85] It accounts, too, for his declaration that: "If I am asked why I believe in God, I answer that it is because I believe in myself, for I feel it impossible to

[83] Newman, *Present Position of Catholics*, 279: "From what I have said, it is plain that First Principles may be false or true; indeed, this is my very point, as you will presently see. Certainly they are not necessarily true; and again, certainly there *are* ways of unlearning them when they are false: moreover, as regards moral and religious First Principles which are false, of course a Catholic considers that no one holds them except by some fault of his own..." These words date from 1851. By the time Newman came to write the *Grammar of Assent* (1870), he expressed himself much more cautiously regarding the problem of defectiveness in first principles, and recognized the possibility of inculpable error. See *Grammar of Assent*, 157-158, 162-163, 169. The 'decisiveness' of Newman's position in the 1851 lectures must be viewed in the light of the apologetic character of the lectures, and his status as a convert, that is to say, his concern not to seem to call into doubt traditional thinking.

[84] Newman, *Philosophical Notebook*, 2:59: "[As] our consciousness of thought is a reflex act implying existence (I think, therefore, I am), so this sensation of conscience is the recognition of our obligation the notion of an external being obliging, I say this, not from any abstract argument for the force of the terms (e.g., 'a law implies a lawgiver') but the peculiarity of that feeling to which I give the name of Conscience."

believe in my own existence (and of that fact I am quite sure) without believing also in the existence of Him, who lives as a Personal, All-seeing, All-judging Being in my conscience."[86]

Newman's subject is a subject under obligation, a practical or acting subject. According to one critic of the modern and postmodern 'critique of subjectivity', Vincent Descombes, this subject has no place in the contemporary discussion.[87] For most modern and postmodern thinkers, "the 'physical' or 'empirical' entity" [i.e., Newman's humanized subject], cannot be identified "as the source of the operations that he believes... to be his."[88] This view of things finds its strongest expression in Foucault's anti-subjectivism, in his claim that the only subject worthy of the name is the endless fiction we create in resistance to the powers-that-be. Descombes observes that, at this point, "the 'critique of the subject' appears in fact paradoxical, since it ends by saying that we really shouldn't attribute to someone his acts and gestures, unless by way of a 'conventional fiction'. But," he continues, "if we can never point to a human subject when it is a matter of answering the question *Who?*, it is, philosophically speaking, no longer possible to take practical questions seriously." The upshot is that "the philosophical subject in its paradoxical version, if it is consistent, will stop short of developing a reflection upon the practical," by which Descombes means the ethical and the political.[89]

Clearly, this modern philosophical abstraction is far removed from Newman's thoroughly 'ethicized' subject whose motto is,

[85] Newman, *Apologia*, 4. I have discussed the relationship between Newman's claim here and his early "mistrust of the reality of material phenomena" in Merrigan, *Clear Heads and Holy Hearts*, 29-47.

[86] Newman, *Apologia*, 182.

[87] Descombes, "Apropos of the 'Critique of the Subject' and of the Critique of this Critique," 123.

[88] *Ibid.*, 129.

[89] *Ibid.*, 130.

"Life is for action,"[90] and whose identity is determined (or defaced) precisely by the commitment to action. The latter point is the subject of the following section.

3. *The Dynamic Subject*

We can be brief here. From everything that has been said, it is clear that Newman's subject is a dynamic entity, a soul engaged in a continual journey towards the Mystery of justice and love first disclosed in conscience. The nature of that journey is dictated by the character of its object. Of that object, Newman remarked, "We fear Him while We love Him."[91] Przywara regarded this tensile union as the "quintessence" of Newman's religious vision, and saw in it an explanation for Newman's description of the Christian life as an attempt to reconcile "opposite virtues." [92]

For Newman, the religious subject is engaged in a process of continual change. One might even speak of a process of endless 're-creation'. However, there is real continuity here, namely, the continuity provided by the One who continually calls the subject to authentic selfhood in love. From Newman's point of view, one might well grant Foucault's claim that the 'subject' has no ground

[90] Newman, *Grammar of Assent*, 67.

[91] John Henry Newman, *Parochial and Plain Sermons*, 8 vols. (London: Rivingtons, 1868). See 5:28. See also 3:35, 184, 188; 4:148-149; 6:90-91; 7:105-107; 8:14.

[92] Erich Przywara, *Augustinus: Die Gestalt als Gefüge* (Leipzig: Jakob Hegner, 1934) 66. An English translation of pp. 42-72 of the foregoing work appeared as "St. Augustine and the Modern World," trans. E. I. Watkin, in *A Monument to St. Augustine: Essays on Some Aspects of His Thought Written in Commemoration of His Fifteenth Centenary* (London: Sheed and Ward, 1930) 249-286 at 280. Przywara explains that the 'fear' of God is experienced precisely as 'reverence.' See Newman, *Parochial and Plain Sermons*, 2:282; see also 3:184, 188; 4:148-149; 6:90-91; 7:105-107.

in himself. He is always being constituted by the 'other' — the others *for* whom he is responsible, and the Other *before* whom he is responsible. His being, therefore, is essentially gift (or grace) and task (or call), something to be actualized in every authentic response to the voice of conscience. Outside of this response — that is to say, on every occasion when conscience is neglected or its claims denied — the subject is ungrounded, indeed, fragmentary, prey to the disparate longings arising from within, or created for him by an increasingly aggressive consumerist society. For Newman, then, in contrast to Freud, the foundational experience that shapes selfhood is not always, everywhere the same. It exists as a potential to be activated, and once it is activated, it is the gateway to a life of perpetual motion towards the ground of his being.[93] In that sense, one might even say that Newman's subject, like that of postmodernity is always 'provisional'.

93 See, in this regard, the discussion in Crosby, *Personalist Papers*, 110-111: "The God of conscience does not just abruptly appear, merely superimposed on moral obligation, but rather 'grows' out of obligation, so to say... namely, that the imperativity of obligation hardly makes sense apart from the divine ground of it. God is already 'contained' in the moral imperativity; so that if we thrive in our personal obligation in relation to moral obligation, we cannot fail to thrive when we proceed to understand that relation in an explicitly religious way. This is verified in the experience of every religiously awakened person, who finds that *the God appearing in conscience does not take over the place in me occupied by my self, repressing me as person; just the contrary, my conscience as religiously potentiated gives me an incomparable experience of my selfhood and subjectivity.* Thus this God appears in conscience *completely apart from and even in opposition to the psychodynamics of the superego*; whereas the superego interferes with and represses my distinct personhood, I am never so alive as person as in the presence of the divine person who makes himself felt in conscience" [Crosby's emphasis]. See also Merrigan, "'Numquam minus solus quam cum solus': Newman's First Conversion and Its Significance for His Life and Thought," 99-116; "Newman and Religious Experience," *Divinising Experience: Essays in the History of Religious Experience from Origen to Ricœur*, ed. Lieven Boeve & Laurence P. Hemming (Leuven: Peeters, 2004) 132-145.

Seen in this light, one of Newman's most cherished prayers takes on a new light. It seems a fitting text with which to conclude these reflections on the human subject who has never before in history been blessed with such possibilities and never seemed more uncertain of what he was to do in the face of them.

> I know, O my God, I must change, if I am to see Thy face!... Oh, support me, as I proceed in this great, awful, happy change, with the grace of Thy unchangeableness. My unchangeableness here below is perseverance in changing. Let me day by day be moulded upon Thee, and be changed from glory to glory, by ever looking towards Thee, and ever leaning on Thy arm... All will turn to evil if I am not sustained by the Unchangeable; all will turn to good if I have Jesus with me, yesterday and today the same, and for ever."[94]

[94] John Henry Newman, *Meditations and Devotions* (London: Burns & Oates, 1964) 58. See the title page of Erich Przywara, *Wandlung: Ein Christenweg* (Augsburg: Benno Filser, 1925). See also Erich Przywara, *Kant Heute* (Munich: R. Oldenbourg, 1930) 109 where Przywara writes: "Welt und Menschheit der Wandlung im unwandelbare Gott, das ist der erste Zug in Newmans Weltbild," and where he inquires whether "die Newmansche 'Wandlung'" is not "ein wahres Wiederaufleben des 'actus in potentia' der Werdebewegtheit... der Metaphysik des Aquinaaten...?" Przywara echoes these Newmanian themes in his own *Kirchenjahr: Die christliche Spannungseinheit* (Freiburg im Breisgau: Herder, 1923) 67, 73-74.

WHAT IS LIVING AND WHAT IS DEAD IN NEWMAN'S GRAMMAR OF ASSENT?

John MILBANK

I

One can read Newman's *Essay in Aid of a Grammar of Assent* as in one respect a thoroughgoing critique of English culture, which is compared unfavourably to the culture of Catholic Europe. At the heart of this comparison stands a contrast between a predilection for the abstract and verbal on the one hand, and a foregrounding of the visual or imagistic on the other. And yet, in arguing for the superiority of the latter emphasis, Newman draws on the resources of British intellectual tradition — on empiricist philosophy and the British proto-romantic and romantic exploration of the role of the imagination. In both cases though, he turns these traditions against themselves: a radicalised empiricism is deployed to defend the miraculous, mysterious and transcendent, while the Coleridgean understanding of the imagination is newly seen to require a displacing of the primacy of the merely literary in favour of the pictorial, the devotional, the lyrical, hymnic and liturgical.

If one were to argue, as one well might, that the British traditions of empiricism, scientific experiment and imaginative vision linked with mysticism have strong pre-Reformation roots, then it could be suggested that the coherence of Newman's cultural mission lies in a demand that the British genius further realise itself by returning to its Catholic origins. And this is something which I personally would wish to endorse.

However, I shall argue in what follows that the *Essay* is a seriously inconsistent treatise. It is not possible to read it always as building to an *apologia* for the Catholic faith rooted in a radical empiricism and an insistence on the primacy of the visual imagination. In the latter emphases lie the book's continued interest, yet disappointingly it frequently lapses into an *apologia* based upon a more conventional empiricism in which, surprisingly, the abstract and the notional reassert their dominant sway. This is the strand in Newman's thought which one might describe as 'all too British' or perhaps even 'all too English'. And it is here that one can situate the central paradox of Newman's intellectual biography — namely the redeployment of quintessentially Anglican empiricist arguments, derived in large part from Bishop Butler, in order to assert the claims of the Church of Rome. This particular mode of apologetics has — as many others, particularly David Nicholls and Fergus Kerr, have argued — the unfortunate result of engendering an overly rationalistic, yet equally overly fideistic, voluntaristic and authoritarian account of the role of the Papacy.[1]

Here I must hasten to say that the question of whether Anglicans should become Catholics, and of the validity of Papal claims, are not at all at present the issue for me. Rather, it is the *mode* of Newman's assertion of the Catholic case that is in question, along with the depth of his grasp of a Catholic ecclesiology. So I am going to argue that the *Essay* points the way to a profound and interesting apologetic and yet confuses this with a superficial and dangerous one.

[1] Fergus Kerr and David Nicholls (eds.), *John Henry Newman: Reason, Rhetoric, and Romanticism* (Bristol: Bristol Classical Press, 1990).

II

Broadly speaking, the more interesting approach is, I think, articulated in the first four chapters of the *Essay*, and then in Chapter Nine on the illative sense. This claim implies that the more implicitly theological Newman becomes, the more he retreats to a more wooden and traditional empiricism: reasons for this I shall indicate later.

In the first four chapters, Newman adumbrates his crucial distinction between real and rational assent. However, in a prior move, 'assent to terms' is seen as far more fundamental than assent to proofs or to inferences.[2] Arguments about logical consistency may be interminable, but they are in principle publicly resolvable, since they concern consistency with formal procedures under agreed rules. This is less clearly the case with our apprehension of first terms, which is required in order that an argument be actually *about* anything whatsoever. Here Newman repeats in his own manner the antique insistence on the primacy of *topica* over *dispositio* in both rhetoric and dialectics. Outside the realm of the apodeictic or the tautologically analytical, argument is subordinated to a desire either to persuade someone to do something — in rhetoric — or else, in dialectics, to get someone actually and immediately to see the truth for themselves. Argument and inference can here only perform the role of a midwife.

So with 'assent to terms' Newman is concerned with our theoretical assent to 'what is the case' prior to argument and with our assent to more complex states of affairs in instances where following a chain of logical links allows us to grasp a series of causes and relations: his example is our final intuitive grasp that John is

[2] John Henry Newman, *An Essay in Aid of a Grammar of Assent*, "Introduction" by Nicholas Lash (Notre Dame, IN: Notre Dame University Press, 1979) Chapter Two, pp. 32-35.

'great-uncle-in-law to Richard' once we have apprehended that John is Richard's wife's father's aunt's husband.[3] The latter apprehension is deemed by Newman to be 'notional', but the former 'real'. Yet this example shows, I think, how for Newman the two forms of assent are always involved in the thinking process and are mutually complementary.

One can try to grasp what he means here by contrast with a Hobbesian, Lockean or Humean philosophy. In that mode of empiricism, the raw 'givens' of understanding are atomistic items of sensory information combined, at least in Locke's case, with certain *a priori* norms of reasoning. This tradition sustained a nominalist suspicion of abstract terms, because the latter might tend to sediment false inferences or generalisations from the basic givens, and to hypostasize generalisations as real universals, having a supposedly 'thingy' consistency.

Now the concealed contradiction of such a philosophy is that empiricism ought to be agnostic as to what may exist and should always wait on the deliverances of experience. However, if one has decided that all that is incontrovertibly given are isolatable items of sensory experience, whose arising in our mind can be explained according to the laws of motion, then one has foreclosed the question of what may be encountered, in terms of an entirely dogmatic ontology. Empiricism is reductionist not when it disputes metaphysics, but rather when it embraces it in a particularly virulent form by asserting that all that can be, or at least all that can be known, is that whose genesis can be broken down into the *combinatorium* of isolated units - which, one might propose, if they are to be uncontaminated by any scholastic notion of intrinsic form or substance must in the end fractalize away into atoms of nothingness.

[3] *An Essay in Aid of a Grammar of Assent*, Chapter Three, p. 36.

Yet the empirical impulse *as such* does not encourage such reductionism. Thus other manifestations of this impulse in British culture have encouraged an openness to the extraordinary, the unclassifiable and the irreducibly prolix, as well as to the recognition (in contrast to Cartesian physics) of mysterious and yet clearly operating forces in nature like gravity and electricity. In the case of Thomas Reid and the Scottish commonsense tradition, empiricism was somewhat disconnected from sensory atomism, and linked rather with a recognition that we are originally confronted with unfathomably complex realities and have no warrant for supposing that the mind (as opposed to the brain) builds up such pictures from multiple initially discrete elements.[4] Reid rightly insisted that the process by which certain sensations lead us to acknowledge certain features of the external world, such as space, motion, extension and colour is actually 'unfathomable'. He argued

[4] Thomas Reid, *An Inquiry into the Human Mind on the Principles of Common Sense* (University Park, PA: Pennsylvania State University Press, 1997). See, for example, Chapter 5, Sections VI-VII, p. 67; Chapter 6, Section VI, p. 90; Section XXIII, p. 189. One is struck by the fact that Reid failed to see that the linguistic and pragmatist dimensions of his epistemology are already present in Berkeley; this is because he too easily accepted, or perhaps helped to foster, the standard idealist reading of the Bishop of Cloyne's notions. In point of fact both thinkers later strongly influenced American philosophy, especially C. S. Pierce — and for similar reasons. For both these philosophers from the Celtic margins rejected the metropolitan barbarism of English and Edinburgh empiricism. See John Milbank, "The Linguistic Turn as a Theological Turn," *The Word Made Strange* (Oxford: Blackwell, 1997) especially pp. 97-105. One can mention also that, without a scholastic notion of 'form' as common to material things and to knowledge, Reid's doctrine sounds too near to one of pre-established harmony and has to remain agnostic as to the finite causal aspects of human understanding. Yet, on the other hand, if Aquinas's species as the mode that intelligible 'form' takes in our mind is not a 'picture' of a material object (and it is not) then the Aberdonian's reflection that our sensations and ideas are 'signs' joins up with Aquinas's view that the form in our mind evolves into an 'inner word' which mysteriously conveys back to us the presence of the material thing that we know.

in consequence that these mysterious inferences 'common' to our sensing must operate by a kind of interpretation of natural signs according to regular rules established by God. In this way he suggested that only a theistic metaphysic overcomes scepticism as to the existence of an external world, and that our trust in our senses is very akin to the trust we accord to the testifying words of other people. In both these two respects Newman's reflections echo those of Reid (whatever the case may be as to the question of influence).

And Newman, like Reid, and perhaps still more emphatically, insists that thought primarily considers complex — even inexhaustibly complex — phenomena. Like Reid again, he suggests that in this respect thought always remains close to the joint operation of the senses and paradigmatically to the sense of sight. Even the ability of thought to abstract away from the immediate present has always as its accompanying vehicle the operation of the imagination.[5] We remember first of all vivid objects; on this basis we imagine other concrete instances and only on that foundation do we arrive at the abstractly general.

It follows that Newman's empiricist suspicion of abstract terms is not at all like that of Hobbes, Locke, and Hume — if anything it is more like that of Wittgenstein. For Newman is not advocating a nominalist priority of the individual thing as pure atom. Rather, in a fashion comparable to Gerard Manley Hopkins' reinterpretation of the Scotist *haeccitas,* he is insisting that the concrete individual

[5] *An Essay in Aid of a Grammar of Assent*, 37-43, p. 41: "And by means of these particular and personal experiences, thus impressed upon us, we attain an apprehension of what such things are at other times when we have not experience of them; an apprehension of sights and sounds, of colours and forms, of places and persons, of mental acts and states, parallel to our actual experiences such that, when we meet with definite propositions expressive of theory our apprehension cannot be called abstract and rational."

case is always more complex, pregnant and mysterious than any term abstracted from it. In a sense though, this position, as later with Wittgenstein, *does* involve following the line of nominalist suspicion to the very end, even if this end undermines the very contrast of nominalism with realism. For one crucial part of Newman's case seems to be that the most innocent seeming atomic terms are *themselves* contaminated by abstraction and universality. Thus he notes that counting seven items is only true if one has already perceived or decided that there are seven items which are denumerable — or as we would now say, seven things that fall within the same mathematical set. Newman mentions that one can count seven or more species of animals, but no species of angels whatsoever — and that 'God' cannot be counted as an item at all.[6] The implication of these statements is that the classical empiricist programme desires ontology to correspond to simple arithmetic, whereas, to the contrary, the latter could only apply after one has made certain arbitrary incisions in the real whose character may well be 'catachrestic' as Newman the rhetorician puts it. If classical empiricism is to hold, then it must remain inescapably Cartesian, in so far as the only paradigm for the accumulation to the complex from the simple must be an arithmetic or a geometric one. In the case of his allusions to the geometric field, Newman again shows a dim glimmering of the revolutionary developments of his own century, mostly far away from Oxford; for example, he points out that the statement that two straight parallel lines do not enclose a space is not a statement about reality, but only about a formal

[6] *An Essay in Aid of a Grammar of Assent*, 75-76. "Unless numeration is to issue in nonsense, it must be conducted on conditions. This being the case there are, for what we know, collections of beings to whom the notion of number cannot be attached, except catachrestically, because, taken individually, no positive point of real agreement can be found between them, by which to call them."

system abstracted from reality.[7] Yet classical empiricism, which is in the end but a variant of Cartesianism, would seem to require that physical reality be Euclidean.

Therefore, where classical empiricism would wish to isolate basic given elements such as space, efficient cause, appetite, will and so forth, Newman sees only abstracted and conventional notions to which words have been affixed. He even suggests that alternative valid lenses through which we view physical process will necessarily entail incompatible implications, yet still be equally legitimate or even required — this sounds like a premonition of a 'quantum' perspective.[8] Where Locke and Hume thought universals were 'only words', Newman insists that concepts for individual items are also 'only words' and moreover, that as incorporated into grammar they can only make sense if they already compare and relate different items. To say 'this is a stone' is already to deploy the words 'this' and 'stone' as universal categories, as Hegel had already insisted.[9] Newman's reflections here exceed in their critical rigour the conclusions not only of Locke but also of William of Ockham, who had considered that all concepts and signs are only 'true' if traceable back to an original intuition of an irreducibly singular presence.[10]

[7] *An Essay in Aid of a Grammar of Assent*, 59: "I have defined a straight line in my own way at my own pleasure; the question is not one of facts at all, but of the consistency with each other of definitions and their logical consequences."

[8] *An Essay in Aid of a Grammar of Assent*, 60 "Notions are but aspects of things; the free deductions from one of these aspects necessarily contradict the free deductions from another."

[9] G. W. F. Hegel, *Phenomenology of Spirit*, trans. A. V. Miller (Oxford: Oxford University Press, 1977) A. II, 67-79.

[10] See Pierre Alféri, *Guillaume d'Ockham: Le Singulier* (Paris: Éditions de Minuit, 1989) 265-299, 362-402, 453-454. Whether or not Ockham's position is a realist one, or admits of a sceptical reading, saving the invocation of the divine guarantee of the truth of our intuitions, remains a matter of scholarly dispute. In the case of our thoughts of God, for Ockham, our predications are not backed

Newman's perspective here could perhaps be construed as an ultra-nominalism which discovers that the artifice of universalising is involved in all predication and is unavoidable (since the raw particulars that would provide genuine foundations are unavailable) even though it must be viewed with extreme suspicion. This would entail outright scepticism. His swerving away from such an extreme is linked to the fact that he did not regard 'notional assent' as simply secondary and inferior to 'real assent'. For while he certainly viewed abstract notions with some suspicion, as tending to provide merely a 'thin' account of reality, he never takes the nominalist step of claiming that abstractions are only generalisations from many particulars or else must be taken as if they were such (in the case of an ultra-nominalism which has concluded that the legitimating data are always already contaminated by abstraction). To the contrary, he time and again declares that abstract notions select certain *aspects* of concrete reality — hence one aspect of physical space is indeed Euclidean. He clearly did not think that these aspects were arbitrary pragmatic ploys in a kind of Nietzschean fashion, because he declares that *real* assent to an envisaged or imagined state of affairs is always 'fertile in aspects'.[11] Indeed it

up by any intuition, yet the intention of our naming of God is grounded in a faith in his absolute unknown singularity whose unlimited power and will is, indeed, the ultimate ontological basis for a created reality composed only of singular existences, in principle infinitely re-arrangeable, except for the requirement of non-contradiction.

11 *An Essay in Aid of a Grammar of Assent*, 47: "...real apprehension has the precedence, as being the scope and end and the test of notional; and the fuller is the mind's hold upon things or what it considers such, the more fertile it is in its aspects of them, and the more practical in its definitions;"; 66: "the doctrines [of the British national religion] are not so much facts, as stereotyped aspects of facts and it is afraid, so to say, of walking round them;" 77: "Our notions of things are never simply commensurate with the things themselves; they are aspects of them...;" 87: "inference, unlike apprehension, is necessarily concerned with surfaces and aspects;" 291: "This is what is meant by originality in thinking; it is

is this term 'aspect' — which so remarkably seems to anticipate Husserl (as well as Heidegger and Wittgenstein) — that provides the crucial mediating link between real and notional assent.[12] If a notional term picks out an aspect and real assent goes on discerning further and further aspects of a complex circumstance, then, just because real assent does not grasp all aspects at once, it must be always already to some degree be involved in notional abstraction. The ontological concomitant of this gnoseology would be that, for Newman, as earlier for Berkeley, a concrete thing is composed of many abstract elements, rather as a word is made up of the letters of the alphabet.[13] One can suppose that, for Newman, in a created universe the likeness and inter-relation between things is not a kind of accidental and secondary upshot, but rather reflects the original architectonic of the divine wisdom.

Newman's position then in the first four chapters is less nominalist than authentically realist in the best medieval sense, whether of Aquinas or of Scotus. Universals, or aspects as notions, are real only in our minds, but this mental reality is rooted in and allowed to exist by, the formal synthetic complexity of substantially existing things. In a more modern mode, however, Newman adds that the rich discernment of universal relevance in a particular situation is not disabled but rather encouraged by an increased concentration on this very specificity. Here it is always the *imagination* which is able to hold together the many facets of a situation and to extend by analogy this synthesis to other real or possible instances. Conversely, the act of notional abstraction does not attain to genuine productive universality, but rather to a kind of phantom

the discovery of an aspect of a subject matter, simpler it may be, and more... intelligible than any hitherto taken."

12 See Stephen Mulhall, *On Being in the World: Wittgenstein and Heidegger on Seeing Aspects* (London: Routledge, 1990).

13 See John Milbank, "The Linguistic Turn as a Theological Turn."

concreteness — it tends to produce a technologically manageable world where a simplified particularity can be easily produced in substitution for the rich original organic world which suggests to us ever new universal lessons.

Newman is here certainly indebted (by whatever routes) to Coleridge and Wordsworth and through this indebtedness tends to qualify an Aristotelian account of abstract universals with a Platonic or neoplatonic account of productive and concrete universals. This can be seen in the way in which he understands real and notional assent to be complementary and mutually corrective. When aspects are apprehended as abstracted terms one achieves a 'broad but shallow' grasp of reality. When, on the other hand, aspects are grasped visually and imaginatively, as manifested in a single instance — like greenness, height, light, circularity, dependence, growth, seasonality, teleology and beauty in one oak tree — then one gains a 'deep but narrow-minded' apprehension of things.

Neither intellectual strategy is adequate on its own and Newman argues for their complementarity by making some psychological and sociological observations. The inventors, discourses, leaders, and scientific geniuses of the world often do badly at school, he declares, precisely because they tend to see something new in a single intuition, but are bad at orderly arrangement and generalisation. Yet the latter capacities are not simply humdrum things to be sneered at, precisely because the full truth of the aspects of a particular thing concerns its regular relations to other things. The intuitive genius may ignore what generally holds and as a result go wildly astray in his conclusions because he is locked in 'one small circle of knowledge'. And to some degree, knowing what generally holds can only be accomplished as a collective task down the generations. Thus the individual imagination, if it is to operate with genuine insight, requires a balancing by abstracting reason, common sense and cultural tradition. Depth may indeed be linked to obsession and even (here Newman agrees with Coleridge) to obscurity, but it requires to be linked with the relative superficiality and yet breadth of a clearer and more regular reasoning.[14] Romanticism seems to modulate into a proto-modernism at this point.

I have been arguing that the key to Newman's account of assent and the relation of real to notional assent is the concept of 'aspect'. But why, a critic could ask here, can one not simply reduce notional aspects to observed states of affairs? Such a reduction would be equivalent to the Fregean extreme extension of the programme of classical empiricism — beyond even Ockham, the aspects or 'qualities' of things do not really inhere in things because there are no qualities and no substances, only accidental *congeries* of atomic circumstances. If, in this way, there are no aspects or qualities, but only states of affairs, then it follows, as Frege tended to suggest, that analytical logic can fulfil all the tasks of philosophy.[15] Once one views the world with a demystified gaze, there can be no arguments concerning what is the case, or at least what is deemed to be the case, since this is simply a matter for empirical scientific investigation. Philosophy now only impinges on the real in terms of the category of reference and thus can be reduced to a logical function: a is b if and only if it is the case that a is b; b need never be seen as an intrinsic aspect of a thing without which it would not exist at all (or at least not in the same fashion), in such a way that would require from philosophy the articulation of an extra-logical ontology.

[14] *An Essay in Aid of a Grammar of Assent*, 47, 76-80.

[15] See Claire Ortiz Hill, *Rethinking Identity and Metaphysics: On the Foundations of Analytic Philosophy* (New Haven, CT: Yale University Press, 1997); Claire Ortiz Hill and Guillermo E. Rosado Haddock, *Husserl or Frege? Meaning, Objectivity and Mathematics* (Chicago, IL: Open Court, 2003).

By insisting, to the contrary, that assent to the real and to basic terms is an inherently *problematic* matter, Newman refused in advance this Fregean position and therefore the entire programme of analytic philosophy in the strict sense. He would have seen its logical discriminations as important but ultimately trivial, since he asserts that the question of apprehension lies both before and after that of logic or inference. And the real ground for this assertion lies in his view that we apprehend reality primarily in terms of bundles of aspects that hold together beyond more arbitrary synthesis. In the twentieth century Husserl, Heidegger and Wittgenstein have provided better justifications for this assertion, which all amount to the point that we do not first see raw items or combinations of such items, but rather first apprehend something as shown in something else which in some sense belongs to it and yet not exclusively. We originally apprehend a river as flowing and sparkling and making music, for example. But Newman already insisted that our primary perception of things is moral, aesthetic and pragmatic as well as detachedly observational. He correctly reasoned, in consequence, that any bracketing out of moral and aesthetic responses as ontologically irrelevant is an arbitrary decision.

It is therefore arguable that Newman already offered something like a phenomenology: intuition has primacy over discourse and presents us with all the serious, grown-up philosophical problematics. However, his insistence on the surplus of real over notional assent would prevent any sort of Husserlian idealist confinement of phenomenological conclusions. And just because that is for Newman impossible — because it is assumed that what is presented to us remains irreducible to how we experience its presentation on pain of surrendering its otherness and reality — he can also retain, unlike Husserl yet without sceptical despair, an awareness that nothing apprehended is *sheerly given*, but is always interpreted, acted upon, decided upon by us creatively and imaginatively.

Newman notes how the experience of 60° Fahrenheit is never sensorially neutral, yet may be subjectively one of either heat or chill; how some people do not distinguish red or green; how some see a curve as convex that others see as concave; likewise how the same upright letters can seem to different children to lean one way or the other.[16] We always see *as* — with a qualitative supplement that is always already bent by our responses. Hence Newman offers in effect a phenomenology which is also a hermeneutics and a pragmatics and therefore he avoids a Husserlian foundationalism as much as a Fregean one.

By starting to develop a radical empiricism, Newman draws on deeper insular resources against the more superficial, philistine ones. However, he is convinced that the development must point us back to the continent and to Rome. Why should this be the case? Interestingly, Newman isolates two aspects of British culture — the literary and the scientific — which from Matthew Arnold through to C. P. Snow came to be regarded as antagonistic rivals. Yet Newman appears, beyond Arnoldean insight, to hint at a deep underlying kinship between the two. *Both,* he seems to suggest, are somehow abstractive and notional, for both tend to substitute regular systems — numerical, experimental or grammatical — for reality, and live only within those systems and their endless possibility for manipulation. Science is comforting because it offers us a regular control; literature is consoling because it secures a world where humane ideas can fictionally hold or be abstractly perfected by the rearrangement of a system of signs.[17]

Against this twin complicity of technology and literary humanism — offering us both material comfort and a smug sense of self-revelation — Newman suggests that the mass of the population cannot be moved to act for the better by such bloodless machines.

[16] *An Essay in Aid of a Grammar of Assent*, 291-292.

[17] *An Essay in Aid of a Grammar of Assent*, 88-89.

Rather, people will only fundamentally assent with their whole being to images and dramas that are at once concretely real and yet imbued with the imaginatively enhanced. Here Newman's strategy is at its most daringly post-secular: Christianity may have lost its hegemony forever he concedes, yet this must leave a problematic cultural vacuum. Cultures are *not* formed either by 'science' — by facts drained of value — *nor* by 'literature' — by values drained of factuality. For Newman, presumably, the secular literary/scientific split was not inevitable, but rather the result of a religious development — Protestantism — which had already encouraged the loss of the integration of fact and value in image, theatre and narrative. Crucial here to Newman's entire cultural strategy was his youthful recognition that the magisterial Reformation has rendered belief incredible precisely by insisting that the age of miracles is closed, such that in consequence the sacred drama and radically empirical possibility of the irruption of the *exceptional event* is a thing of the past.[18] Once the deep sacred past had been claimed by evolution, it became doubly crucial, as Newman realised, to claim the present also for the continuation of sacred drama or the 'scenic' as he terms it. (Indeed, Robert Bruce Mullin has shown that the shift towards the charismatic and holiness movements within the Protestant churches was the fruit of a similar neo-Catholic transformation.)[19]

Likewise, for Newman, the religious manifestation of the British literary obsession as Biblicism offers no vivid epiphanies but only a vague sense of the providential, which itself will be eroded by Biblical criticism, if the literal authority of the sacred word is all that we can rely upon. Instead, Newman suggests that we need to

[18] J. H. Newman, *Two Essays on Biblical and Ecclesiastical Miracles* (London: Longmans and Green, 1890).

[19] See Robert Bruce Mullin, *Miracles and the Modern Religious Imagination* (New Haven, CT: Yale University Press, 1996).

see that the Biblical histories concern a personal apprehension of the intertwining of the mythical with the historical which the canons of written history will tend to reject, since they concern only thinned-out aspects of events which all can recognize without benefit of subjective inspiration.

In these respects one can see Newman as carrying forwards strands of the Oxford Movement which were not simply conservative or reactionary but post-secular and critically counter-cultural. Frequently, he insists that intellectual understanding is not the pursuit of a method, nor an act of technical manipulation, but the ineffable judging or creative response of a living mind. In the face of modern physical reductionism, his metacritical response is to insist on the mysterious manifestations of the psychic as constituting our primary reality and as undergirding the unpredictable drama of human history. This psychic excess over any technical medium Newman also seems to extend to an excess of thinking over language. Here, arguably, he breaks with the romantic sense (as mediated to Britain by Carlyle) that we are always trapped within a shadowy world of signs within which the subject can only ironically and negatively assert himself. However, just as Newman denies that real aspects are purely available in isolation from notional ones, so also he is not necessarily saying that there are any concepts independent of verbal mediation. Rather, he is perhaps suggesting, in a fashion that recalls Kierkegaard, that if language discloses the real this can only be affirmed by an entirely subjective judgement which enacts the intrinsic but incomprehensible bond that exists between the psychic and the ontological. This bond is for Newman more manifest in the iconic and sacramental taken along with language than it is by language alone, since the imagistic directly conjoins the conceptual and the semiotic with the plenitude of the concretely real.[20]

[20] *An Essay in Aid of a Grammar of Assent*, 87: "Belief is concerned with 'things concrete' 'which variously excite the mind from their moral and imaginative

For this reason statues, pictures, totems and processions stand at the centre of culture as much as narratives and recitals. But for Newman, British culture has lost this vital dimension and hence has become increasingly incapable of such real passionate religious commitment as remains possible in the south of Europe. Perhaps he would not have been surprised by the way in which during the first five years of the twenty-first century a new irruption of the religious in world affairs has coincided with the re-direction of the course of events by singular incidents whose visual impact, albeit of a negative order, moves more than any arguments or demonstrations — the twin towers dissolving in flames, terrorists torturing hostages on video, David Kelly on his last walk in the Oxfordshire countryside.

In the end, Newman's work in the first four chapters of the *Essay* and in the chapter on the illative sense shows a deep kinship with that of other genuine counter-enlightenment, rather than merely conservative, thinkers like Vico, Jacobi, and Hamann.[21] Like them, as his frequent mathematical examples tend to show, he resists above all the algebraicization of the real in both a literal and an extended sense. In supposedly grasping the real, science must inevitably substitute its own system of signifying equivalents of the real for the real itself — just as geometry, says Newman, can be algebraicized, even though algebra will not let us know that there is no

properties';" 90: "It is well to freshen our impressions and convictions from physics, but to create them we must go elsewhere;" 91: "to act you must assume, and that assumption is faith." (One should note here that it is in fact arguable that Carlyle, in *Sartor Resartus*, which is already beyond German Romanticism, was exploring this conjunction as a kind of tension when he ironically takes 'clothes', which are altogether material and yet utterly ornamental and signifying, to be the paradigm for culture.)

[21] See John Milbank, "Knowledge: The Theological Critique of Philosophy in Hamann and Jacobi," *Radical Orthodoxy: A New Theology*, ed. J. Milbank, C. Pickstock, and G. Ward (London: Routledge, 1999) 21-38.

real fourth dimension and will merely mention certain things like the square root of minus a, which it cannot intuit, whereas the intuition of an equivalent spatial phenomenon is possible for geometry.[22] In a fashion somewhat akin to the reflections of the later Husserl, Newman fears that the reduction of science to repeatable procedure will lose the original intuitions on which it is based and that this will further disguise the fact that this intuition was but one of many possible intuitions, all inevitably abstracting from a real plenitude. If, by contrast, the sciences remember that they begin with a compelling icon and a commitment in excess of *given* warrants — since warrants are never sufficient to justify commitment — then the analogous reasonableness of religious vision and commitment may come into view. Evidential warrants never demand assent in any human field for Newman, for one can always suspend one's certainty as to the referential bearing of any formal system, as well as withhold one's psychological commitment to it. From this perspective, religious assent is not exceptional and aberrant but rather normative — for it is given precisely where the real is deemed to coincide with human passions and interests. This arises in the case of dramatic events and their representations which exemplify in concrete form the compellingly attractive and uplifting.

III

And yet… when Newman turns more directly to the religious case, he seems partially to forget the radical character of his critique of modern intellectual norms and to fall back upon specifically modern modes of religious apologetic. He rejects, indeed, Paleyian arguments from design in nature, since such inferences, being too complex, can support no true assent to an immediate

[22] *An Essay in Aid of a Grammar of Assent*, 57.

apparition. Yet he endorses Butlerian or Manselian or quasi-Kantian moral proofs for God's existence whose inherent structure is really in no better case. In the early part of the book Newman seems to insist on the concrete co-belonging of the true, the good and the beautiful; yet in his treatment of the ethical he rejects the moral sense tradition dating back to Shaftesbury which sustained a link between goodness and aesthetic harmony and thereby preserved an irreducibly social dimension to morality which does not prise questions of conscience apart from those of appropriate social roles. Following instead the purer stoicism of Bishop Butler, Newman views the moral response as proceeding from the entirely inner voice of conscience which prescribes a non-negotiable duty and is concerned with persons not things — he concomitantly (but questionably) denies that we can have any true passions for the latter. This approach tends to divorce practical recognition of the good from the interpretation of theoretical states of affairs and from judgement about what will promote social harmony. Where the latter, more classical approach is taken, one's vision of reality, including transcendence, will tend to be inseparable from one's understanding of what ought to be done. But for Newman at times, our sense of the beautiful and of empirical truth is self-contained and does not point beyond the circle of immanence. This leaves the inner voice of conscience alone as that which points us towards God, now divorced from a wider 'reading' of the world, while the voice of conscience of itself 'vaguely reaches forwards to God'. Newman also resorts to more extrincisist arguments for which the fact of conscience supports a strongly probabilistic *inference* as to God's existence, such that the latter alone can explain why we should be subject to an inward moral imperative.[23]

[23] *An Essay in Aid of a Grammar of Assent*. For the integration of the true, good and beautiful, see p. 87: "Belief... being concerned with things concrete, not abstract, which variously excite the mind from their moral and imaginative

Despite his insistence on the primacy of revelation for all real religion, Newman offers here a weak natural theology based upon the supposedly universal human recognition of 'conscience', even though he acknowledges that Plato and Aristotle knew nothing of conscience, but only acknowledged 'moral sense'. Of course, after Nietzsche, all such arguments seem absurd — but it would have been open to Newman in his own terms to see that the modern deontological system of conscience is simply one limited and perhaps dubious notional system. Instead, at the end of the book

properties, has for its objects, not only what is true, but inclusively what is beautiful, useful, admirable, heroic..." For the question of moral proof of God see pp. 97-98: the first principle of such a proof "which I assume and shall not attempt to prove... is... that we have by nature a conscience." For the separation of the moral and the aesthetic see p. 99: "... taste and conscience part company: for the sense of beautifulness, as indeed the Moral Sense, has no special relations to persons, but contemplates objects in themselves; conscience, on the other hand, is concerned with persons primarily, and with actions mainly as viewed in their doers, or rather with self alone and one's own actions, and with others only indirectly and as if in association with self. And further, taste is its own evidence... but conscience does not repose on itself, but vaguely reaches forward to something higher than itself..." Here not just the aesthetic is subordinated, but also a 'lower', more aesthetic, social and situated aspect of morality. Newman sounds much more 'Kantian' than 'Hegelian' here. See also pp. 100-101 for the denigration of objects. For Newman's 'extrinsicism' see p. 101: "These feelings [of conscience] in us are such as require for their exciting cause an intelligent being... conscience... sheds upon us a deep peace, which there is no sensible, no earthly object to elicit... If the cause of these emotions does not belong to the visible world, the object to which his perception is directed must be supernatural and divine." Here any extrinsic argument confirms the pictures of an all-seeing and retributive judge which conscience naturally (we are told) tends to elicit. Newman sounds at this point far more like Pelagius than Augustine — failing to argue like the latter, that our deeper, more primordial relation to God and the Good is that of a lover to the beloved (see also p. 311). Newman proceeds (p. 102) to compare the inference from conscience to God to that from images of the external world to its reality, which works in animals more by instinct than by ratiocination. This 'Reidian' as well as Butlerian analogy would be more convincing if one were to remove the sundering of moral from intellectual and aesthetic apprehension.

he offers an entirely un-Catholic and wholly Kantian account of punishment as the formal enactment of intrinsic desert entirely detached from questions of the teleological flourishing of the offender, his victims and the community.

There is supposed to be a parallel between conscience and the illative sense as the faculty which issues in real assent. This then requires, as Newman suggests, that the operation of conscience involve something like Aristotelian *phronesis* — yet such an exercise of moral craft, or of a tacit and impresentable sense of what should be done in particular circumstances, involves a constant reading of the world and *not* simply a listening to an inner voice.[24] There seems to be an inconsistency here, whereas Newman also more coherently approximated the illative sense to an Aristotelian or Thomist exercise of *intellectual* virtue which must be alert to practical goodness as well as to theoretical truth. More clarity on the role of *phronesis* however emerges when it turns out that, for Newman, it is associated not just with practical reasoning but also with the governing of assents to inferences, whereas the illative sense concerns assent to terms, whether real or notional.[25]

In so far as *phronesis* governs inferences, it is clearly to do with judgements as to the probable rather than the certain. Here though, Newman seems un-alert to the radical distinction between a pre-modern sense of the probable as involving a kind of ineffable intuition which approximates to an unreachable truth, and a modern sense of the probable as concerning a *calculable* approximation to certainty — the modern sense was encouraged by the development of calculus, but in the 19th century enjoyed new applications to physics, biology and sociology.[26]

[24] *An Essay in Aid of a Grammar of Assent*, 277.

[25] *An Essay in Aid of a Grammar of Assent*, 278.

[26] See Ian Hacking, *The Emergence of Probability* (London: Cambridge University Press, 1975). David J. Lepew and Bruce H. Weber, "Genetic Darwinism

This confusion emerges in Newman's contestation of the Lockean claim that assent must keep pace with the strength of inference. The contestation contains several strands. First of all Newman denies that, as a matter of fact, this is psychologically true — assent can lag behind or exceed inference. In the second place, Newman sees this psychological reserve as epistemologically justifiable — inference is never complete and its real applicability never entirely certain, while practical exigencies nevertheless demand that we also commit ourselves in excess of evidential warrant. We reason in broken syllogisms — enthymemes where the middle term is loosely analogical, not univocal — scarcely ever perfect ones. In the third place, Newman points out that our most basic real assents to our own existence, our having had parents, the roundness of the globe and the physical insularity of Britain and so forth, do not correspond to evidence or inference but rather concern the sorts of assumed and all-encompassing facts that are the traditional province of ontology.[27]

All these responses to Locke are entirely cogent and unseat his 'manly' reasoning which Newman supposedly admired. Yet this is not so clear when Newman turns from the question of foundational 'assents' to that of 'inferences'. All too woodenly 'male' is Newman's Butlerian extension of the range of Lockean 'convergent probabilities' as legitimating a full act of 'complex assent' — that is, a certain conviction concerning something not immediately given such as a physical reality which we 'simply' assent to, yet nevertheless reasonably justified in terms of a supposition that it is immediately given elsewhere and to someone else or in potential to ourselves in another time and place. For in this case real

and the Probability Revolution," *Darwinism Evolving* (Cambridge, MA: MIT 1997) 167-335.

[27] *An Essay in Aid of a Grammar of Assent*, 136-156. On Enthymemes see p. 153.

assent is not really taking that 'leap' which alone affirms the binding of the psychological with the ontological, but rather is simply affirming a sure train of inference as so nearly certain that it can be taken as truly certain. Hence Newman's invocation of Butler's claim that we can affirm a somewhat uncertain event as real if denial of its reality would tend to render incoherent a chain of preceding or consequent and incomprehensible events seems to have little to do either with Aristotelian *phronesis* or with the real assents of the illative sense. The same applies to his statement that 'a proof is the limit of convergent probabilities'.[28]

The essential modernity of Newman's version of probability is also shown in his endorsement of the modern legal admission of circumstantial evidence as opposed to confession and testimony — and his failure to see that this frequently issues in miscarriages of justice. Nevertheless, there is a real confusion here, and Newman fully sustains *phronesis* as regards inferences, when he writes that sometimes 'the reasons of [a person's] conviction are too delicate, too intricate' to be objectively traced. Thus they are 'in part invisible; invisible except to those who from circumstances have an intellectual perception of what does not appear to the many. They are personal to the individual'.[29]

Given this stark tension in the work, one can legitimately ask just how important for Newman is modern probabilism in the sphere of religion? To answer this final question one must consider briefly Newman's reflections in the *Essay* on the nature of the Christian doctrine of God. The attributes of God and the conception of the

[28] *An Essay in Aid of a Grammar of Assent*, 254. In general for 'Informal inference' see pp. 230-260. And see p. 253 for Newman's telling affirmation that his notion of informal inference is like the method of proof in Newtonian science, where likeliness becomes truth in the way a polygon infinitely tends towards a circle.

[29] *An Essay in Aid of a Grammar of Assent*, 259-260. On circumstantial evidence, see pp. 256-258.

three persons of the Trinity, all taken one by one, can, Newman declares, be the object of a real religious, devotional and imaginative assent. However, this is less clear in the case of the unity of the divine attributes, or the thought of the Trinity taken as whole. Here, Newman rightly says, there can be no total proof of the co-belonging of the divine attributes and so of the divine simplicity, nor can there be any adequate imagination of the divine three-in-one.

In this instance a predominantly notional, and so theological rather than religious conception, preserves an *apophasis* in relation to God. Yet while Newman seems to affirm that there must be some glimmer of intuition as to the divine simplicity, he explicitly denies this in the case of the divine trinity. This doctrine is entirely notional and cannot be the object of any act of real imaginative assent, even dimly and remotely. Here Newman, knowing little of the traditional doctrine of the divine names (for all his earlier interest in allegory) seems to lack the concepts necessary to think a remote participatory insight into the unknown, or an obscure seeing of the invisible.[30]

[30] *An Essay in Aid of a Grammar of Assent*, 30. Here Newman rightly says that the unity of the divine attributes cannot finally be 'proved', except in relation to a certain remote intuition of the divine simplicity; for the doctrine of God and the Trinity, see pp. 95-123. With regard to the dogma if the Trinity, Newman says at p. 115 that "... the question is whether a real assent to the mystery, as such, is possible; and I say it is not possible, because although we can image the separate propositions, we cannot image them together." Again at p. 116 "we see Him [God] at best only in shadows, but we cannot even bring those shadows together, for they flit to and fro, and are never present to us at once." At p. 112 he wonders if the doctrine of the Trinity can in any way be "really apprehended" and at p. 115 he suggests that this can only be the case implicitly, via submission to the Word of God in the Church.

[31] *An Essay in Aid of a Grammar of Assent*, 131: "that the church is the infallible oracle of the truth is the fundamental doctrine of the Catholic religion." But of course it isn't and there is no simple 'fundamental' doctrine. See also p. 129.

Now, given Newman's general insistence on the necessity of real apprehension for any affirmation of ontological truth, this appears to render the depths of Christian doctrine unreachable by the ordinary religious imagination. As Newman often suggests, this must in consequence (including the doctrine of the Trinity) be believed primarily on grounds of submission to ecclesiastical authority. In consequence, for Newman, the overwhelmingly important act of real assent in the religious sphere is to the authority and infallibility of the Catholic Church.[31] But this surely seems crass — real assent to such authority should rather be seen as indissociable from a certain intuitive insight into the compelling truth of all that the Church teaches, just as acceptance of infallibility cannot be divorced from recognition of the presence of the Holy Spirit in the Eucharist and in every Christian congregation. One cannot deny that Newman at his best pointed towards such a perspective, and that his attraction to Catholicism concerned precisely what he saw as its greater sense of divine teaching as working gradually and organically through the developing collective insight of human beings into symbolic mysteries. Nevertheless, it seems ironically true that he better presented such a vision in his Anglican phase, dominated by his 'Alexandrianism'.[32] In the *Grammar*, by contrast, he too much presents real assent to Catholic authority as a kind of isolated starting point and independent foundation.

Here his original evangelical anxiety over the waning authority of the Bible leads him to abandon his sophisticated validation of the cultural primacy of tradition, the visual, the imaginative, and the active, in favour of a substitution of a foundationalist Papalism for a foundationalist Biblicism. As with a now crude conception of science, so with a now crude conception of religion: one begins

[32] See Rowan Williams, "Newman's *Arians* and the Question of Method in Doctrinal History," *Newman after a Hundred Years*, ed. Ian Kerr and Alan G. Hill (Oxford: Oxford University Press, 1990) 263-285.

with a few certainties and from then on it is a matter of a combination of probabilistic inference combined with unquestioning submission to intrinsic authority. It is here telling that Newman assumes the absolute truth of the Newtonian account of motion on grounds of cumulative probable evidence, whereas his suspicion of absolute schemes might have led him to suggest a relativisation of a theory based upon the postulation of an ideal counter-factuality.[33]

Supposedly, recognition of the Roman Church is a matter of real assent: one is overwhelmed by its sheer consistent thereness. Certainly this is linked for Newman with the necessary role of testimony for true affirmation in all of human life and hence also with the way in which assessment of personal character is bound up with the acceptance of truth. Nevertheless, his almost exclusive focus on our inward relation to God and on intimate friendship means that he provides no very convincing account of how the truth of Catholic doctrine is bound up with a new and attractive mode of corporate being. Nor does he manage, in the manner of Augustine, to link our reliance on testimony to our obscure anticipation of the full presence of that which we seek to know. Given these *lacunae* it is not surprising that, in the *Apologia,* Newman offers also a series of probabilistic arguments for Papal authority: that it is likely that God would have established it, that it could not have survived without supernatural aid etc. He even appears to suggest in the *Grammar* that the variation of subjective judgment requires an absolute personified and supernaturally sanctioned barometer. But such a view reduces the instance of variation in subjective judgement to the arbitrary, rather than allowing it to be variously disclosive of the real. At this point Newman's subtle

[33] *An Essay in Aid of a Grammar of Assent*, 345.

philosophical explorations collapse into a simple apologetic alliance of scepticism with fideism.[34]

Some English people might suppose here that Newman is succumbing to a continental Baroque authoritarianism. Yet the irony is that he is rather too inattentive to a third English cultural bias that complements the literary and the scientific. This is the *politicisation* of religion consequent on the Reformation, which, while it positively sustained the sense of the Church as a real society, also tended to subordinate the entirety of religion and theology to questions of a regular legal government of spiritual realities: one sees this in Hooker, in Butler, and in F. D. Maurice. In Butler it takes its most debased form of discernment of supposed analogies between the system of nature on the one hand and the system of religion on the other. Nature is seen as on the whole rewarding virtue and punishing vice, while the necessary sufferings of some for the benefit of others — clearly on the model of political economy — is seen as parallel to the Christian doctrine of vicarious atonement.[35] Despite his disparagement of the British obsession with an abstract and general doctrine of providence, Newman at the end of the *Grammar* endorses this parallel in a way that aligns

[34] *An Essay in Aid of a Grammar of Assent*, 324, 328, 336, and 344-345. At p. 345 Newman *does* speak of Christianity's elevation of women, protection of the poor, destruction of slavery, encouragement of culture. But he needed to give a more elaborated account of these themes in terms of their links with the nature of the Church as the true society and the Christian vision of God and his relation to the Creator. His follower, W. G. Ward, for all his ultramontanism, was much stronger at this point; J. H. Newman, *Apologia pro Vita sua*, ed. Ian Kerr (London: Penguin, 1994).

[35] *An Essay in Aid of a Grammar of Assent*, 316: "I will but add, that, since all human suffering is in its last resolution the punishment of sin, and punishment implies a Judge and a rule of justice, he who undergoes the punishment of another in his stead may be said in a certain sense to satisfy the claims of justice towards that other in his own person" J. H. Butler, *The Analogy of Religion* (London: Routledge, 1885) Part II, Chap. V, pp. 184-204.

him with his pro-capitalist market evangelical contemporaries rather than with those High-Church Anglicans who stressed the priority of incarnation over atonement and concomitantly the need for a social epiphany in the present that did not sacrifice some human beings to others, nor the present to the future.[36]

Newman's Catholic understanding of salvation might seem radically to distance him from the evangelical supporters of political liberalism. Yet, to the contrary, his Tridentine tendency to see justification as finally a matter of individual merit independently responsive to grace, only perfects the idea that vicarious suffering is finally educative for the individual who receives its benefits but must responsibly claim them on behalf of his own self-directed destiny.[37]

So if, in the end, Newman discovers that the real location of spiritual government lies on the continent and in the shape of the Catholic Church, he has made this discovery in terms of an all too English projection which after all does not consistently break with Lockean empiricism nor with a necessarily related Lockean liberalism.[38] In the face of radical uncertainty and the arbitrariness of individual wills, the individual must be directly confronted with an unquestionable authority which is at once an undeniable fact and also something to be accepted on the grounds of probabilistic reasoning.

[36] Boyd Hilton, *The Age of Atonement: The Influence of Evangelicalism on Social and Economic Thought 1795-1865* (Oxford: Oxford University Press, 1988). This is a too little known book, whose new relevance to our own time is obvious.

[37] J. H. Newman, *Lectures on the Doctrine of Justification* (London: Rivingtons, 1874). And see David Nicholls astute assessment in Kerr and Nicholls (eds.), *John Henry Newman*.

[38] See Terence Kenny, *The Political Thought of John Henry Newman* (London: Longmans, 1957).

Was Newman therefore simply overwhelmed by his own inherited habits of mind, combined with a fear of an irreversible decline of Christianity? To a degree one must answer yes. But more profoundly, one can conclude that he did not sustain and extend his remarkable adumbration of a radical empiricism because he did not sufficiently realise (unlike, by contrast, Coleridge) that such a view requires an elaboration of its implicit metaphysical assumptions. Thus at the heart of Newman's refusal of algebraicization lies the claim that the mind, not logical processes, concepts or words is the real seat of comprehension. This then allows him to say that the mind may rationally decide or judge something in an ineffable way that cannot be fully explicated, without thereby lapsing into arbitrariness or unreason. But such a view assumes that intelligence and the soul are ontological realities which are the prime sites of the truth of Being and hence in some way intrinsically linked to Being as such. Aristotle, Plotinus and Proclus provided, in differing ways, such accounts of the soul and its relation to reality, and Coleridge had known that in insisting on the primacy of the imagination and of concrete apprehension he was ultimately indebted to the Proclean tradition.[39] Newman, by contrast, was still more of a philosophical amateur. This is shown most noticeably at the start of the chapter on the illative sense. Here he refuses after all to endorse the idea that a certainty in excess of evidence and inference concerns 'intuition' or something like a recognition of 'intellectual forms', and insists that he is concerned only with the practical operation of assent, not with its metaphysical possibility. Yet without some account of the latter, there is no reason why we should not account for our mental operation in terms of naturalistic vagaries.

[39] See Jean Trouillard, *La Mystagogie de Proclus* (Paris: "Les Belles Lettres", 1982) 44-53.

Newman, as his correspondence reveals, remained troubled by the lack of a 'test' to distinguish a commitment to the vivid yet illusory from the vividness of truth. Nicholas Lash incisively comments here that it is just as well that Newman never devised such tests, for this would obscure Newman's profounder point, that, to cite Lash, 'such security… is, in the last analysis, received as a gift'.[40] A gift, in its surprising rightness and acceptability, has to be its own guarantee, and if Newman says that only mind as mind, beyond method, techniques and criteria can recognize the truth, then this is tantamount to saying that it is, precisely and literally, the faculty for receiving and recognizing spiritual gifts. Truth as gift is its own warrant; it must be self-authenticating. But if it is received by mind as that which is properly at home in mind and yet also as something that derives at times from non-cognitive and non-reflective being, then there must be some common medium between this non-cognitive being on the one hand, and mind on the other, through which truth can be transferred and sustained.

Newman himself suggests as much in his concept of 'aspects' which may be both real and notional and are thereby transferable from things to mind. But does he not sometimes say that such aspects are 'intuited', and should one not think of aspects as being qualities of intelligible forms? Without such a scholastic notion, how can the concrete thing be any more than a random bundle of disparate elements? By failing to endorse the intuition of intellectual form, Newman becomes himself prey to the suspicion that real assent is but an animal and arbitrary habit which requires an authoritarian regulation if anarchy is not to ensue. In the end therefore, his thought is inconsistently poised between a radical empiricism that could re-invigorate ancient realism and an all too

[40] Nicholas Lash, "Introduction" to *An Essay in Aid of a Grammar of Assent*, 19.

modern positivism, not without kinship with the positivism of those exceedingly modern Catholic traditionalists Joseph de Maistre, Donoso Cortes and Carl Schmitt.

The irony is that he embraced too much of an inauthentically Catholic post-Tridentine Catholicism, just because he remained too influenced by the modernising currents of British empiricism, and, just like Edward Pusey (as Peter Nockles has rightly argued) also insufficiently attentive to the deeper currents of Anglican thought — one thinks of Ralph Cudworth, the Caroline divines, the non-jurors, the Aberdeen Circle, Robert Louth, John Wesley, George Berkeley, and Coleridge himself — who retained links to a pre-Tridentine Catholicism, while also elaborating critiques of a reductive empiricism linked to that peculiarly British blend of the empirical and the Platonic.[41]

But at his best, Newman was also a most remarkable heir of this more authentic Britishness and *beyond* his forebears rightly saw that it could only attain its fulfilment by returning to its European and Catholic roots.

[41] Peter B. Nockles: *The Oxford Movement in Context* (Cambridge: Cambridge University Press, 1994). In his earlier works on Arianism however, Newman had echoed Cudworth against his 18th C. German commentator Mosheim, implicitly defending the former's view that the spirit of mystical pagan philosophy was by no means entirely antagonistic to Christian theology and also Cudworth's prodigious insight that there is in Plato himself a 'Trinity' closer to the that of the Christian Trinity than the subordinationist triads of the Neo-Platonists. Even though, as Rowan Williams says, this led Newman into the 'opposite error' to that of Mosheim — namely blaming Antioch not Alexandria for Arianism — this does not — as Williams also rightly indicates — at all negate the importance of the perspectives which Newman derived from Cudworth. See "Newman's *Arians* and the Question of Method in Doctrinal History," and J. H. Newman, *The Arians of the Fourth Century* (London, 1883) 44

"THE WINTER OF MY DESOLATION" CONSCIENCE AND THE CONTRADICTIONS OF ATHEISM ACCORDING TO JOHN HENRY NEWMAN

Michael J. BUCKLEY, S.J.

Among the historic advances bringing into realization both the promise and the menace of the nineteenth century, Friedrich Nietzsche and John Henry Newman identified a momentous reversal in religious convictions.[1] Something absolutely fundamental was dying. Both discerned an irretrievable decline in the religious confidence and doctrinal commitments that had for fifteen hundred years specified the character of Christian Europe and whose dissolution constituted now for the individual believer and for the religious culture of the West a defiant, even insurmountable crisis. Both recognized that this disintegration bespoke not another episodic appearance of chronic religious alienation nor the momentary revivification of an ancient disbelief. A profound cultural reversal, unique in Christian history, was claiming the nations of Europe. It was a revolution, gathering continual increase in its distinguished adherents as an educated skepticism about creed and denominational allegiances almost imperceptibly matured into an open and outspoken dismissal of any reality of God.[2] Nietzsche and Newman

[1] "From the time that I began to occupy my mind with theological subjects I have been troubled at the prospect, which I considered to lie before us, of an intellectual movement against religion, so special as to have a claim upon the attention of all educated Christians." John Henry Newman, "On Final Causes," as in *The Theological Papers of John Henry Newman on Faith and Certainty*, ed. J. Derek Holmes (Oxford: Clarendon Press, 1976) 156.

foresaw that this denial was to break upon the subsequent century and eventually tell upon all the portions of what had once been Christendom.

For Nietzsche, this was the greatest event in human history, the death of God — the coming to acceptance that "the belief in the Christian god has become unbelievable."[3] For Newman, this dark foreshadowing of an even darker future formed "the winter of my desolation," as the world moved with increasing momentum toward the repudiation of what he held most tenaciously within it: "And in these latter days, in like manner, outside the Catholic Church things are tending, — with far greater rapidity than in that old time from the circumstance of the age, — to atheism in one shape or another. What a scene, what a prospect, does the whole of Europe present at this day! and not only Europe, but every government and every civilization through the world, which is under the influence of the European mind!"[4] It was, he judged, an unprecedented disruption: "that the writers and thinkers of the day do not even believe there is a God... Christianity has never yet had experience of a world simply irreligious.[5]

[2] Newman to Mother Mary Imelda Poole (December 27, 1872): "I think either Antichrist is coming, or that a great and purifying trial, which may last centuries, is coming on the Church. The course of God's Providence is as glorious as it is awful. I hear, as you do, dreadful accounts of the fallings away among our own people, I mean English people. A lady writes me word this morning, 'It is quite the exception now to meet in Society a believer'." *The Letters and Diaries of John Henry Newman*, ed. Stephen Dessain, *et al.*, [Vols. 1-6 (Oxford: Clarendon Press, 1978-1984) 11-22; (London: Nelson, 1961-1972) 23-31; (Oxford: Clarendon Press, 1973-1977)] 26: 222. Hereafter referred to as *L.D.*.

[3] Friedrich Nietzsche, *The Gay Science*, 3: #125; 5: #343, trans. with commentary by Walter Kaufmann (New York: Vintage, 1974) 183-184, p. 279.

[4] John Henry Cardinal Newman, *Apologia Pro Vita Sua: Being a History of His Religious Opinions*, ed. Martin J. Svaglic (Oxford: Clarendon Press, 1967) 218-219. Hereafter referred to as *Apo.*

[5] John Henry Cardinal Newman, "The Infidelity of the Future" (Sermon at the opening of St. Bernard's Seminary, Olton, 2 October 1873), *Catholic Sermons of Cardinal Newman* (London: Burns and Oates, 1957) 123.

It was difficult even to speak with great precision about what was taking place. Univocal terms with which to name this cresting disbelief were hard to come by. "Atheism" had for centuries denoted immorality, in a manner that one today might speak of a person as "godless." So in 1846, George Jacob Holyoake, the last man tried and imprisoned in England for the blasphemy that was atheism, coined the term "secularist" indicating an allegiance to a code of duty pertaining to this life, founded on considerations purely human, and intended mainly for those who find theology indefinite or inadequate, unreliable or unbelievable."[6] In 1869, some twenty-five years later, Thomas Huxley invented and subsequently presented to the Metaphysical Society "agnostic" to distinguish his scepticism from dogmatic denial or affirmation.[7] Newman's studies

[6] George Jacob Holyoake, *English Secularism, A Confession of Belief* (Chicago, IL: Open Court, 1896) 35. The description continued: "Its essential principles are three:

1. The improvement of this life by *material* means.
2. That science is the available Providence of man.
3. That it is good to do good. Whether there be other good or not, the good of the present life is good, and it is good to seek that good."

[7] Thomas Henry Huxley, "Agnosticism," as in *Science and Christian Tradition*, Collected Essays, 5 (London: Macmillan and Co., 1893-1894) 5: 237-239; (reprinted Greenwood Publishing Group, May 31, 1970). Of the origin of the name "agnostic" to cover this attitude, Huxley gave the following account:

"When I reached intellectual maturity and began to ask myself whether I was an atheist, a theist, or a pantheist; a materialist or an idealist; a Christian or a freethinker; I found that the more I learned and reflected, the less ready was the answer;... The one thing in which most of these good people were agreed was the one thing in which I differed from them. They were quite sure they had attained a certain 'gnosis', — had, more or less successfully, solved the problem of existence; while I was quite sure that I had not, and had a pretty strong conviction that the problem was insoluble..."

"This was my situation when I had the good fortune to find a place among the members of that remarkable confraternity of antagonists, long since deceased, but of green and pious memory, the Metaphysical Society. Every variety of philosophical and theological opinion was represented there, and expressed itself with

of the early Church had recorded how ambiguously had run his own chosen term, "atheism." Neither the meaning of the term nor its applications were precisely fixed, and the range of its indeterminacy contributed to the confusion of the religious controversies and passions in which it was enlisted.

For the ancient pagans, as Newman noted, "atheists" were those who denied polytheism; for the Christians, those who affirmed it. So Julian the Apostate charged that Christians preferred "atheism to godliness." Indeed, "atheism" was "a popular imputation upon Christians as it had been before on philosophers and poets, some of whom better deserved it."[8] As if in rebuttal, Christians charged that atheism belongs with the Gentiles who did not know the true God. Atheism — "godlessness" — came to denote, confusedly in the polemic exchanges, either those disowning or denying God, or those disowned by God, or those denying the gods of popular

entire openness; most of my colleagues were *-ists* of one sort or another; and, however kind and friendly they might be, I, the man without a rag of a label to cover himself with, could not fail to have some of the uneasy feelings which must have beset the historical fox when, after leaving the trap in which his tail remained, he presented himself to his normally elongated companions. So I took thought, and invented what I conceived to be the appropriate title of 'agnostic'. It came into my head as suggestively antithetic to the 'gnostic' of Church history, who professed to know so much about the very things of which I was ignorant; and I took the earliest opportunity of parading it at our Society, to show that I, too, had a tail, like the other foxes. To my great satisfaction, the term took." R. H. Hutton in the New English Dictionary, but in a slightly differing account confirms Huxley's authorship. Hutton wrote that the word "was suggested by Huxley at a meeting held previous to the formation of the now defunct Metaphysical Society at Mr. Knowles's house on Clapham Common in 1869, in my hearing." See Bill Young, "The Origin of the Word *Agnostic*," *The Secular Web* (June 2004).

http://www.infidels.org/library/modern/reason/agnosticism/agnostic.html.

Essays (London: Macmillan and Co., 1893-1894, in *Collected Essays*, 5: 237-239.

[8] John Henry Cardinal Newman, *Select Treatises of Saint Athanasius*, Volume 2, "Being an Appendix of Illustrations" (London: Pickering and Co., [2]1881) 2: 357.

religion their appropriate worship, or those denying Jesus Christ as God.

But by the fourth century, Athanasius could apply the term not simply to pagans, but to a fellow, albeit heretical, Christian, claiming of Arius that "he is on all sides recognized as godless (atheist,) Arius," as the same distinguished Alexandrian Father of the Church had similarly characterized Asterius and Valentinus. Eustathius had marked the Arians in general as "anthropous atheious," and Arius himself complained that the Patriarch Alexander had driven him and his followers from Alexandria as if they were atheists.[9] The word ranged in and out of inter-Christian controversies. Newman registered all of this ambiguity, recalling in a letter to John Allen that in the previous century even the great Joseph Butler had been accused of "making atheists" by his mode of argumentation, while Newman associated David Hume with Epicurus as a "teacher of atheism."[10] For Newman himself, however, "atheism" seems to mean any of the forms in which one effectively asserts that "there is no God," and he saw very little difference between such an assertion and the proposition that "nothing definite can be known about Him."[11]

Part One: The Problem

Newman experienced the problem set by this growing atheism not as a personal temptation, but as a searching contradiction. For the existence of God, he stated repeatedly, was as certain to him as was his own existence.[12] "If I am asked why I believe in a God, I answer that it is because I believe in myself, for I feel it impossible

[9] Newman, *Select Treatises of Saint Athanasius*, 2: 354.

[10] Newman to John Allen (January 8, 1846), *L.D.*, 11:85-86. See also *The Idea of a University*, ed. I. T. Ker (Oxford: Clarendon Press, 1976) 49-50. Hereafter referred to as *Idea*.

[11] *Idea*, 49.

to believe in my own existence (and of that fact I am quite sure) without believing also in the existence of Him, who lives as a Personal, All-seeing, All-judging Being in *my conscience*."[13] Yet there was an epistemological paradox admittedly present within this conviction: "Of all points of faith, the being of a God, is to my own apprehension, encompassed with most difficulty, and yet borne in upon our minds with the most power."[14] "Most difficulty… Most power." This incongruity proved the experiential soil for the profound religious antinomies in the world of the nineteenth century.

For in the culture around him, what Newman called "the world of men," he experienced the starkest contravention of his primordial conviction: "The world seems simply to give the lie to that great truth, of which my whole being is so full."[15] This opposition did not induce the suspension or the destruction of belief, but it did evoke a profound confusion — the kind of dislodging confusion, as he noted, that one would feel before a world become incoherent, as if the external world had denied Newman's own existence or as if one had glanced into a mirror and seen no reflection of his face. A mirror? Because the world, which should reflect its Creator, instead denied the existence of God, as Newman found, in its "pervading idolatries, the corruptions, the dreary hopeless irreligion, that condition of the whole race, so fearfully yet exactly described in the Apostle's words, 'having no hope and without God in the world'."[16]

This contradiction constituted the "profound mystery, which is absolutely beyond human solution." Atheism for Newman was not

[12] *Apo.*, 216.

[13] *Apo.*, 180 (italics added).

[14] *Apo.*, 215.

[15] *Apo.*, 216.

[16] *Apo.*, 217. Newman is citing *Ephesians* 2:12.

a warring of diverse arguments or even divergent positions within a religious controversy, conflicts into which he readily entered and in which he felt at home.[17] It exceeded anything that could be called either schism or heresy. It embodied the most absolute contrariety between foundational religious claims: between the waning of belief and the voice of conscience in which Newman found the reality of God as given inescapably. It was a world not so much in disagreement as deeply inconsequent.

To understand something of the telling strength of this antinomy, one must recall that Newman insisted upon the indefectibility of human certitude. Assent is a judgment that such-and-such is the case. Certitude is reflex or complex assent, the "consciousness of knowing, as expressed in the phrase, 'I know that I know'." Certitude is thus "an assent to an assent, what is commonly called a conviction." Now Newman contended, that judicious women and men are in their convictions only infrequently in error: "Among fairly prudent and circumspect men, there are far fewer instances of false certitude than at first sight might be supposed. Men are often doubtful about propositions which are really true; they are not commonly certain of such as are simply false. What they judge to be a certainty is in matter of fact for the most part a truth."[18] This assertion was fundamental to the entire enterprise of *A Grammar of Assent*, that the way that human beings de facto do reason is the way they should reason, that there is a connaturality between the mind and reality such that in general either human convictions about truth are correct or else one will not be able to rest in them. It was of critical importance to register "what Certitude is, not simply as it must be, but in our actual experience of it."[19]

[17] *Apo.*, 217.

[18] John Henry Newman, *An Essay in Aid of a Grammar of Assent*, ed. Ian Ker (Oxford: Clarendon Press, 1985) 129. Hereafter referred to as *G.A.*

[19] *G.A.*, 133.

And this experience indicates three conditions that assent become certitude: [1] that it follows on investigation and proof, [2] that it is accompanied by a specific sense of intellectual satisfaction, [3] that it is irreversible. "If the assent is made without rational grounds, it is a rash judgment, a fancy, or a prejudice; if without the sense of finality, it is scarcely more than an inference; if without permanence, it is a mere conviction."[20] But certitude is the assent to an assent, and one of its characteristics is its stability.

The difference between simple assent and conviction told in the character of religious belief: certitude was indefectible not only in its truth but in its lasting, unshakeable character. While "assents may and do change; certitudes endure. This is why religion demands more than an assent to its truth; it requires a certitude, or at least an assent which is convertible into certitude on demand. Without certitude in religious faith there may be much decency of profession and of observance, but there can be no habit of prayer, no directness of devotion, no intercourse with the unseen, no generosity of self-sacrifice. Certitude then is essential to the Christian."[21] At a minimum authentic religious belief was the stuff of certitude.

It is true that great numbers of human beings pass through life without either serious doubt or certitude, even "on the most important proposition that can occupy their minds." Their judgments are only those of simple assent, the beliefs and opinions by which human beings live, which usually forms the fabric of the ordinary, the day-by-day beliefs and sometimes the texture of their allegiances — human beings who "having very little intellectual training, have never had the temptation to doubt, and never the opportunity to be certain." The faith of the medievals was such, but it possessed what was essential for religious assent, i.e., a material or

[20] *G.A.*, 168.
[21] *G.A.*, 144.

interpretative certitude. Their religious belief had only to be questioned in order to develop into that explicit reflex assent that could be called certitude. One might term all authentic religious belief a latent certitude.[22]

How, then, could religious faith fail in Europe — fail not in this or that instance, nor simply with the superficial and thoughtless, but fail with serious and reflective thinkers such as George Eliot, Matthew Arnold, and Newman's great friend William Froude, fail from group to group, even from national culture to national culture, and that religious belief fail which was as evident to Newman as his own existence? Does one deny that religious belief with its interpretative certitude had been present in the centuries past? Certainly Newman did not. Yet all over Europe, one saw religious belief decline through the centuries that formed modernity and in so many instances finally fail. This failure constituted for Newman the scandal of the nineteenth century. How was it possible that propositions accepted for thousands of years, acts of assent to religious truth which were at least material certitudes, convictions for which men and women went to their deaths through the centuries, religious knowledge as well as religious belief that were so much of the texture of the culture — how could all of this fail, and fail so pervasively and with such rapidity as these shadows lengthened over Europe? How was it possible that the intellect, as a matter of fact, could not keep the religious truth it had for centuries preserved? The question, again, is not just Newman's. Nietzsche's madman asked the same question: "How did we do this? How could we drink up the sea? Who gave us the sponge to wipe away the entire horizon?"[23] This for Newman constitutes the contradiction that demanded resolution.

[22] *G.A.*,138-139.

[23] Nietzsche, *The Gay Science* 3: #125, p. 181.

Part Two: The Ambiguity of Intellect

Newman located the rising destruction of religious belief proximately in the corruption of reason, but this diagnosis mirrored in its complexity the very oppositions it was invoked to explain.

No one celebrated the human intellect more wisely and more lyrically than Newman. "Right reason" could come to the knowledge that God exists, that the soul is immortal, that future retribution awaits the evil. Indeed, these are the basic beliefs of "natural religion," and reason even unaided by grace but exercised with integrity could discover them.[24] Knowledge could be its own end and the university has for its purpose neither art nor utility nor even duty, but intellectual culture: "Here it may leave its scholars, and it has done its work when it has done as much as this. It educates the intellect to reason well in all matters, to reach out towards truth, and to grasp it."[25] But in the brilliant promise of intellect lay its liabilities for cancerous self-destruction.

Newman discovered very early in his life that the intellect could corrupt as well as enhance the human spirit. Under the influence of the Oriel Noetics, especially Richard Whately, Newman found himself in 1827 gradually "beginning to prefer intellectual excellence to moral," a realization to which he was awakened by a partial breakdown and the death of his youngest sister, Mary.[26] Right reason could indeed lead one to natural religion. But such reason seems an abstraction before "Reason, considered as a real agent in the world, and as an operative principle in man's nature, with an historical course and with definite results."[27] It takes a very different — a disordered — course; it "considers itself from first

[24] *Apo.*, 218; *G.A.*, 251-263; *Idea*, 157.

[25] *Idea*, 114.

[26] *Apo.*, 26.

[27] *Idea*, 157.

to last independent and supreme; it requires no external authority; it makes a religion for itself."[28] Such was the critically realistic or — if you will —the pessimistic assessment of Newman, a judgment that remained throughout his life. The arrogance of reason obtains when the human intellect charts the divine insistently within the coordinates of its own capacities and experiences, i.e., when it considers itself so naturally and adequately equipped for the knowledge about God that it refuses to admit any disclosures of the divine that transcend these human parameters. This was "rationalism" for Newman, "a certain abuse of Reason; that is, a use of it for purposes for which it never was intended, and is unfitted. To rationalize in matters of Revelation is to make our reason the standard and measure of the doctrines revealed."[29]

Religious rationalism collapsed the distinction between capacities for the human and capacities for the divine. Feuerbach and Freud were advancing a strikingly similar reduction of content of the divine to the human, that the divine was nothing more than the human either writ large or writ paternal and extending this analysis to claim that this was the underlying object in all religious belief, a projection of the human onto an imaginary subject. Newman did not deny that such an event took place, especially in the overextensions of reason. Indeed he saw it as the project of rationalism and the cancerous destruction of all authentic faith.

Accept this, that the mode of the human is to determine the understanding of God, and you have the arrogance, the disorder of intellect. Even if this disordered intellect accepts a religious faith, it does so on its own terms. God is reduced to fit the human

[28] *Idea*, 157.

[29] John Henry Newman, "On the Introduction of Rationalistic Principles into Revealed Religion," Tract 73 as in *Tracts for the Times* (1836), largely reprinted in *Newman the Theologian*, ed. Ian Ker (Notre Dame, IN: University of Notre Dame Press, 1990) 75.

capacities to understand. God is like a human being — only bigger. Here also, the human reason is still liable to the blindness of self-interest, to the deception and energies of the passions, to historical conditioning and unattended motivations — and liable to them in proportion as it considered its own excellence as proof against them.

In considering reason within the concrete history of "fallen man" as well as of salvation, Newman wrote: "I am considering the faculty of reason actually and historically; and in this point of view, I do not think I am wrong in saying that its tendency is towards a simple unbelief in matters of religion. No truth, however sacred, can stand against it, in the long run." He spoke repeatedly of "the all-corroding, all-dissolving scepticism of the intellect in religious inquiries."[30] Rationalism or liberalism — "the anti-dogmatic principle" — was very simply not the appropriate use of reason, but its abuse, its abstraction from the broader contexts of religious life and authority and its employment beyond its orientation and capacity, for the reduction of revealed Mystery to a manageable and obvious set of affirmations. The human mind is made the measure of the reality of God, nothing can be told it which it cannot comprehend and ground for itself, and that which remains obscure and unmastered is discarded. "And this, it is to be feared, is the spirit in which multitudes of us act at the present day."[31]

The effect is inevitable: the pretensions of a finite intellect to an adequacy and an autonomy that is preposterously unwarranted gradually devolve from its initial and rationalistic claims into the ineluctable fate of the rationalist, a bitter and pervasive scepticism. The sceptic is often little more than the deeply disappointed rationalist.

Reason moves most damagingly in this latter direction when it corrodes the human conscience. It is here that Newman finds the

[30] *Apo.*, 218.

[31] Newman, "On the Introduction of Rationalistic Principles into Revealed Religion," 76.

possibilities of atheism. For the *natural* informants or evidence for the existence of God available to all human beings are three: the human conscience, the voice and testimony of humankind, and the system and course of the world.[32] And the greatest of these was conscience.[33] Indeed, were it not for conscience, an assessment of the other two informants, i.e., of the course of the world and the directions of human beings, would have left Newman an atheist or a pantheist or a polytheist.[34] The fundamental natural witness to the reality of God was conscience. It is here above all that one looks for the substantiation of the conviction that God exists.[35] If conscience is corrupted or misunderstood or deadened or neglected, there is nothing that can take its place.

For Newman, the fundamental religious battle is joined in the nineteenth century between conscience and what he called "the ordinary sin of the intellect." For the corruption of conscience is a constant threat in a civilized age, "its besetting sin." Not that one denies conscience, but rather that one transposes or translates it into another, a weaker idiom: "conscience tends to become what is called a moral sense; the command of duty is a sort of taste; sin is not an offence against God, but against human nature."[36]

[32] For a remarkable parallel to this triad, cf. Nietzsche, *The Gay Science*, 3: #357, pp. 304-310.

[33] *G.A.*, 251: "By Religion I mean the knowledge of God, of His Will, and of our duties towards Him; and there are three main channels which Nature furnishes for our acquiring this knowledge, viz. our own minds, the voice of mankind, and the course of the world, that is, of human life and human affairs... And the most authoritative of these three means of knowledge, as being specially our own, is our own mind whose informations give us the rule by which we test, interpret, and correct what is presented to us for belief, whether by the universal testimony of mankind, or by the history of society and of the world."

[34] *Apo.*, 216.

[35] *G.A.*, 72-83.

[36] *Idea*, 165.

So Newman could write to Henry Parry Liddon this short note in which he named both the kind of adversary and the kind of devolution consequent upon the weakening and destruction of conscience: "What you say about Arnold's new book is most painful. But if the generation will give up as superstitious the moral and religious instincts of the mind, not the most logical arguments in behalf of their truth will serve to re-establish them. I have often thought how soon I might get over the sense that murder, as such, is a sin (I am not speaking of the natural horror one has of cruelty — or of murder as in particular cases an injustice) but of murder as such — after I have killed half a dozen persons. I suppose some nurses *(not* farming nurses) have not any great horror at the idea of killing children. And thus the idea of God may go."[37] To understand the emergence of atheism, then, one must understand the religious character of the human conscience and its corruption. For Newman contended that just as the witness the senses make possible the apprehension of the visible world, so the judgment of conscience serves for the existence of God.

Part Three: Conscience

One recognizes conscience intuitively, that is, through the same internal self-appropriation by which the mind comes to awareness of memory, sensation, and reasoning, i.e., as an act of the mind. A distinction of terms is essential here. One has "faith" in what is external, what is other; but one "intuits" what is internal and part of one's consciousness: "I would draw a broad line between what is within us and without us, and apply the word 'faith' to our reliance <certainty> of things without and not within us... Surely there

[37] Newman to H. P. Liddon (March 2, 1873), *L.D.*, 26:268. Newman is referring to Matthew Arnold's *Literature and Dogma: An Essay towards a Better Apprehension of the Bible.*

are things prior to faith. I apply the word 'intuition' to such... Taking the acts of the mind to bits, therefore, knowledge of my existence is the fourth act; though I call all four one complex act of intuition. Here we have real intuition, but I have faith, not intuition, of the external world."[38] One intuits conscience, and one believes in the external fact that conscience delivers — as an object not of intuition but of faith — that is, the existence of God. This external fact is more intimately connected with what is intuited than anything else."[39] The existence of God is an object of faith in one of Newman's peculiar meanings of this word, i.e., the conviction which arises from what is internal [conscience] about an external fact [God] and which is "different in evidence <proof> from every other external fact."[40]

Newman is quite consciously transposing the grounds for demonstrating the existence of God from the external world to the inner, conscious world of the thinking subject. In this, he is following the current of fundamental thinking set in motion by John Locke and reaching its crest in the nineteenth century with Kant and Hegel — though Newman was neither a Kantian nor a Hegelian. But he agrees with that whole intellectual world in what Richard McKeon would call its "selection," the fundamental area that must be explored and out of which one would derive the crucial categories and predicates of thought. With Newman's "epistemological selection," one investigates the processes of thought to establish warrants for the assertion about things. Intuition is prior to faith.

Like "experience" for William James, "conscience" for Newman is a double-barreled word. It denotes both the recognition of

[38] John Henry Newman, *The Philosophical Notebook of John Henry Newman*, ed. Edward Sillem, 2 vols. (New York/Louvain: Nauwelaerts, 1969-1970) 2:71. Hereafter referred to as *P.N.*

[39] *P.N.*, 2:43.

[40] *P.N.*, 2:41; see also p. 39.

the moral content of a situation — in the ethical judgment both of what is right and good and what is wrong and evil — or the consequent and experienced imperative, the demand that one should do the right or good and avoid the wrong or evil. "The feeling of conscience" is thus twofold — but the two are indivisibly one. Conscience is, then, "a moral sense and a sense of duty." The first is a judgment of reason and functions as the principle or source of morals or ethics; the second is a "magisterial dictate" and functions as the principle of religion.[41] The first is the rule of right conduct; the second is the summons to and the sanction of right conduct. Newman believed that this second contained the primary and most authoritative aspect of conscience as well as bore the ordinary sense of the word. For "half the world would be puzzled to know what was meant by the moral sense [the first use of the term]; but every one knows what is meant by a good or bad conscience."[42]

Conscience as dictate was experienced metaphorically as "a voice, or the echo of a voice, imperative and constraining, like no other dictate in the whole of our experience."[43] The experience of this dictate comprises two moments: antecedent to choice, in its sense of obligation that such and such is to be done or avoided; subsequent to choice, in the "sanction to that testimony [of conscience] conveyed in the feelings which attend on right or wrong conduct."[44] Newman's argument "from conscience" for the existence of God comprises both of these moments in the recognition of obligation, i.e., of what is to be done or should have been done, and also the emotions or feelings that it elicits. He argues that in the unsurpassable and absolute character of the command, one experiences

[41] *G.A.*, 73, 76; *P.N.*, 2:47.
[42] *G.A.*, 74.
[43] *G.A.*, 74-75.
[44] *G.A.*, 74.

the sovereign moral government of our lives *quo majus nihil*; in the emotions that attend the command — whether fulfilled or dismissed — one experiences that this government is personal, i.e., it is the government by a person. Let us consider each of these.

The phenomena or intimations of conscience are the experiences of moral obligation or responsibility: "You should do this; you should omit that." Human perception identifies these intimations of conscience as the reverberations of an admonition in some way other than the subject, i.e., in these dictates, conscience is registering the commanding — even sovereign — direction given by another. One is not simply identifiable with his or her conscience. Neither did one create or excite this sense of obligation — any more than one created or excited the experience of an external world. One found it — or, if you prefer, one was found by it. Conscience recognizes something or someone that is other. "What I am insisting on here," wrote Newman, "is this: that it [conscience] *commands*; that it praises, <it> blames, it threatens, it implies a future, & it witnesses of the unseen. *It is more than a man's own self.* The man himself has not power over it, or only with extreme difficulty; he did not make it, he cannot destroy it. He may silence it in particular cases or directions; he may distort its enunciations; but he cannot, or it is quite the exception if he can, he cannot emancipate himself from it. He can disobey it; he [-can] <may> refuse to use it; but it remains. This is Conscience."[45] It is irreducibly other.

Conscience is also irreducibly morally and religiously supreme. One recognizes — note: recognizes without demonstration or proof — that the claim of conscience is superior to every other claim in one's life. It must be followed no matter what the opposition. It is in this sense absolute — as opposed to hypothetically or conditionally

[45] *P.N.*, 2:53.

necessary. It is not another precept in the universe or in consciousness, but supreme over all. Human beings recognize in conscience a moral imperative that should rule over all of their other choices and actions. Thus, conscience in its dictates is the supreme governor.

It is also pervasive. It is present in every option a human being confronts and in every choice a human being makes: to permit, to forbid, to command, to urge. And if conscience is both sovereign and pervasive, then the source of conscience must be in this way sovereign and pervasive. But is its source personal; is it of a person?

In his University Sermon of 1830, Newman seems to have contended that a natural religion founded on conscience could reveal "no points of his [God's] personal character.[46] But he came to perceive that it is the instinct of the human mind to recognize in the data or commands of conscience "an external Master" as it is the instinct of the mind, indeed, "of brute nature" to recognize in the data of sense perception an external world.[47] And this instinctive perception of the personal in the imperatives of conscience seemed to him to be expressed most clearly in the emotions that surrounded the dictates of conscience.

Before a choice is made, one feels the sense of responsibility or obligation for the choice that is to be made; after choice, one feels the sense of satisfaction or shame. "Responsibility" — to whom? "Shame" — before whom? An experience of responsibility or fear or shame implies "that there is One to whom we are responsible,

[46] John Henry Newman, *University Sermons: Fifteen Sermons Preached Before the University of Oxford, 1826-1843*, introd. D. M. MacKinnon and J. D. Holmes (reprinted from the third edition, London: SPCK, 1970) 2:22-23. See the remarks of Ian Ker in *G.A.*, 359 (n. 73) and of Edward Sillem in *P.N.*, 2:31 (n. 2).

[47] *G.A.*, 76; see also pp. 71-72.

before whom we are ashamed, whose claims upon us we fear."[48] One does not feel shame before a stone or a horse or a dog; one feels no remorse even about breaking a merely human precept. When one has violated the claims of conscience in a serious matter, however, there is nothing visible necessarily to which we feel this sense of unalloyed responsibility or before which we feel shame and fear, no one or no thing visible whose claims we, through these emotions, recognize as definitive.[49]

Conscience in this manner is like no other experience that human beings undergo, and its reference to the personal other is embodied concretely in this manifold range of spontaneous human emotions: "reverence and awe, hope and fear, especially fear, a feeling which is foreign for the most part, not only to Taste, but even to the Moral Sense, except in consequence of accidental associations."[50] In these emotions, one recognizes that the Other, the source of the imperative, has already been accepted as personal. One may be mortified if his actions have been ugly, but he feels responsible and guilty if his actions have been immoral.

> These various perturbations of mind which are characteristic of a bad conscience, and may be very considerable, — self-reproach, poignant shame, haunting remorse, chill dismay at the prospect of the future, — and their contraries, when the conscience is good, as real though less forcible, self-approval, inward peace, lightness of heart, and the like, — these emotions constitute *a specific difference* between conscience and our other intellectual senses, — common sense, good sense, sense of expedience, taste, sense of honor, and the like, — as indeed they would also constitute between conscience and the moral sense, supposing these two were not aspects of one and the same feeling, exercised upon one and the same subject-matter.[51]

[48] *G.A.*, 76.

[49] *G.A.*, 76.

[50] *G.A.*, 75.

[51] *G.A.*, 75 (italics added).

These emotions are such as to indicate that their "exciting cause," to which they refer, must be personal.

Newman is not saying that conscience or the imperatives of conscience are God — they remain finite and human and fallible — but he is saying that these are the shadow and the evidence of God, the phenomena or the impressions or the experience from which the intellect instinctively moves to the assertion of God.[52] They are the created effect of God, the finite participation in and experience of the sovereignty of God. One has the experience in this command of an undeniable absolute. While conscience is not God, it is, nevertheless, repeatedly named "an echo of God." For finite as it is, it makes a claim upon our lives that is supreme and unsurpassable and omnipresent.

Thus in summary for Newman, both the superiority and pervasiveness of the claim of conscience over every other claim disclose the matchless supremacy of this Other to which conscience points, while the attendant emotions evoked by conscience disclose that this Other is already and implicitly recognized as personal.

How is Newman arguing here? Is he saying that we feel obligation and consequently we imply that there must be an all powerful source? Is Newman's God still the God of inference, but now the evidence from which inference moves is the sense of duty? Or is he saying that God is given in the very act of obligation itself? In scholastic terminology, is obligation a *signum quod* of the divine reality or a *signum in quo* — is obligation like smoke from which we infer fire or like a handshake in which we experience friendship?

The answer to this question is not always clear in Newman.[53] But his mind seems to have come down upon the second

[52] *P.N.*, 2:53.

[53] For the difficulty in understanding Newman's position, see Newman to W. G. Ward (November 26, 1859) *L.D.*, 19:247. See also *P.N.*, 2:53.

alternative with his acknowledgement of "instinct," namely, that by a "singularly congenial" movement, an instinct of the mind "recognizes" God in the imperative of conscience in a manner which parallels, for Newman, the "faith" in an external world. The evidence that there are things external to us is the impression the phenomena make upon our senses, "and our warrant for taking these for evidence is our instinctive certitude that they are evidence."[54] It is through instinct that human beings affirm an external world; it is through instinct that they affirm that God is given in their conscience. This instinctual recognition would explain Newman's contention in the *Apologia* that there were "two and only two absolute and luminously self-evident beings, myself and my Creator."[55] "Self-evident?" The word is important. Through intuition, the self is given; to the faith that arises out of the instinctive recognition of conscience, God is given. [56]

In his *Philosophical Notebook*, Newman summarized his argument: "If then our <my> knowledge of our <my> existence is brought ** home to me by my consciousness of thinking, and if

[54] *G.A.*, 71. Similarly, human beings come by instinct to recognize the character of particular authors — a Cicero or a Jerome — from the phenomena of their writings. See *G.A.*, 72.

[55] *Apo.*, 18.

[56] James Collins records that in Newman's private notes, he lists four main reasons for his choice of the proof from conscience, the first of which is indicated here. But Collins adds: "Second, the proof from conscience is not a purely theoretical process and does not stop at a purely abstract truth. Instead, it makes us aware of God at the center of our freedom. It is personal, not only in its point of departure, but also in apprehending God precisely as a personal judge and providential guide. Hence this inference ordinarily yields both a speculative truth and a practical commitment of the finite person to God as a person. It is the source of a moral and religious relationship with God and thus overcomes the deficiencies of the proof from design." See James Collins, *God in Modern Philosophy* (Chicago, IL: Henry Regnery Company, 1959) 362-363, 444 (n. 47). See *P.N.*, 2:67.

thinking includes as one of its modes conscience or the sense of an imperative coercive law, & if such a sense, when [analyzed, i.e. when] reflected on, involves an inchoate recognition of a Divine Being, it follows that such recognition comes close upon my recognition that I am, and is only not so clear an object of perception as is my own existence."[57]And again to W. G. Ward: "Conscience, or the sense of moral obligation on my mind is such, as distinctly to carry with it the sense of an Obliger; or that the *immediate* shape with which it comes to me is, not that of a divine truth, but of a divine command or will. The immediate form need not be the ultimate basis. I have only said that my conscience is to me a proof of a God, just as a shadow is a proof of a substance. The shadow does not depend upon the mere arbitrary *will* of the substance for its shape, but on the *nature of* the substance."[58] Conscience always entails a keen sense of obligation and responsibility. God is given to human experience aboriginally as the whence of obligation and the whither of responsibility.

Newman believed that the argument from conscience was the demonstration available to all of humankind, that it lay at the basis of natural religion. Just as the burden of the *Grammar of Assent* was to assert the justification of the belief of the uneducated, so the argument from conscience extended this justification by making as a principle of religion what was common to all human beings, the unlearned and the learned.[59] And the *Grammar* insisted upon this

[57] *P.N.*, 2:63.

[58] Newman to W. G. Ward (November 26, 1859) *L.D.*, 19: 247.

[59] *G.A.*, 251. It is interesting that Hegel, for vastly different reasons, locates the transition of Spirit into religion in the form of conscience: "Der sich selbst wissende Geist ist in der Religion unmittelbar sein eignes reines *selbstbewußtsein*. Diejenigen Gestalten desselben, die betrachtet worden, — der wahre, der sich entfremdete und der seiner selbst gewisse Geist — machen zusammen ihn in seinem Bewußtsein aus, das seiner Welt gegenüber tretend in ihr sich nicht erkennt. Aber im Gewissen unterwirft er sich wie seine gegenständliche Welt

point: "Our great internal teacher of religion is, as I have said in an earlier part of this Essay, our Conscience. Conscience is a personal guide, and I use it because I must use myself; I am as little able to think by any mind but my own as to breathe with another's lungs. Conscience is nearer to me than any other means of knowledge. And as it is given to me, so also it is given to others; and being carried about by every individual in his own breast, and requiring nothing besides itself, it is thus adapted for the communication to each separately of that knowledge which is most momentous to him individually, — adapted for the use of all classes and conditions of men, for high and low, young and old, men and women, independently of books, of educated reasoning, of physical knowledge or of philosophy."[60] Whatever one says about the manner of the divine self-disclosure through conscience, so concrete, so sharp is this image of God, gained in this manner, that it can elict real assent.

Why is this voice, the voice of conscience an "echo" of the voice of *God*? Because it is so absolute, so sovereign. It is not God, but it participates in the absoluteness of God. It is "the main guide of the soul," governing as sovereign everything a person does, surpassing in its government every other claim, and at the same time pervading an entire life — no time and no place escapes its commands. Sunshine implies a sun, even if unseen; knocking on the door implies the presence of one asking for admittance, so

überhaupt, so auch seine Vorstellung und seine bestimmten Begriffe und ist nun bei sich seiendes Selbstbewußtsein. In diesem hat er für sich, als *Gegenstand vorgestellt*, die Bedeutung, der allgemeine Geist zu sein, der alles Wesen und alle Wirklichkeit in sich enthält; ist aber nicht in der Form freier Wirklichkeit oder der selbständig erscheinenden Natur." Georg Wilhelm Friedrich Hegel, *Phänomenologie des Geistes*; nach dem Texte der Orginalausgabe herausgegeben von Johannes Hoffmeister (Hamburg: Felix Meiner, 1952), #677, pp. 474-475.

60 *G.A.*, 251.

do these commands "necessarily raise our minds to the idea of a Teacher, an unseen Teacher."[61]

[*A Tentative Excursus*: If one wished to ask a metaphysical rather than an epistemological question: How, one might inquire, does conscience relate to the causality of God? How does it come forth from God in a manner so precise that it can serve to lay upon human beings the authority of God? As we have insisted, Newman is rich in metaphors and similes, calling it the "echo of a voice," the "reverberations of an external admonition," "the shadow" of the substance of God; he compares it to the knocking on the door by someone requesting entrance and to the sunshine or light given by the sun. God not only gives conscience its being, but uniquely specifies its nature. It participates in His absolute authority, without being God. Conscience seems a created participation in or expression of God as sovereign good:, sovereign, as supreme moral ruler; good, as that of which every other created good is exemplified. If this is true, then the activity of conscience resembles in its ontological structure the character of contemplation in John of the Cross, i.e., "the overshadowing" of the attributes of God.[62]]

Objection

But isn't Newman simply divinizing the superego [*Über-Ich*] of later Freudian psychoanalytic theory, the agency among the triadic agencies of the mind whose functions are both the supervision and the judging and punishing of human deeds? Freud equates the

[61] John Henry Cardinal Newman, *Sermons Preached on Various Occasions* (new impression, London: Longmans, Green and Co., 1927) 65. See *P.N.*, 2:53 and Newman to Ward (November 26, 1859), *L.D.*, 19:247.

[62] See John of the Cross, "The Living Flame," Stanza 3 with Commentary, as in Kieran Kavanaugh and Otilio Rodrigues, *The Collected Works of Saint John of the Cross* (revised edition, Washington, DC: Institute for Carmelite Studies, 1991) 673ff.

judging feature of superego with conscience, and, can, like Newman, speak of the "voice of conscience."[63] How similar is the doctrine of Newman to the superego's influence as detailed by Freud: "I feel an inclination to do something that I think will give me pleasure, but I abandon it on the ground that my conscience does not allow it. Or I have let myself be persuaded by too great an expectation of pleasure into doing something to which the voice of conscience has objected and after the deed my conscience punishes me with distressing reproaches and causes me to feel remorse for the deed."[64] Both Newman and Freud have conscience as dictate. And could not Newman's list of the consequences of a bad conscience be equally at home with the catalogue of emotions assigned to Freud's superego: "self-reproach, poignant shame, haunting remorse, chill dismay at the prospect of the future?"[65] Further, the personal is present in these exercises of the superego, maintains Freud, because the superego originates in the internalization by the child of the parental superego or ego-ideal, and it "observes, directs and threatens the ego in exactly the same way as earlier the parents did with the child."[66] Indeed Freud sees the superego as the mechanism that binds aggression, that shapes the renunciation of the outward expression of aggression and turns it inwardly into guilt. "In Freud's oedipal perspective, the renunciation of the instincts (sex and aggression) is motivated by castration anxiety (fear)" that shapes the characterizes the superego.[67]

63 Sigmund Freud, *New Introductory Lectures on Psycho-analysis*, trans. and ed. James Strachey (New York: W. W. Norton and Co., 1964) 74-75.

64 Freud, *New Introductory Lectures*, 74-75.

65 *G.A.*, 75.

66 Freud, *New Introductory Lectures*, 77.

67 I am grateful here to Professor Diane Jonte-Pace of Santa Clara University for these summary comments on the origins of the superego and Freud's own criticism of a superego morality.

There is no time adequate here to give this objection the careful examination it deserves, but a number of characteristics might offer some indications that this objection does not pose a definitive end to Newman's finding the presence of God within the dictates of conscience. Perhaps one could distinguish Newman's conscience and Freud's super-ego in terms of four parameters: conscious awareness, rationality, freedom, and dominant emotions. Let us look briefly at each.

One must first recognize, that the Freudian superego or ego-ideal was itself — as conditioning can often be — primarily "unconscious and inaccessible to the ego."[68] This means more than simply producing unconscious effects. It means, as Freud wrote in *The New Introductory Lectures to Psycho-Analysis,* that "large portions of the ego and super-ego can remain unconscious and are normally unconscious. That is to say, the individual knows nothing of their contents and it requires an expenditure of effort to make them conscious."[69] In its unconscious state, Gregory Zilboorg emphasizes, Freud's superego is the "precipitate of all the demands and commands and particularly of the taboos connected with what is known as 'the oedipus complex'."[70] In contrast, Newman's imperative of conscience is emphatic in its consciousness, following as

[68] Sigmund Freud, *The Ego and the Id,* trans. Joan Riviere, ed. James Strachey (New York: W. W. Norton, 1960) 36.

[69] Freud, *New Introductory Lectures*, 87. "We call a psychical process unconscious whose existence we are obliged to assume — for some such reason as that we infer it from its effects — but of which we know nothing. In that case we have the same relation to it as we have to a psychical *process in* another person, except that it is in fact one of our own. If we want to be still more correct, we shall modify our assertion by saying that we call a process unconscious if we are obliged to assume that it is being activated *at the moment,* though at *the moment* we know nothing about it." *Ibid.*, 88.

[70] Gregory Zilboorg, "Superego and Conscience," *Conscience: Theological and Psychological Perspectives*, ed. C. Ellis Nelson (New York: Newman Press, 1973) 218.

it does in its indivisible unity with the first moment of conscience, the rational judgment between good and evil. This prior moral judgment is — for all of its attendant emotions, Newman underlines — "a judgment of the reason."[71] Indeed, conscience as a moral sense is "an intellectual sentiment."[72]

Reason as such has virtually no role to play in the formation or the agency of the superego. It is more a conditioning or compulsion from without, an introjection especially of the father's authority. Indeed, "Freud usually discusses the superego as oedipal, involving fear of punishment, castration anxiety, and renunciation".[73] But it is brought about and strengthened more generally by the conditioning of parental and societal expectations. One is conditioned to accept certain things and reject others. This stands in contrast with Newman's rational dictate bearing upon that whose goodness or rationality one has consciously and reasonably recognized. When the super-ego develops into a pathological extreme, it resembles in its exaggerations compulsive hand-washings, obsessive actions to which one is driven by a sense of guilt and whose values obtain simply as a displacement of object and an escape from unrecognized guilt. In some contrast, Newman's moral commands are a second moment of conscience, the experience of absolute obligation following upon the moral differentiation of good from evil. Moral judgment and moral imperative are distinct aspects of conscience, but only that; the act that unites them into a unity is conscience, and conscience is indivisible.[74] Newman emphasizes that moral judgment and moral imperative are two aspects "of one and the same feeling, exercized upon one

71 *G.A.*, 73.

72 *G.A.* 5: #1, p. 75.

73 Once more, let me thank Professor Diane Jonte-Pace for this summary articulation of the origin of the superego in the oedipal experience

74 *G.A.*, 73.

and the same subject-matter."[75] Perhaps it is precisely in this indivisibility that the superego and Newman's conscience so strongly and evidently differ. The imperatives of conscience follow upon the rational recognition of good and evil — not upon the uneasy feeling and compulsive susceptibilities evoked from previous conditioning. If the judgment of right and wrong is not of reason, it is not of conscience for Newman. In fact, the moral judgments of conscience and the dictate consequently upon them can sometimes be at loggerheads with compulsive emotions of attraction or repulsion generated by conditioning. Conscience can even contradict the superego.

In the superego, it is the historical past that dominates, and the precepts and prohibitions about the present or the future come out of the earliest object choices desired by the id.[76] These dictates bring as prohibitions into the present the parental ego-ideals and the guilt and threat one has undergone repeatedly in the past when these ideals were threatened or not realized. Newman's conscience speaks to freedom, to an experience of self-responsibility or self-determination, while the superego speaks to and evokes constraints and past conditioning. The person, moved by conscience to act, feels called, summoned, directed to follow the actions she recognizes as right or good. As she confronts this choice, she will have a radical sense of her own freedom, of her responsibility for what she deliberates about and chooses; indeed, the responsibility for her entire life.

[75] *G.A.*, 75. Newman has placed the contradictory in a contrary to fact sentence.

[76] Freud, *The Ego and the Id*, 31: The origin of the super-ego is "the outcome of two highly important factors, one of a biological and the other of a historical nature: namely, the lengthy duration in man of his childhood helplessness and dependence, and the fact of his Oedipus complex, the repression of which we have shown to be connected with the interruption of libidinal development by the latency period and so with diphasic onset of man's sexual life."

As conscience and the superego are different in the character of their command, so they are different in the emotions they principally evoke. For Newman's conscience, the principal emotion was fear; for Freud's superego, the principal emotion was shame and guilt. In the *Idea of a University,* Newman was at pains to distinguish his sense of conscience and its religious significance from the disgust, humiliation and shame that come over the cultivated, but conditioned mind when it realizes its self-betrayal into vice. "When the mind is simply angry with itself and nothing more, surely the true import of the voice of nature and the depth of its intimations have been forgotten, and a false philosophy has misinterpreted emotions which ought to lead to God. "Fear implies the transgression of a law, and a law implies a lawgiver and judge," but the tendency of "intellectual culture is to swallow up the fear in the self-reproach, and the self-reproach is directed and limited to our mere sense of what is fitting and becoming. Fear carries us out of ourselves, whereas shame may act upon us only within the round of our own thoughts."[77] John Glaser has, consequently, pointed out that the characteristic of the superego is its narcissism: the need to be right, correct so that one is approvable, lovable. The shame resulting from the violation of previous conditioning entails the fear of isolation, of being abandoned because one is not lovable. "The thematic center is a sense of one's own value."[78]

One need not deny that conscience in Newman's sense can be and often initially is mingled and confused with the superego — just as true worship and prayer often embody many false and superstitious practices without themselves being superstitious, or as a false prophet can for a time be indistinguishable from a true

[77] *Idea*, 165.

[78] John W. Glaser, "Conscience and Superego: A Key Distinction," *Theological Studies* 32 (1971) 38. The remarks above on the difference between conscience and super-ego are very indebted to Glaser's article.

prophet. Even further, one need not deny that the conditioning that is the superego can command and habituate one to practices that conscience will demand and confirm. But it is obviously of crucial importance to distinguish them. Newman argues that the experience of responsibility and fear are both interpersonal, i.e., that both of these feelings essentially involve another person: "If, as is the case, we feel responsibility, are ashamed, are frightened, at transgressing the voice of conscience, this implies that there is One to whom we are responsible, before whom we are ashamed, whose claims upon us, we fear."[79] Such feelings as moral obligation before duty and fear before transgression "require for their exciting cause an intelligent being." The absolute character of the imperative indicate the sovereign character of this other. So the mind spontaneously recognizes "the phenomena of Conscience, as a dictate, avail to impress the imagination with the picture of a Supreme Governor, a Judge, holy, just, powerful, all-seeing, retributive, and is the creative principle of religion."[80] If conscience, containing both this experience and its recognition, stands as the principle, the source of all religious affirmation, then it becomes critically important for Newman's reading of the rise of atheism. It is important to note that Newman — in contrast with the *quinque viae* of St. Thomas or the solar system with Newton or the contingency of matter with Samuel Clarke or physical design with Paley — offers as the principal evidence for the reality of God an experience that is intrinsically religious. God is given with conscience. Conscience would have to be corrupted in order to corrupt belief in the reality of God. That means that the loss of a sense of God can fundamentally only be moral.

[79] *G.A.*, 76.
[80] *G.A.*, 76.

Part Four: Rejected Alternatives

But what about other sources in nature that would offer warrant or demonstration for the existence of God? Truth to tell, Newman reposed very little credence in the other two natural informants about God, ones commonly cited in the apologetic manuals of his time, and this reserve indicates how much foundational importance he was ascribing to the witness of conscience.

The first of these was that of universal consensus, one embodied in the rites and devotions and practices extant in the history of religions. One must here identify religion in its primitive state, founded on a sense of sin, structured with precepts that reflect this origin, and requiring expiation, reconciliation, and some great change in human conduct. Such religion was the natural, albeit primitive, expression of conscience.[81] Later developments, the religions of civilized times and those of philosophy, are not developments of this primordial religion but its perversion or contradiction, "recognizing a moral sense — ethics — but ignoring conscience." This is but "artificial religion," issuing only out of a development of the human intellect, "a one-sided progress of mind," and a contradiction to the fundamental religious principle, conscience.[82]

The third natural informant, celebrated in the theologies that issued from the mechanics of the previous century and synthesized in such works as Paley's *Natural Theology* lay with the world of nature, the system of the universe, its order and precision. It includes both human life and human affairs. But what actually strikes the mind confronted with the course of nature is not the presence of God, but His absence — the dismay "that His control of this living world is so indirect and His action so obscure. This is the first lesson that we gain from the course of human affairs.

[81] *G.A.*, "Natural Religion," 251-254.
[82] *G.A.*, 254-255.

What strikes the mind so forcibly and so painfully is, his absence, (if I may so speak) from His own world."[83]

It is true, as Edward Sillem notes, that Newman admitted the demonstrative value of arguments from the material universe, but "he held, that if these arguments are not regarded as *corollaries* to the argument from conscience, they are of no religious value."[84] Before the world of nature alone, one confronts not the voice of God as in conscience, but the silence of God. "It is a silence that speaks. It is as if an other had got possession of His work."[85] For in this world of system and pattern, God does not appear and a thousand "why's" come out of human experience with nature: Why does God not give us more immediate knowledge of His reality? Why does He allow events to move in their observed way without divine order? Why is He not more forthcoming about Himself, His will, His providence? God does not appear. "On the contrary, He is specially 'a Hidden God;' and with our *best* efforts we can only glean from the surface of the world some faint and fragmentary views of Him."[86]

Only human conscience can give answers to the questions posed by nature, not nature itself. Before this hiddenness of God in nature and in the course of human events, Newman saw only two alternatives: either God did not exist or God has disowned His creation. For Newman, it was a "great question whether atheism is not as philosophically consistent with the phenomena of the physical world, taken by themselves, as the doctrine of a creative and governing Power." The religious question is whether physical phenomena teach human beings or remind human beings of the

[83] *G.A.*, 255-256.

[84] *P.N.*, 2:32 (n. 6). Sillem lists the various places in Newman's writing where one can find substantiation for this claim.

[85] *G.A.*, 256.

[86] *G.A.*, 256.

reality of God. If they do not, the lack lies with the dispositions of the person, with his or her failure to bring to bear those moral principles by which these data may be interpreted religiously.[87] The religious interpretation must be made to tell in the theological assessment of nature because "I believe that the study of Nature, when religious feeling is away, leads the mind, rightly or wrongly, to acquiesce in the atheistic theory, as the simplest and easiest."[88] Even if one is successful in inferring from the data of the physical sciences the existence of divine power and divine skill, none of them can teach God as Moral Governor: "The essence of Religion is the idea of a Moral Governor and a particular Providence; now let me ask, is the doctrine of moral governance and a particular providence conveyed to us through the physical sciences at all?"[89] This gave the consistent direction to his apologetics: "For myself, as my writings show, I have never based the belief in a God on any argument from merely external nature, but simply as implied in the fact and deducible from the existence of conscience, nor do I see any difficulty in the notion of the existence of a being endued with reason (at least in its lower degrees) yet without a conscience." Indeed, Newman would go further and make conscience the condition for the possibility of belief: "*Because* he had no conscience, he would have no idea of a God."[90]

This reservation ran contrary to the physico-theologies of the time, i.e., to the argument from Newton's universe and Paley's

[87] John Henry Newman, "Faith and Reason, Contrasted as Habits of Mind," in *Fifteen Sermons Preached Before the University of Oxford* (London: Longmans, Green, and Co., 1909) 194.

[88] John Henry Newman, "Secular Knowledge without Personal Religion tends to Unbelief," in *Discussions and Arguments on Various Subjects* (London: Longmans Green, and Co., 1899) 300.

[89] Newman, "Secular Knowledge," in *Discussions and Arguments on Various Subjects*, 303.

[90] Newman to George William Cox (January 28, 1865), *L.D.*, 21:395-396.

watch which had made the arguments from the material universe primary. But against those heady days of a foundational unity between science and religion, Newman had learned a lesson from ancient philosophy, "this remarkable fact in the history of heathen Greece against the former supposition, that her most eminent empirical philosophers were atheists, and that it was their atheism which was the cause of their eminence."[91] And in what did their atheism consist, the atheism of Democritus and Epicurus? The denial of providence, of final causes within the universe, of God or mind dwelling within and directing the universe. Newman relied upon Bacon's analysis for this tendency towards atheism among mechanical philosophers or physicists: "Physical philosophers are ever inquiring *whence* things are, not *why*; referring them to nature, not to mind; and thus they tend to make a system a substitute for a God."[92] Contrary to the attempts to search science and physical investigations for foundational assertion about the existence of God, Newman counseled: "From religious investigations, as such, physics must be excluded, and from physical, as such, religion; and if we mix them, we shall spoil both. The theologian, speaking of Divine Omnipotence, for the time simply ignores the laws of nature as existing restraints upon its exercise; and the physical philosopher, on the other hand, in his experiments upon natural phenomena, is simply ascertaining those laws, putting aside the question of that Omnipotence."[93]

The celebrated attempts of the seventeenth and eighteenth century to found religion on physics received from Newman what must pass as one of his most sardonic comments: "There are religious experimentalists, though physics, taken by themselves, tend

[91] Newman, "Secular Knowledge," in *Discussions and Arguments on Various Subjects*, 298.

[92] *Ibid.*, 299.

[93] *Idea*, 189.

to infidelity; but to have recourse to physics to *make* men religious is like recommending a canonry as a cure for the gout, or giving a youngster a commission as a penance for irregularities."[94] It is not that all argument from the world of nature and from its order is intrinsically false; it is that few are capable of such an argument and fewer still to build religious belief upon it.

The results could be paradoxical: Make religion — as one does in these physico-theologies — the conclusion of inference and you will undermine it: "To most men argument makes the point in hand only more doubtful, and considerably less impressive. After all, man is *not* a reasoning animal; he is a seeing, feeling, contemplating, acting animal. He is influenced by what is direct and precise... Life is not long enough for a religion of inferences."[95] Science and literature may strengthen one's religious beliefs, but the foundations for such convictions must be what is direct and precise within human experience, and for human beings what is most direct, what is most given in and by conscience.[96] Writing from Rome in 1847, Newman summarized to J. D. Dalgairns his very nuanced evaluation of the apologetics of the time: "(1) I hold reason *can* prove the being of a God — that such a conclusion is the legitimate result of reason well employed... *but* this is very

[94] Newman, "Secular Knowledge," in *Discussions and Arguments on Various Subjects*, 299.

[95] *G.A.*, 66-67.

[96] Perhaps, again, the opponent in so many ways most parallel in his reflections to Newman is Friedrich Nietzsche: "Why atheism today? The 'Father' in God is thoroughly refuted, likewise the 'judge' and the 'rewarder'. Also his 'free will' — he does not hear us, and even if he heard us he could not help. The worst of it is that he seems to be incapable of communicating clearly. Is he unclear? — This is what I have found out from many questions and conversations as to the cause of the decline of European theism. It seems to me that the religious instinct is growing powerfully, but is rejecting theistic gratification with deep distrust." *Beyond Good and Evil*, translated with an introduction by Marianne Cowan, A Gateway Edition (Chicago, IL: Henry Regnery Company, 1955) #53, p. 60.

different from saying that reason is the *mode* by which individuals come at truth. (2) Next I have denied that the argument *from design* is philosophically true — has the Holy See condemned this? if so, of course I retract it — but else I say the philosophical argument of reason for the being of God is, not from external nature, but from the *law of conscience*."[97]

If Europe, then, was to lose its sense of God, that loss must come through a corruption of conscience. "Conscience may be *deadened*," Newman wrote to Baron Friedrich von Hugel. The accepted practices of the vendetta, for example, could as the customs of the country leave one in "invincible ignorance" that cruelty was wrong.[98] As early as his study of the *Arians of the Fourth Century,* Newman had maintained that "infidelity is a positive, not a negative state; it is a state of profaneness, pride, and selfishness; and he who believes a little, but encompasses that little with the invention of men, is undeniably in a better condition than he who blots out from his mind both the human inventions, and that portion of truth which was concealed in them." In this way, one could understand how Origen was willing to deal in friendly interchange with the pagan philosophers in Alexandria, but avoided deliberate heretics and apostates. Ignorance of God is not simply ignorance, an error of understanding or judgment. The loss of a sense of God could only be moral.[99]

Part Five: The Infallible Church

All of this could happen because the intellect alone was not enough to secure the primacy of conscience and its mediation of

[97] Newman to J. D. Dalgairnes (February 14, 1847), *L.D.*, 12:34.

[98] Newman to Baron Friedrich von Hügel (January 26, 1879), *L.D.*, 29:14.

[99] John Henri Newman, *The Arians of the Fourth Century* (London: Longman, Green, and Co., [5]1888) 85-86.

the existence of God. After sin and within the fallen state of human beings, nothing less than a divine intervention could steady human beings in their recognition of a divine voice within the moral imperative, or could bring them continually and resolutely before that which was already present within them. So much countered this mediation of God through conscience: the voice of conscience was a demand for an austere subjection and obedience even in the face of passionate self-interest, deception, the myriad conflicts within motivation; the liberty claimed in some intellectual movements and championed by much in the culture was an antomony or a spontaneity of human reason that in the absorptions of personal gratification, indulgence and self-complacency could become illusion and rebellion. Before such massive counters, Newman was pessimistic about the success of conscience to remain intact.

What could destroy conscience as the voice of God, as the primordial witness to God? The gradual erosion of religion through the overextended claims of the autonomous reason, the reduction of God and the things that pertain to God to the dimensions of human understanding and expectations. At first nothing changes: the external practices are maintained and the moral content of an ethical code unaltered. But gradually and imperceptibly a sea change in the understanding of conscience occurs. It is no longer a response to the demands of another; it becomes a response to what one demands of herself. As mentioned previously, conscience in its religious usage can evoke fear as well as shame. Conscience as cultivated moral sentiment can evoke only shame: "Fear carries us out of ourselves, whereas shame may act upon us only within the round of our own thoughts." The autonomous reason severs a dependence upon God at this deepest level of human choice, leaving intact the moral life itself virtually unchanged initially. The moral life is no longer an obedience to the command of God. Gradually, then, over time and with the increased exile of religion to formalities and the peripheries of life. It seems appropriate here to cite a text already considered: "conscience tends to become what is called the moral sense; the command of duty is a sort of taste; sin is not an offence against God, but against human nature."[100] Perhaps one could say that infidelity, in Newman's sense of that word, can begin when the superego subsumes the place of conscience.

For conscience does not cease to exist, but it becomes self-respect. When one offends against it, shame is evoked by a sense of being a fool rather than a sinner. The religious character of conscience dies by a substitution, done so easily under the imperialism of the intellect, of an autonomous moral sense or taste, responsible only to itself, for an obligation commanded and sanctioned by another. Moral life becomes only ethical, not religious; conscience became, quite literally, godless. Edward Gibbon drew the outlines of such an individual figure with his depiction in Julian, of a "godless intellectualism" that was "an historical fulfillment of his own idea of moral perfection."[101]

As Europe moved towards its increasing distance from real convictions about the religious, about the divine and effective presence or imperative within human life, various expedients had been attempted "to arrest fierce willful human nature in its onward course, and to bring it into subjection." But what could have the "force and the toughness necessary to be a breakwater against the deluge?"[102] The political establishment of national churches in various countries in Europe was attempted, but this was giving way before its own ineffectuality.[103]

Education was another expedient, and in 1841 Sir Robert Peel and Lord Brougham had launched a program which maintained

[100] *Idea*, 165.
[101] *Idea*, 169.
[102] *Apo.*, 219.
[103] *Apo.*, 219.

"that the claims of religion could be secured and sustained in the mass of men, and in particular in the lower classes of society, by acquaintance with literature and physical science, and through the instrumentality of Mechanics' Institutes and Reading Rooms." Newman found this a dream and a delusion. It reduced religion to conclusions and opinions, neither of which will sustain human conviction under the demands and allurements of life. Both strategies substituted notional assent about propositions for the concrete realities to which religious and real assent is given: "The heart is commonly reached, not through the reason, but through the imagination, by means of direct impressions, by the testimony of facts and events, by history, by description. Persons influence us, voices melt us, looks subdue us, deeds inflame us. Many a man will live and die upon a dogma: no man will be a martyr for a conclusion."[104]

Newman would extend the same judgment to Sacred Scripture itself, even while insisting that its source is God and its reading grace. It has proven historically idle to attempt to make of the bible an instrument for which it was never intended, i.e. a continual response to the skeptical human intellect, infinite in the varieties of doubts that it fosters and passionate in the urgency with which self-seeking can give those doubts form and substance. "A book, after all, cannot make a stand against the wild living intellect of man, and in this day it [Scripture] begins to testify, as regards its own structure and contents, to the power of that universal solvent, which is so successfully acting upon religious establishments."[105] Philosophic and literary religion becomes liberalism, the anti-dogmatic religious movement against which Newman spent his life; scriptural religion became evangelicalism, which played directly into the hands of the liberals."[106] There had to be a

[104] *G.A.*, 65-66.

[105] *Apo.*, 219.

[106] *Apo.*, 39-40. "I thought little of the Evangelicals as a class. I thought they played into the hands of the Liberals."

divine intervention that was more than human inference and sentiment on one side and a book on the other. In terms of this, Newman understood the incarnation of the Son of God and the continuation of his authoritative teaching in an infallible Church.

What did Newman mean by an infallible Church? "I would rather word the question thus," he wrote, "'Can I be certain that God is true and that God has spoken?' And I prefer to put it in this shape, because I understand what is meant better, while I think it is the real interpretation of any thing which I hold myself about the Church's infallibility."[107]

The present infidelity was a "moral epidemic, and it is likely to have its course. While it lasts, argument is useless… Personal experience of the power of the Gospel is our great, or our only defense from scepticism. Argument is of little use. Beyond this inward evidence, an Infallible Church is the main external safeguard — But when minds are wilful, there is no safeguard at all.[108]

This conviction brought Newman to an understanding of the moral need for an infallible Church, paradoxically one of the most scandalous features of the Catholic Church for Victorian England. The Church was the continuation of the presence of Christ, an abiding reminder of the religious, of the involvement of God at the deepest level of human life, an involvement that was both sustaining, transforming, and correcting the movement of the intellectual and passionate appetites of human beings. For the Church — with all of the distinctions and *caveats upon* which Newman could insist and at great length — could speak on fundamental religious issues in the name and by the authority of God.

For Newman, it was the charism of infallibility which gave the Church its meaning, its manner of teaching and action, and its

[107] Newman to Frank Scott Haydon (April 24, 1858), *L.D.*, 18:333-334.

[108] Newman to J. R. Bloxam (February 20, 1883), *L.D.*, 30:186. See also *Apo.*, 219-220.

peculiar mission to the world. "Supposing then it to be the Will of the Creator to interfere in human affairs, and to make provisions for retaining in the world a knowledge of Himself, so definite and distinct as to be proof against the energy of human scepticism... there is nothing to surprise the mind, if He should think fit to introduce a power into the world, invested with the prerogative of infallibility in religious matters. Such a provision would be a direct, immediate, active, and prompt means of withstanding the difficulty;... And thus I am brought to speak of the Church's infallibility, as a provision, adapted by the mercy of the Creator, to preserve religion in the world, and to restrain that freedom of thought, which of course in itself is one of the greatest of our natural gifts, and to rescue it from its own suicidal excesses."[109]

As a response to the religious self-destruction of human kind, then, Newman articulates both a transcendental and categorical witness to the reality of God. Transcendentally, there is the authoritative witness of conscience, innate and supreme in every human being, pervasively present through every human choice, and strengthened and perfected because interiorly transformed by the grace of the indwelling Spirit. Categorically, there is the authoritative witness of the church, the extension or body of Christ, proclaiming with certitude the fundamental creed and morality of the Christian community and the involvement of God within human life — "the great elementary truths" — in such a way as legitimately to demand a response in absolute faith, a community sent to and safeguarded in its definitive proclamation by divine mandate and the Spirit of Christ.

Only such a power, contended Newman, could counter those beginnings of error, of religious skepticism and self-interest, and gradual disengagement, whose organic and ultimate effect is to

[109] *Apo.*, 219-220.

undermine all religious belief in any divine involvement within human life. On the other hand, one could diminish the religious nature of conscience by destroying any such authoritative ecclesial voice by which it could be sustained and safeguarded. And this diminishment of an authoritative church, the substitution of religious sentiment for dogma, had marked European scepticism. The rise of complete disbelief, the rise of atheism, was but the organic development of such a diminishment.

For just as there is an organic development of doctrine, so there is an organic devolution of belief. The *Grammar of Assent* traced out one such movement as example: "The third [person] gradually subsided into infidelity, because he started with the Protestant dogma, cherished in the depth of his nature, that a priesthood was a corruption of the simplicity of the Gospel. First, then, he would protest against the sacrifice of the Mass; next he gave up baptismal regeneration, and the sacramental principle; then he asked himself whether dogmas were not a restraint on Christian liberty as well as sacraments; then came the question, what after all was the use of teachers of religion? Why should any one stand between him and his Maker? After a time it struck him, that this obvious question had to be answered by the Apostles, as well as by the Anglican clergy; so he came to the conclusion that the true and only revelation of God to man is that which is written on the heart. This did for a time, and he remained a Deist. But then it occurred to him, that this inward moral law was there within the breast, whether there was a God or not, and that it was a round about way of enforcing that law, to say that it came from God, and simply unnecessary, considering that it carried with it its own sacred and sovereign authority, as our feelings instinctively testified; and when he turned to look at the physical world around him, he really did not see what scientific proof there was there of the Being of God at all, and it seemed to him as if all things would go on quite as well as at present, without that hypothesis as with it; so he dropped it, and became *a purus, putus* Atheist."[110]

The only external power that can inhibit the beginnings of such decline, one that could insist upon the intimate and demanding intervention of God within human life, is an historical church which can definitively and continually over the centuries formulate or proclaim the Christian creed and authoritatively decide if a new articulation of the faith of this community is its faithful translation into another idiom. Only a community under such a mandate to preach and to summon to belief and assured of an indwelling divine assistance could morally ask for faith in its most fundamental doctrine.

This is not the place to explore the relationship in Newman between ecclesiology and belief, but only to note that they are inextricably united. Both conscience and the church, in variously different ways and modalities, speak authoritatively to the Christian awareness and in so doing mediate — again in vastly different ways and modalities — the reality of God. Dismiss either of them, maintained Newman, and there is no logical pausing in religious disintegration until one reaches total disbelief in the existence of God. This was the pattern that Newman saw in the atheism emerging in his own time and reaching a pervasive presence in the century which was opening before him.

[110] *G.A.*, 160-161.

NEWMAN'S PATHS TO ROME
THE CULTURAL GEOGRAPHY OF LIBERAL ASSENT

Keith HANLEY

In making sense of Newman's career and the leading structures of his thought one simplifying figure recurs both in his own works and in many commentaries on them — what Meriol Trevor, in the abridgement of her full biography, representatively called *Newman's Journey*.[1] He was the acknowledged leader of what became known as "the Movement party," on an outlandish Romewards trajectory, but his own way there was marked by slow progress, various stages and some reversals. On the one hand, as Leslie Stephen wrote of "Newman's Theory of Religious Belief," the route followed was dictated throughout by conscience and authority to arrive at the one true destination: "For the intellect," Stephen summarised, "when not subordinated to conscience and enlightened by authority, is doomed to a perpetuity of fruitless wandering."[2] Geoffrey Faber writes of *Apologia* that propelling Newman's journey all along had been a desire for absolute resolution:

> He must, he says, for years have had an habitual notion... that in some sense or other he was on a journey. He was being impelled on that journey by something in himself which would not let him stand

[1] Some other examples of this guiding motif are Jean Honoré, *Itinéraire Spirituel de Newman*; William Zehringen, "'The True Key to My Whole Life': The Soul's Journey in John Henry Newman's *Apologia pro Vita sua*," *Chicago Studies* 37 (1998) 151-177; and Vincent Ferrer Blehl, *Pilgrim Journey: John Henry Newman 1801-1845* (London: Burns and Oates, 2001).

[2] Leslie Stephen, *An Agnostic's Apology, and Other Essays* (London: Smith, Elder, 1893) 170.

> still. And this was not ambition nor a desire for intellectual consistency; it was the search for an absolute spiritual rule. In Leo's voice [at the Council of Chalcedon, and then on the Monophysites] he first recognized the veritable accents of power, severe, uncompromising, peremptory.[3]

Yet on the other hand, as W. David Shaw writes, Newman often warns "that faith cannot be defined in advance of his exploring expedition into 'unknown country'."[4] Newman's journey, therefore, is characterised by both exploration and absolute resolution — *a closure that only becomes defined by processes of exploration.*

What I intend to do then in the following essay is to mark clearly some of the major signposts in this movement of exploration, or more precisely, the different tensions between exploration and exact resolution, according to the theme of the journey, as that would have played on the mind of a nineteenth-century Englishman such as Newman. I am suggesting that the notion of place (*locus* and *civitas* alike) and the especially enormous spiritual and historical weight accorded to the place of Rome in the British imagination of that time, and the particular way in which place and authority would eventually coalesce for Newman in the Roman Church, be taken as crucial for understanding and interpreting him. In other words, Newman's search for a tensionless state of mind in matters of faith can be seen as a kind of intellectual geography. What I will show is that this search occurs by way of some rather complex feelings and intellectual sentiments which can only be usefully located somewhere between the domain of the oedipal and the artistic, and never achieving the sort of full resolution he had

[3] Geoffrey Faber, *Oxford Apostles: A Character Study of the Oxford Movement* (Harmondsworth: Penguin, 1954) 388.

[4] W. David Shaw, *Victorians and Mystery* (Ithaca, NY/London: Cornell University Press, 1990) 235.

sought. What we have is an unfinished map, as it were, because Newman's sense of place and his authority commitments remained buoyant and open-ended even rather late in his life since the theme of the journey, the unfinished journey, never left him. The motifs of travelling and arriving, place and destination, might well be seriously considered in gaining an insight into his final, or nearly final, thinking on faith.

Travelling to Rome

If the journey has been most neatly expressed as "the Path to Rome," it was a path whose imaginative axis from England was far from unilinear or unidirectional. As the object of the English gaze, Catholic Rome had established itself from 1300, the first Holy Year, as the leading pilgrimage centre in Europe. The only apostolic see, Rome looked for allegiance from all quarters to its single, centralised bishop. After the official break between England and Rome, the flowering of Renaissance humanism replaced its sacred construction as the supreme spiritual centre, and in the course of the seventeenth century the Grand Tour, by which the heirs of the English governing classes established their elite rite of passage to political hegemony by accessing the cultural experience of the classic lands of the Mediterranean, restored the status of Rome as the fount of western culture. It remained in the eighteenth century a minority interest, yet when the peace after the thirty years war was declared in 1763 English people of the upper and middle classes crammed into Rome. From that time, English travellers had begun to approach it with an increasing sense of the superiority of their own national power, and compared national characteristics more and more in their own favour. They had, in their own Protestant minds, culturally colonised Rome as its patrons and consumers. But during the Napoleonic period, 1797-1814, this eighteenth-century aristocratic and classical educational pattern was itself revolutionised by the military occupation of the French. The French army entered Rome in 1798 and exiled Pope Pius VI to Florence and Valence; in 1808 Rome was appropriated by the French Empire, and Napoleon was excommunicated by Pius VII. For the rest of the century until 1870, when the Papal States lost their sovereignty after the Italian army entered Rome and it became annexed to Italy, the city had become a symbol of political and ideological contention. For the forces of revolutionary modernism, it had come to stand for the desacralised capital of a modern state; for the forces of reaction, the beleaguered Vatican had become an ahistorical international centre of supreme spiritual power.[5]

Throughout Newman's lifetime, then, "Rome" — in inverted commas — was a signifier of indeterminate powers, among which that of a triumphalist missionary church was waxing despite, and arguably due to, its loss of temporal power. In 1818, the English College in Rome, which had been requisitioned by Napoleon's army, reopened and ten students arrived, including Nicholas Wiseman, the future Archbishop of Westminster. His path from Rome crossed that of Newman's in the other direction in the 1830s, when Wiseman made a tour of England, an expedition which was eventually to result in the restoration of the hierarchy and Wiseman himself becoming the Archbishop of Westminster. On the atlas of nineteenth-century European Christianity, the opposed gazes of Catholic Rome and Protestant Britain were exchanged between two opposed power centres — of tradition and progress, the origin and future of the civilisation, the universal church and the British Empire. But of course these oppositions were themselves not unconflicted: there is a chiasmus between political liberals in both

[5] My synoptic history owes much to Brian Barefoot, *The English Road to Rome* (Upton-upon-Severn: Images, 1993).

countries and between traditionalists, and Newman had to tread his own way between their ideological incompatibilities.

Recovering the British gaze towards Rome, there is a variety of anxiously engaged response along the spectrum of Christianities along which Newman himself passed. For the Protestant traveller to Rome in the age of reform, Rome offered unsettlingly mixed meanings. An exemplary Evangelical encounter with Rome is that of Dorothea Brooke in Chapter 20 of *Middlemarch*, set in the early 1830s, "sobbing bitterly," as she considers "her own spiritual poverty"[6] in her boudoir on the Via Sistina.[7] "[A]fter" what George Eliot refers to as "the brief narrow experience of her girlhood she was beholding Rome, the city of visible history, where the past of a whole hemisphere seems moving in funeral procession with strange ancestral images and trophies gathered from afar."[8] In fascinated alienation, Dorothea was confronted with a "stupendous fragmentariness," threatening but disturbingly potent, while the Gregorian panoply resulted in chaotic unintelligibility:

> To those who have looked at Rome with the quickening power of a knowledge which breathes a growing soul into all historic shapes, and traces out the suppressed transitions which unite all contrasts, Rome may be the spiritual centre and interpreter of the world. But let them conceive one more historical contrast: the gigantic broken revelations of that Imperial and Papal city thrust abruptly on the notions of a girl who had been brought up in English and Swiss Puritanism, fed on meagre Protestant histories and on art chiefly of

[6] George Eliot, *Middlemarch*, World's Classics, ed. David Carroll (Oxford: Oxford University Press, 1986) 158.

[7] For the rich imaginary archaeology of this street, see Augustus J. C. Hare, *Walks in Rome*, 2 vols (London: George Allen, 1903): "The columns and precious marbles of the Domus Pinciana were removed to Ravenna by Theodoric; but some of the mosaic floors that have felt the feet and been swept by the garments of these people of other days are still lying in situ beneath No 57 Via Sistina..." (1:32).

[8] *Middlemarch*, 158.

> the hand-screen sort;... The weight of unintelligible Rome might lie easily on bright nymphs to whom it formed a background for the brilliant picnic of Anglo-foreign society; but Dorothea had no such defence against deep impressions.[9]

Finding self-expression in "Rome" was, of course, easier for the High Church imagination. A pioneer, whom Newman acknowledged from the Romantic movement, was Wordsworth,[10] who in his journey to Rome in 1835 had paralleled Newman's advance to the Anglo-Catholicism which both had begun to embark upon. The context of liberal church reform was that for which both were seeking imaginative restoration and spiritual authority which had historically emanated from Rome.[11] Wordsworth evidences a fresh appreciation of Catholic history and customs in the series of *Memorials of a Tour in Italy, 1837*, some of which reappeared in a pamphlet entitled *Contributions of William Wordsworth to the Revival of Catholic Truths* in 1842. A sonnet bears the title "At Rome. — Regrets. — In Allusion to Niebuhr, and Other Modern Historians," which insists on sustaining the fabulous content of "Rome" in the face of contemporaneous methods of source-criticism:

> What is it we hear?
> The glory of Infant Rome must disappear,
> Her morning splendors vanish, and their place
> Know them no more?...
> One solace yet remains for us who came
> Into this world in days when story lacked
> Severe research, that in our hearts we know

[9] *Ibid.*, 158-159.

[10] See Newman, *A Letter Addressed to the Rev. R. W. Jelf, D.D.* (Oxford: John Henry Parker, 1841), where Wordsworth is described as a leading influence on the "great progress of the religious mind of our Church" (27).

[11] For a fuller account of Wordsworth's tour, see Keith Hanley, "Wordsworth's Grand Tour," *Romantic Geographies: Discourses of Travel 1775-1844*, ed. Amanda Gilroy (Manchester: Manchester University Press, 2000) 71-92.

> How, for exciting youth's heroic flame,
> Assent is power, belief the soul of fact.[12]

An important part of that historical recuperation is represented by its culminating religious discourse.

The next stage in approximation was the convert imagination, which was to lead to full dogmatic "assent." It was a more complex path than that of the born Catholic. For Hilaire Belloc, the title of whose 1902 popular travelogue of his walk from the Valley of the Upper Moselle to the Eternal City, *The Path to Rome*, was to establish the phrase popularly, Britain was planted back firmly in its European context on the imperial map. Belloc's book alluded to a sacred European geography which followed the Roman road from the time of the imperial city of the Caesars to that of the Apostles, and which for him still bore the primary meaning of pilgrimage:

> I will start from the place where I served in arms for my sins; I will walk all the way and take advantage of no wheeled thing; I will sleep rough and cover thirty miles a day, and I will hear mass every morning; and I will be present at High Mass in St. Peter's on the Feast of St Peter and St Paul.[13]

His actual journey followed the old imperial map, on which the road network was designed for military communication, running dead straight from camp to camp. It was a direct route: the Upper Moselle valley points directly towards Rome; while the Vosges mountains, from where this river flows, are unchallenging:

> But after crossing the Belfort Gap and advancing towards the Jura, Belloc soon found himself in extreme difficulties when he tried to cross the Alps in a straight line... The Alps defeated him. He had to

[12] *The Poetical Works of William Wordsworth*, ed. Ernest de Selincourt and Helen Darbishire, 5 vols. (Oxford: Clarendon, 1940-1949) 3:213, ll. 4-7, 10-14.

[13] Hilaire Belloc, *The Path to Rome* (Harmondsworth: Penguin, 1958) vii.

> follow a tourist route for some miles of the way... The straight line from Toul and the Moselle valley to Milan does, when protracted, rather surprisingly continue almost exactly through Piacenza, Siena, Viterbo and Rome. This was the route that Belloc now followed as nearly as he could.[14]

For Belloc, half French and half British, Rome was the true centre of a Catholic Europe, and all roads still led there. Belloc had been educated at the Birmingham Oratory School, where Newman in his late seventies had taught him Latin, and been so everyday a presence as to be known popularly as "Jack." No-nonsense Belloc saw Newman as provincially concerned with differentiating Catholicism from Anglicanism.[15]

G. K. Chesterton, on the other hand, found the Eternal City, especially in its Renaissance and baroque aspects, impossible to naturalise for his convert imagination, from a Unitarian past, as he reveals in *The Resurrection of Rome,* 1930: "I do not" he writes "think it is easy for Englishmen or northerners in general to understand Rome. I do not think it is at all easy for them to like Rome."[16] Unlike the unhesitatingly directed mind of the cradle Catholic, Chesterton often describes the turning which shaped his conversion as a journey which had set outwards on a quest, only to find its destination, paradoxically, as a return homewards. The twin-directionality is resolved in circularity. When he was only twenty-two he first told the tale in *The Coloured Lands*, of the man who took (in his words) "the shortest journey from one place to the same place,"[17] which turns out to be around the world. This recurrent motif became the model for the negotiations which inform his

[14] Barefoot, *The English Road to Rome*, 213-214.

[15] See A. N. Wilson, *Hilaire Belloc* (Harmondsworth: Penguin, 1986) 19.

[16] G. K. Chesterton, *The Resurrection of Rome* (London: Hodder and Stoughton, 1934) 23-24.

[17] G. K. Chesterton, *The Coloured Lands* (New York: Sheed and Ward, 1938) 233.

notion of "orthodoxy," as at the start of his book of that name, 1908:

> I have often had a fancy for writing a romance about an English yachtsman who slightly miscalculated his course and discovered England under the impression that it was a new island in the South Seas...
>
> I wish to set forth my faith as particularly answering this double spiritual need for that mixture of the familiar and the unfamiliar which Christendom has rightly named romance. For the very word "romance" has in it the mystery and ancient meaning of Rome.[18]

Newman's own first visit to Rome, as a tourist in 1833 when he was thirty-three, during his Mediterranean holiday with the Froudes, was made in the context of the Catholic revivalism of the 30s. It was the journey of an unwitting convert-to-be, and deeply conflicted. En route there from the south of Italy, he was disturbed by his affective unmoorings, especially the dominance, and vehemence, of his classical imagination, as at Messina: "Why wedded to the Lord still yearns my heart/Upon these scenes of ancient heathen fame?... Ah! is it blame? — /That from my eyes the tear is fain to start?"[19] But Rome was more complex. The deep impression it made on him initially, as he approached from Naples through the Campagna, was customary for the period — answering his educated expectation: "At length the walls of Rome appear... In the twilight you pass buildings about which you cannot guess wrongly. This must be the Coliseum; there is the arch of Constantine."[20] It confirmed the kind of foreknowledge that Augustus Hare describes in the introduction to his most successful of all Victorian

[18] G. K. Chesterton, *Orthodoxy* (London: John Lane, 1909) 12-13.

[19] "Messina," *Verses on Various Occasions* (London: Burns, Oates, and Co., 1868) 124. Henceforth *V.V.*

[20] To his Sister Harriett, March 4, 1833, *Letters and Correspondence of John Henry Newman During His Life in the English Church*, ed. Anne Mozley, 2 vols. (London: Longman, Green, and Co, 1891) 1:359. Henceforth *A.M.*

vade mecums, *Walks in Rome*, 1871, quoting Montaigne, Niebuhr, and Dr Arnold to the effect that:

> When travellers... arrive at Rome and go to the Coliseum, it is to visit an object whose appearance has been familiar to them from childhood, and, long ere it is reached, from the heights of the distant Capitol they can recognise the well-known form; — and as regards S. Peter's, who is not familiar with the aspect of the dome, of the wide-spreading piazza, and the foaming fountains, for long years before they come to gaze upon the reality?[21]

If Newman first approached Rome as a classically trained and pious Anglican, there was also in his case the added imaginative fulfilment of his Alexandrian studies. His responses were complicated and developing ("Rome grows more wonderful every day"[22]) within an overall traditionalist admiration for its multiple histories, ancient and recent, torn by the knowledge of conflict and fall: a "wonderful place," where "the effect of every part is so vast and overpowering — there is such an air of greatness and repose cast over the whole," as well as "traces of long sorrow and humiliation, suffering, punishment and decay."[23] As for the evidences of corruption he had also expected, and believed he had encountered, as Ian Ker argues, "The only explanation he could provide at the time was that there was an important distinction between Rome as a place (according to Protestant mythology one of the four beasts of the Apocalypse) and as a church...".[24]

On several levels at this time, Newman was in transit. The journey was both deeply ambiguous and life-changing. He recoiled, for example, at its superstitions, which he was later to condone, and

[21] *Walks in Rome*, I:1.

[22] *A.M.*, 1:359.

[23] To Frederic Rogers, March 5, 1833, *A.M.*, 1:362-363.

[24] Ian Ker, *The Catholic Revival in English Literature, 1845-1961* (Notre Dame, IN: University of Notre Dame Press) 17.

observing the Pope at High Mass he experienced an ambivalence which in some ways never changed: "I could only say in very perplexity my own words, 'How shall I name thee, Light of the wide west, or heinous error-seat?'"[25] It was particularly difficult at that moment to locate himself in his own nation, amid the extreme political polarities at home. When the shocking proposals in Lord Grey's Irish Church Reform Bill reached Newman in Rome, he was caught between two stools. He began to move towards a version of English Roman Catholicism, more Catholic than their clergy's, that should refute the advantages of emancipation and reform and proceed uninterruptedly from a past which was inscribed in the scenes he was witnessing. Alienated from his own nation, and what Keble was to term its "apostasy," he nonetheless did not foremostly and actively belong to the mythic and imaginary south to which he was deeply and helplessly attracted: "I was drawn to [Sicily] as to a loadstone,"[26] he wrote.

Indeed, instead of travelling home with the Froudes, he turned back south on a solitary return visit to Sicily which, after dangerous sickness, helped to clarify a providential scheme in his destiny: "I was sure God had some work for me to do in England,"[27] work which had been impelled by convictions confirmed by this tour, but to be fulfilled elsewhere. He was taking back with him a sense of restoration which was now deeply indebted to the Roman church. In "The Good Samaritan," Palermo, 13 June, he addressed Rome: "O that thy creed were sound!/For thou dost soothe the heart, thou Church of Rome,/By thy unwearied watch and varied round/Of service, in thy Saviour's holy home."[28] The church is hailed as

[25] *The Letters and Diaries of John Henry Newman*, ed. Charles Stephen Dessain et al., 8 vols. (Oxford: Clarendon Press, 1978-99) 3:268. Henceforth *L.D.*

[26] To his Sister Harriett, Feb. 16, 1833, *A.M.*, 1:344.

[27] *John Henry Newman: Autobiographical Writings*, ed. Henry Tristram (London/New York: Sheed and Ward) 136.

[28] *V.V.*, 146.

"a foe," who tends his "wounds with oil and wine."[29] His best known formulation of these awarenesses, "The Pillar of the Cloud," written during his journey back to England, records his actual movement away from the south of Italy, but also describes the path which was eventually, though unknown to him at the time, leading him back towards Rome as the source of doctrinal authority. The poem was written as his ship lay becalmed, poised midway across the Mediterranean, in the straits between Sardinia and Corsica. At the time, something definitive seemed to have been concluded, and he hoped never to have to travel again: "– one step enough for me."[30] The reference to the exodus in "The Pillar of the Cloud" equates England with the Promised Land, but the poem's sense of destination actually came to mean something different from what he then realised, in the light of his subsequently fuller journey.

His second visit resulted from his conversion, when, having received minor orders, he went to the College of Propaganda to study in 1846. It was a highly self-conscious and representative journey in his mind, a resolution of the English schism, and his delayed progress derived from his desire to bring with him the whole Church of England: "To understand Scripture and history was to become Catholic and children of the Reformation would find their way home."[31] Yet Newman's relations to the institutions of the Roman church were never to escape a certain awkwardness. During the journey there he surprisingly asserted that Milan was "a most wonderful place — to me more striking than Rome."[32] He was obliged to dress the part, with a feeling however of the absurdity of its demands: "Buckles at the knees, buckles on the

[29] *Ibid.*, 147.

[30] *Ibid.*, 148.

[31] Quoted by J. R. Glorney Bolton, *Roman Century, 1870-1970* (London: Hamish Hamilton) 53.

[32] To W. G. Penny, Sept. 24, 1846, *L.D.*, 11:249.

shoes, a dress coat with a sort of undergraduate's gown hanging behind, black stockings which must be worn without a wrinkle, and a huge cocked hat — that I should have lived so long to be so dressed up!"[33] He was a fish out of water, and both an insider and outsider. His attraction to the Oratorians was a highly selective acquiescence in Rome — he identified with St Philip Neri, a Florentine, and his great peroration on him in *On the Scope and Nature of University Education* turns out to be on an alien within Rome to whom all bowed: "And who was he, I say, all the while, but a humble priest, a stranger in Rome… and yet… he has achieved the glorious title of Apostle of Rome."[34] The ambivalence was mutual. Notoriously, Rome was not to come to his aid in the Achilli case. The third visit, in 1856, resulted from the clash of the two English oratories, and his insistence on his original commission. His eventual assimilation involved enabling change. The final visit, in 1879, to receive the cardinal's hat, may be said to represent his ultimate arrival, after several false starts and digressions, on the solicited condition that he would not be required to reside at Rome.

Newman's religious map had been the conflicted map of the Cisalpine Catholic, double-centred both at home and abroad, opposed to the neo-Ultramontane vision, centred in the Vatican. Thus he occupied the position of a liberal within his adopted church. In 1859his article, "On Consulting the Laity in Matters of Doctrine," was delated to Rome for heresy, while he was referred to by Mgr George Talbot, led by Cardinal Henry Manning, as the representative of "a dangerous party rising in England,"[35] but the continuities in his thought can be recovered from reversals of his different positions over time. As an Anglican, he denounced liberalism as "the Anti-dogmatic

[33] To Richard Stanton, Nov. 6 1846, *L.D.*, 11:267.

[34] John Henry Newman, *On the Scope and Nature of University Education*, ed. Wilfred Ward (London: Dent, 1965) 207.

[35] *L.D.*, 23:242 n. 1.

principle"[36] and its developments, while his own ideas on developmentalism were to be seen as tarred with the same brush. As Wilfred Ward notes:

> He had opposite dangers to face in the earlier and the later period. At Oxford he feared that Christianity would be swept away by the tide of rationalistic liberalism which lost sight of the profound truths contained in the Christian tradition and derived from revelation. In later years his fear was exactly the opposite.[37]

Mapping the Universe

Inflected in Chesterton's view of orthodoxy as the "romance" which is "Rome," with its interplay between the familiar and the unknown, is the content of a circuit within which truth can only be reconfirmed by exploration; but until truth has been thoroughly explored its meanings can never be fully apprehended. This was the model of knowledge which Newman worked with in the series of five lectures which made up *On the Scope and Nature of University Education*, delivered in 1852, and which was to be his conception behind the Catholic University in Dublin. There and elsewhere, the sea voyage of discovery is a dominant figure for the enterprise involved, and he uses it reflexively as the figure for his composition of the lecture series itself:

> I have felt like a navigator on a strange sea, who is out of sight of land, is surprised by night, and has to trust mainly to rules and instruments of his science for reaching the port... it is not till the morning comes and the shore greets us, and we see our vessel making straight for harbour, that we relax our jealous watch, and consider anxiety irrational.[38]

[36] *Apologia pro Vita sua*, ed. Martin J. Svaglic (Oxford: Clarendon Press, 1967) 329.

[37] Quoted in Ward's Introduction, *On the Scope and Nature*, ix.

[38] Discourse VIII, "Duties of the Church Towards Liberal Knowledge," *On the Scope and Nature*, 184-185.

His lectures, he felt, had themselves demonstrated that the full voyage of knowledge is bound to come full circle and "be sure to come home," as he reiterates in the lecture on "Christianity and Scientific Investigation," which was published in the enlarged edition, *The Idea of a University*, 1873:

> It is the very law of the human mind, in its inquiry after and acquisition of truth, to make its advances by a process which consists of many stages, and is circuitous.
> The analogy of locomotion is most pertinent here. No one can go straight up a mountain; no sailing-vessel makes for its port without tacking.[39]

It was in Ireland that as first Rector he attempted to institutionalise his own liberal definition of "Rome," amid a number of competing constructions, led by Irish prelates who were at war on this representative issue — pre-eminently the ultramontanist, the Apostolic Delegate Archbishop Paul Cullen of Dublin, and the nationalist Archbishop John MacHale of Tuam, insisting on the authority of the Irish bench of bishops. Both demanded the rule of the ecclesiastics over the educated layman. The idea of the Catholic University was not, for Newman, specifically Irish, though it was meant to incorporate Irish national culture within its scope, and he adhered to the University Committee's original agenda: "The university is destined for the benefit not merely of the Catholics in Ireland but those of the empire."[40] Yet because Newman's programme was from the prelates' viewpoint decentred from both Ireland and Rome, they saw his ambition as one, in Roy Jenkins's words, for "a Catholic Oxford on the banks of the Liffey."[41] Newman himself

[39] *Ibid.*, 225-226.

[40] Quoted in Louis McRedmond, *Thrown Among Strangers* (Dublin: Veritas Publications, 1990) 49.

[41] In Roy Jenkins, "Newman and the Idea of the University," in *Newman: A Man For Our Time*, ed. David Brown (London: SPCK, 1990) 147.

saw his own version as the first internationalist intellectual home of English-speaking Catholics, and planned a never-to-be–realised tour of principal American cities. The attempt to incorporate the diverse interests in a higher vision of cultural disinterestedness he found extremely taxing, and he wrote of the lectures: "I am writing them intellectually against the grain more than I ever recollect doing anything."[42] Newman came to detest nationalism, but he was unembarrassed by the contemporary Christian paternalist ideas of imperialism which he deployed in "Christianity and Scientific Investigation." Just as Ireland was an integral but separate part of the British Empire, so the intellectual map of western culture would find a place for, and defend the interests of, all principal areas of learning:

> What an empire is in political history… such is a university in the sphere of philosophy and research. It is, as I have said, the high protecting power of all knowledge and science, of fact and principle, of inquiry and discovery, of experiment and speculation; it maps out the territory of the intellect, and sees that the boundaries of each province are respected, and that there is neither encroachment nor surrender on any side.[43]

Perhaps there is even a subliminal acknowledgement of the rights of Ulster Protestantism in that echo of "No Surrender!"

Newman's Catholic version of liberal education derived from a benign interpretation of British imperial policy for guarded self-determination which was aimed above all at relieving the British taxpayer of financial liabilities at home. He had to keep pace with the dynamism of imperial expansion, while at the same time he resisted becoming swept along by its reductive and utilitarian agenda. A significant case in point was his material exploitation of, and

[42] Quoted in Meriol Trevor, *Newman: The Pillar of the Cloud* (London: Macmillan, 1962) 518.

[43] *Scope and Nature*, 211-212.

figurative caution about rail travel. Networking tirelessly for the Irish project, Newman's travelling was busier and quicker than that suggested by the heroic image of sea-voyaging which Victorians such as Kingsley and J. A. Froude had also seen as the characterising vehicle of the golden age of Protestant expansionism and the means of imperial federation. Though part of Newman resisted the reduction of experience involved in train travel, causing him to complain that "I cannot bear this gadding to and fro — it is against the habit of my life — and against our Rule,"[44] steamships after all enabled him to sustain the axis between Dublin and Birmingham, and the railways allowed him to get about and consult a various and large constituency of interested and influential parties. Yet the mental processes of deliberating on his Dublin lectures were slow-going, and had to be so in order to incorporate the many conflicting considerations: hurrying them "would be like attempting to run 50 miles an hour on the narrow gauge."[45] Still, he was shocked and disappointed to find that the Papal States were without a railroad when he visited in 1855, and it was with deep irony, in relation to the dogmatic teaching on infallibility, that he later wrote to a friend:

> You are going too fast at Rome. We do not move at railroad pace even in the 19th century. We must be patient and that for two reasons, first in order to get at the truth, and next in order to carry others with us. The Church moves as a whole; it is not a mere philosophy, it is a communion.[46]

While he wished to retard the immediate pursuit of new directions which the utilitarian age of railway travel promised, in order rather to achieve a sense of arrival as encompassing the challenge and

[44] To Mrs J. W. Bowden, 9 December 1853, *L.D.*, 15:494.

[45] To Mrs J. W. Bowden, 19 July 1851, *L.D.*, 14:313.

[46] Quoted in Bolton, *Roman Century*, 53.

variety of the experience of journeying, he needed to accommodate change and differences. Rome was in danger of careering into the past, whereas he wished to move forward comprehensively and deliberatively. The new modes of travel provided a means for his modernism, linking far-flung places together, and he relied on the new railway routes just opening around Ireland, guided by an attentive use of the new Bradshaw which aimed helpfully to alert the new consumer to the confusion of growing connections. Their potential, however, had to be subdued to his own schedule.

Throughout the university lectures Newman is concerned with mapping and charts, to outline the principles of nineteenth-century Catholic liberal universalism. Discourse V, on "Liberal Knowledge Viewed in Relation to Learning," argues for a judicious kind of guidance which becomes formulated in a series of propositions which all take this form. The Irish university should be seen as the centre of a panoptic gaze which rather than being simply regulatory provides also a representation of different fields of accumulated knowledge:

> I say then, if we would improve the intellect, first of all we must ascend: we cannot gain real knowledge on a level; we must generalize, we must reduce to method, we must have a grasp of principles, and group and shape our acquisitions by them... The same feeling comes upon us in a strange city, when we have no map of its streets. Hence you hear of practised travellers, when they first come into a place, mounting some high hill or church tower, by way of reconnoitring its neighbourhood. In like manner you must be above your knowledge, gentlemen, not under it, or it will oppress you; and the more you have of it the greater will be the load.[47]

He describes a historical geography of western civilisation, with a moving centre over time and place, far beyond the pale of Irish nationalism, and even of a specifically Catholic historiography:

[47] *Scope and Nature*, 117.

> It is not a mere addition to our knowledge which is the illumination; but the locomotion, the movement onwards, of that mental centre to which both what we know and what we are learning, the accumulating mass of our requirements, gravitates. And therefore a truly great intellect, and recognised to be such by the common opinion of mankind, such as the intellect of Aristotle, or of St. Thomas, or of Newton, or of Goethe (I purposely take instances within and without the Catholic pale, when I would speak of the intellect as such), is one which takes a connected view of old and new, past and present, far and near, and which has an insight into the influence of these one on another; without which there is no whole, and no centre.[48]

A map may indeed be drawn, because the connecting philosophy is non-latitudinarian: its destination, rather than its absolutist premise, will be the realisation of the synonymity between truth and Catholic truth:

> Those on the other hand who have no object or principle whatever to hold by lose their way, every step they take… But the intellect which has been disciplined to the perfection of its powers… cannot be at a loss, cannot but be patient, collected, and majestically calm, because it discerns the end in every beginning, the origin in every end, the law in every interruption, the limit in each delay; because it knows where it stands, and how its path lies from one point to another.[49]

Newman's chart puts its faith in freedom of liberal knowledge and development as, according to the title of Discourse IV, "Its Own End:"

> The principle of real dignity in knowledge, its worth, its desirableness, considered irrespectively of its results, is this germ within it of a scientific or a philosophical process. This is how it comes to be an end in itself; this is why it admits of being called liberal. Not to know the relative dispositions of things is the state of slaves or

[48] *Ibid.*, 112.

[49] *Ibid.*, 115-116.

children; to have mapped out the universe is the boast of philosophy.[50]

The Itinerary of Assent

Newman had a very particular relation to authority which dictated a very particular relation to language. His identity depended on the insistence of a set structure of belief, so that he wrote, discussing the Sanction of the Illative Sense in *The Grammar of Assent*: "I am what I am, or I am nothing. I cannot think, reflect, or judge about my being, without starting from the very point which I aim at concluding. My ideas are all assumptions, and I am ever moving in a circle."[51] The entelechal law of self-realisation for Newman is both willed and ineluctable:

> Other beings are complete from their first existence, in that line of excellence which is allotted to them; but man begins with nothing realized (to use that term)... Thus he gradually advances to the fullness of his destiny... each of us has the prerogative of completing his inchoate and rudimental nature, and of developing his own perfection out of the living elements with which his mind began to be. It is his gift to be the creator of his own sufficiency; and to be emphatically self-made. This is the law of his being, which he cannot escape; and whatever is involved in that law he is bound, or rather he is carried on, to fulfil.[52]

What drives such a psychology of belief, I suggest, is a distinctive resolution of the Oedipal story whereby Newman had formatively arrived at a position of integrating antagonism in total deference. A. N. Wilson observes that an "ambivalence towardsfather-figures" is inherent in Anglo-Catholicism, and that Newman displayed it

[50] *Ibid.*, 92-93.

[51] John Henry Newman, *An Essay in Aid of a Grammar of Assent*, ed. I. T. Ker (Oxford: Clarendon Press, 1985) 347.

[52] *Ibid.*, 349.

> in all his dealings with bishops, both in his Anglican and his Catholic incarnations. He governed his whole grown-up life around the belief that bishops were possessed of supreme apostolic authority, while going out of his way to say and write things which they would find unacceptable; and this was true of the author of Tract Ninety as it was of the man who baited Archbishop Cullen of Dublin or fell foul of Manning.[53]

Conjecturally, it is connected with his father's increasing social and economic decline, ending as a publican in Clerkenwell, weighed against his own academic rise, and with the illusory empowerments of precocity assumed by the boy-don in that ménage of intimate politics, the Oxford college. His whole career was to be marked by failure and ostracism from the English Establishment viewpoint, though, following another — his own chosen — course. it was to end triumphantly, even back at Oxford, with his cardinalate.

Repeatedly, Newman confers, on his own terms, the authority to which he is then willing to submit, achieving self-empowerment by submission, much in the fashion of Wordsworth's "Ode to Duty," recalling Newman's own treatment of conscience in *The Grammar*:

> Yet not the less would I throughout
> Still act according to the voice
> Of my own wish; and feel past doubt
> That my submissiveness was choice.[54]

It involves a subtle negotiation with authority which Newman somehow finds inadequate unless it bows to his own demands of it. It was, of course, in patristic orthodoxy, the pronouncements of

[53] In A. N. Wilson, "Newman the Writer," in *Newman: A Man for Our Time, Centenary Essays: Lectures Delivered at Oxford University in 1990*, ed. David Brown (London: SPCK, 1990) 125.

[54] *Poetical Works of Wordsworth*, 4: 85, ll. 41-44.

the Church Fathers, that Newman found the expression of his own self-fulfilling absolutism, and closed the circle.

In a late open letter, published as "A Disturbance of Memory on the Acropolis," Freud writes about the sensation of "Entfremdungsgefühl" (translated as "derealization") which befell him when, as a young man, he and his brother visited this culminating object of their boyhood historical imagination ("'So all this really *does* exist, just as we learnt at school'!"[55]). He simply could not believe he had arrived there ("What I see here is not real"[56]), and examining the "after-effect" he discovers two separate persons in his mind: one was amazed actually to have encountered something he had thought of as doubtful — like someone who actually sees the Loch Ness Monster, and the second was amazed that, instead of his simply rejoicing in the fact, its existence should then have been further brought into question. Freud identifies the connection between this effect and a feeling of depression he had experienced before the final part of the journey as a "too good to be true" feeling,[57] which is further related to the case histories of persons he elsewhere describes as "wrecked by success" and who go to pieces because an overwhelmingly powerful wish of theirs has been fulfilled.[58] Such a character-type is disturbed by a fate which fails to enact the anticipated severe regulations of the super-ego, derived from the punitive agency in childhood. In the letter, Freud interprets the effect in Athens as the result of an ego defence against his guilt over

[55] In Sigmund Freud, *Standard Edition of the Complete Psychological Works*, ed. and trans. under the general editorship of James Strachey, 24 vols. (London: Hogarth, 1953-1974) 22:241. Henceforth *CPW*.

[56] *Ibid.*, 244.

[57] *Ibid.*, 242.

[58] See "Some Character-Types Met with in Psycho-Analytic Work", *CPW*, 14:309-336.

> the satisfaction in having gone such a long way: there was something about it that was wrong, that from earliest times had been forbidden. It was something to do with a child's criticism of his father... It seems as though the essence of success was to have got further than one's father, and as though to excel one's father was still something forbidden.[59]

In sum, Freud suggests, "what interfered with our enjoyment of the journey to Athens," including the sense of cultural superiority over their businessman father, "was a feeling of *filial piety*,"[60] which was the residual upshot of an Oedipal *agon* with his father, in actually accessing the Acropolis, a prized centre of cultural power. Freud's embarrassment with Rome had an added Semitic dimension. Despite his many forays into Italy, he famously had an inhibition from travelling to Rome, which he linked with its being the power centre of Christendom. He had to wait until he was forty-six before he felt himself to be prepared for his first entry into Rome, when he wrote to his friend, Wilhelm Fliess, with whom he had shared his desire to travel there over a long period ("You know my Roman dreams"[61]): "Rome has been an overwhelming experience for me... a high-spot in my life."[62]

In order to relate the insights of Freud's letter to Newman's psychology of belief, it should be recalled how Newman notably sustained a strong sense of "derealization" from his schooldays, as he recounts in *Apologia Pro Vita Sua*: "I thought life might be a dream, or I an Angel, and all this world a deception, my fellow-angels by a playful device concealing themselves from me, and

[59] "Disturbance of Memory," 247.

[60] *Ibid.*, 247-248.

[61] March 2, 1899, in *The Origins of Psychoanalysis*, ed. Marie Bonaparte, Anna Freud, Ernst Kris (London: Imago, 1954) 279.

[62] *Ibid.*, 335.

deceiving me with a semblance of a material world."[63] He tells us that his "inward conversion" at the age of fifteen, with the conviction that he was "elected to eternal glory," followed

> in the direction of those childish imaginations... in isolating me from the objects which surrounded me, in confirming me in the mistrust of the reality of material phenomena, and making me rest in the thought of two and two only supreme and luminously self-evident beings, myself and my Creator....[64]

Newman also wrote: "I used to wish the Arabian tales were true,"[65] and in relation to his being completely ready to accept the flight of the Holy House of Nazareth to Loreto, Lytton Strachey commented wickedly that, "When he came to be a man, his wish seems to have been granted."[66] It was indeed granted when he had sailed from Naples to Messina, and on his first enthralled encounter with Sicily wrote: "From the moment I saw Sicily I kept saying to myself, 'This is Sicily'."[67] At Syracuse, he observed about Taormina:

> I never saw anything more enchanting than this spot. It realised all one had read of in books about scenery — a deep valley, brawling streams, beautiful trees, the sea (heard) in the distance. But when after breakfast, on a bright day, we mounted to the theatre, and saw the famous view, what shall I say? I never knew that Nature could be so beautiful; and to see that view was the nearest approach to seeing Eden. O happy I![68]

On his way back, at Palermo, he wrote again: "It *is* a country. It passes belief. It is like the Garden of Eden."[69]

[63] *Apologia pro Vita sua*, 56.

[64] *Ibid.*, 59.

[65] *Ibid.*, 56.

[66] In *Eminent Victorians* (London: The Folio Society, 1967) 48.

[67] To his Sister Harriett, February 16 1833, *A.M.*, 1:344.

[68] To his Sister Harriett, April 25, *A.M.* 1:397.

[69] To Frederick Rogers, June 5, *A.M.* 1:408.

Newman had himself been unable to travel to Athens from Patras when they had first entered the Mediterranean and crossed the Ionian Sea, but on their way to their culminating destination of Rome via Corfu and Malta, Newman and the Froudes had sailed close to Ithaca, where he significantly associated the sight of the Homeric island with his childhood experience of derealisation:

> I thought of Ham, and of all the various glimpses which memory barely retains, and which fly from me when I pursue them, of that earliest time of life when one seems almost to realise the remnants of a pre-existing state. Oh, how I longed to touch the land, and to satisfy myself that it was not a mere vision that I saw before me![70]

Besides his childhood home, Grey Court House at Ham, near Richmond, which in a letter of 1886 he describes as having appeared to him "as if it was Paradise"[71] in his boyhood and as having remained in his dreams throughout life, there are a tissue of literary allusions here. In "the remnants of a pre-existing state" Newman evokes Wordsworth's "Ode: Intimations of Immortality," and its feeling of

> Those obstinate questionings
> Of sense and outward things
> ...
> Blank misgivings of a Creature
> Moving about in worlds not realised,[72]

which Wordsworth said the poem takes as "presumptive evidence of a prior state of existence."[73] Newman's longing "to touch the land" to convince himself of its actuality is reminiscent of Doubting

[70] To his Mother, December 30 1832, *A.M.*, 1:318; see also *A.M.*, 1:314.

[71] To Thomas William Morton SJ, February 24 1886, *L.D.*, 31:119.

[72] *Poetical Works of Wordsworth*, 4:283, ll. 142-143, 145-146.

[73] Note dictated to Isabella Fenwick, in *ibid.*, 464.

Thomas in John's gospel, and "a mere vision" may possibly owe a hint to Keats's "Was it a vision, or a waking dream?"[74] from "Ode to a Nightingale," but, much less expectedly, in "that I saw before me" there is also an echo of the regicidal Macbeth's dagger: "Is this a dagger which I see before me,/The handle toward my hand? Come, let me clutch thee."[75] Altogether, the unconscious of Newman's text reveals an anxiety to arrive at cultural empowerment innocently: Macbeth does not want to see a real dagger with which to kill the king, the powerful father figure, and the uncertain quality of Newman's other literary resonances allows him overall, like Freud on the Acropolis, to deny an hostility which gaining the place's unproblematic reality might trigger. Yet Wordsworth's spiritual intimations that "heaven lies about us in our infancy!"[76] initiate a complication in Newman's desire for Ithaca. Unlike Wordsworth, who wishes to retain a childlike state of radiant perception and who unwillingly submits to social and cultural maturation, Newman-as-Macbeth wishes to exceed the derealization that he sees before him, "and to satisfy [himself] that it was not a mere vision." The inconsistency is resolved by St Thomas, who points up the nature of the reality which Newman craves to assure himself of, as something more than simply high cultural experience. The indeterminacies of his earliest memories, that is, as well as the later dissolution of Oedipal rivalry, were also creating the condition of Revelation and belief.

Newman returned to the same condition of belief in *The Grammar of Assent*, contrasting Assent and Certitude, and saw

[74] *John Keats: A New Selection*, ed. John Barnard (Harmondsworth: Penguin, 1988) 171, l. 79.

[75] *The Riverside Shakespeare*, ed. Evans G. Blackmore, Harry Levin, Charles A. Shattuck (Boston: Houghton Mifflin, 1974) 1319, II, i, 33-4.

[76] *Poetical Works of Wordsworth*, 4:281, l. 66.

it represented in both the incredulous wonderment of the released Israelites in Psalm 126 and again in the response of the apostles to the Resurrection:

> I gaze on the Palatine Hill, or on the Parthenon, or on the Pyramids, which I have read of from a boy, or upon the matter-of-fact reality of the sacred places of the Holy Land and I have to force my imagination to follow the guidance of sight and of reason. It is to me so strange that a lifelong belief should be changed into sight, and things should be so near me, which hitherto had been visions. And so in times, first of suspense, then of joy; "When the Lord turned the captivity of Sion, then" (according to the Hebrew text) "we were like unto them that dream." Yet it was a dream which they were certain was a truth, while they seemed to doubt it. So, too, was it in some sense with the Apostles after our Lord's resurrection.[77]

What they knew to be true seemed unbelievable, and partly so because it had been so deeply desired, and then disconcertingly granted. In order to experience assent, something of the imaginative and visionary state which the certainty of actualisation cancels has to be recaptured to substantiate the reality of the unseen spiritual world: what originally had been felt because it was yet unseen was to be re-experienced within and beyond what had been made manifest. That way, any guilt derived from the apparent by-passing of the superego or paternal restriction is relieved by the workings of Revelation, as doubt overlaps with belief. The upshot is Pauline, and is developed in Newman's sermon, "The Invisible World," 1837, which is a commentary on 2 Cor 4:18: "While we look not at the things which are seen, but at the things which are not seen; for the things which are seen are temporal, but the things which are not seen are eternal." There Newman observes: "and the world which we do not see as really exists as the world we do see... another world all around us, though we see it not, and more

[77] *Grammar of Assent*, 219-220.

wonderful than the world we see, for this reason if for no other, that we do not see it."[78]

Psychologically, if not logically, when what is certain seems doubtful, what seems incredible may yet be true. The progression involves passing through the shadow of a challenge to filial piety towards assent as, after all, submission to paternal authority — something wonderfully given and received rather than guiltily taken. Jacques Lacan's re-telling of the Oedipal story as language acquisition and identification within the Symbolic Order, or the cultural and social domain of the father, describes a borderland of what he calls "the Mirror Stage," when an infant is from about 6 to 18 months old, which represents the subject's first awareness of unity and wholeness, still connected to the original, blissfully undivided oneness with the mother and not yet engaged in an Oedipal contest for "the Word of the Father." Lacan suggests that, normatively, the Word of the Father is appropriated in a way which leaves a wound of division, whereby the subject will forever be alienated in language — it will only exist in words. The Mirror Stage occupies a zone of pre-Oedipal being, in which the substitution of word for thing is yet to come, and enjoys an indeterminate state after which Freud's derealization hankers, prior to representation and actual content being brought to closure and so completing the subject's inscription in the system of language. Newman's "from the moment I saw Sicily, I kept saying to myself 'This is Sicily'" reiterates the moment of transition which in his case is desired from a complexity of motives. But the ground for assenting to the closure is in excess of the certainty of material literalism — that is, simply touching the place. It depends on the capability of language to continue to represent a pre-existent closure which somehow evades the fate of Oedipal alienation and in some way retains an alternative relation to the mother. Newman accordingly desires

[78] *Parochial and Plain Sermons*, ed. William John Copeland, 8 vols. (London: Longmans, Green, and Co., 1900) 4:200-201.

to inscribe himself selectively in those specific versions of the Word of the Father which authorise that position.

The Mirror Stage, Lacan argues, remains as a register within language and cultural formation which he calls "the Imaginary." It has a narcissistic structure which insists on reflexivity within the domain of the father, as Newman's arresting image for "the unspeakable distress" with which he beholds a godless society in the *Apologia* divulges:

> If I looked into a mirror, and did not see my face, I should have the sort of feeling which actually comes upon me, when I look into this living busy world, and see no reflexion of its Creator.[79]

The alienation occasioned by representational divergence, difference, and the absence of reflexivity threaten the condition for assent, and that state's admittance to a further level of signification. The configuration which generates the set of deepening inner implications becomes a matter for spiritual discipline, bringing the subject into line with an ultimate, permanent and all-powerful structure, which Newman's meditation declares to be the closest representational point to divine reality:

> I know, O my God, I must change, if I am to see Thy face!... Oh, support me, as I proceed in this great, awful, happy change, with the grace of Thy unchangeableness... All will turn to evil if I am not sustained by the Unchangeable; all will turn to good if I have Jesus with me, yesterday and today the same, and for ever.[80]

Words can never carry any more than assent, as their representational capacity is indeed dependent on the separation of word and thing.

Yet language may take the subject to the representational point at which it does invite or command assent. It is suggestive to read in the *Apologia* that Newman's susceptibility to "the mystical or

[79] *Apologia pro Vita sua*, 377.

[80] John Henry Newman, *Meditations and Devotions* (London: Burns & Oates, 1964) 58.

sacramental principle" in Clement of Alexandria and his disciple Origen, when preparing his *Arians of the Fourth Century*, responded to Fathers who reflected his own imaginary insistence:

> I understood [their teaching] to mean that the exterior world, physical and historical, was but the outward manifestation of realities greater than itself. Nature was a parable: Scripture was an allegory: pagan literature, philosophy, and mythology, properly understood, were but a preparation for the Gospel.[81]

Self-reflexively too, Newman found parallels and subtle coincidences in ancient church history — the Monophysites of AD 450 and the Council of Chalcedon represented the unexpected manifestation of his own predicament: "in the middle of the fifth century, I found, as it seemed to me, Christendom of the sixteenth and the nineteenth centuries reflected, I saw my face in that mirror,"[82] so that "The shadow of the fifth century [Rome] was on the sixteenth," as of the nineteenth, "like a spirit rising from the troubled waters of the old world, with the shape and lineaments of the new."[83] Many commentators have noted, with William Barry, that in the *Apologia* Newman presents a life-story which "is full of strange coincidences, accidents which turn out to have a purpose, even grotesque encounters like that with the Jerusalem bishopric, and what De Quincey terms 'echo auguries,' by which one sentence does the work of years and volumes."[84] At critical moments, certain formulations spoke to him as providing just the authoritative declarations he desired: a crucial instance is Wiseman's citation of St Augustine's "Securus judicat orbis terrarum:" "By those great words of the ancient Father, the theory of the *Via Media* was absolutely pulverized."[85] He then

[81] *Apologia pro Vita sua*, 89.
[82] *Ibid.*, 209.
[83] *Ibid.*, 210.
[84] *Newman* (London: Hodder and Stoughton, 1905) 76.
[85] *Apologia pro Vita sua*, 212.

began to know that the end of his questing lay in the pronouncements of the church councils. The long brewing of eventual articulation is indeed the overall plot of the *Apologia*, as he was to describe the process in *The Scope and Nature of University Education*:

> The principles which I am now to set forth under the sanction of the Catholic Church were my profession at that early period of my life, when religion was to me more a matter of feeling and experience than of faith. They did but take greater hold upon me as I was introduced to the records of Christian antiquity....[86]

J. A. Froude attests to Newman's power to convey his progressive rediscoveries, the shock of the old. As Newman preached on the Passion, "it was as if an electric stroke had gone through the church, as if every person present understood for the first time the meanings of what he had all his life been saying."[87] Newman saw a similar effect in Keble: "His happy magic made the Anglican Church seem what Catholicism was and is," especially his poems in *The Christian Year*, which Newman likened to the discovery of Molière's Monsieur Jourdain:

> The established system found to its surprise that it had all its life been talking, not prose but poetry... Beneficed clergymen used to go to rest as usual on Christmas Eve and leave to ringers, or sometimes to carollers, the observance which was paid, not without creature comforts, to the sacred night; but now they suddenly found themselves, to their great surprise, to be "wakeful shepherds;" and "still the day came round," "in music and in light," the new-born Saviour "dawned upon their prayer."[88]

Related to Newman's version of Revelation is his version of Providence: a dispensation conferred, providing him with the medium

[86] Newman, *On the Scope and Nature of University Education*, 4.

[87] In James A. Froude, "The Oxford Counter-Reformation," in *Short Studies on Great Subjects* (London: Longmans, 1899) 4:286.

[88] Newman, *Essays Critical and Historical*, 2:444.

for the realisation of his desire. Lord Acton writes of the linguistic context of the young Newman, a given idiom — "the microscopic subtlety and care in the choice of words, in guarding against misinterpretation and in correcting it, which belonged to the Oxford training, which is a growth of no other school"[89] — which had provided him with the appropriate tools for his way of writing. Equally, his historical moment came to him with the evolutionary thought which was in the discursive air of the age. It offered him the kind of continuity he was looking for — a continuity that he could represent to himself as changeless amid change, so that "Christianity, as a doctrine and worship, will develop in the minds of recipients."[90] On the other hand, he was an "inopportunist" in part because the movement of the European mind was out of pace with enforcing ideas like infallibility. Indeed, in his Dublin inaugural, "Christianity and Letters," Newman takes his own sense of an elect trajectory as the basis of the development of Christian civilisation itself, arguing that Christianity "waited till the *orbis terrarum* attained its most perfect form before it appeared; and it soon coalesced, and has ever since co-operated, and often seemed identical, with the Civilization which is its companion."[91]

Correspondingly, he evolves a style which flows and incorporates as it progresses to his conclusions, a kind of fullness of speech which can then represent the whole history of his search for imaginary self-expression. It was, of course, precisely this denial of difference in opinion amid a claimed continuity that led to accusations of deviousness, and the stylistic effect is the fluency which

[89] *Letters of Lord Acton to Mary Gladstone*, ed. Herbert Paul (London: George Allen, 1904) 46.

[90] *An Essay on the Development of Christian Doctrine* (London: Longmans, Green, and Co., 1920) 57.

[91] In "Christianity and Letters," *The Idea of a University*, ed. Ian T. Ker (Oxford: Clarendon, 1976) 215.

Gerard Manley Hopkins points to in his notion of "chromatism," "the beauty of an infinite curve," opposed to "diatonism," which he sees as represented by Newman's style.[92] The first is fluid and apparently shapeless, and, unlike the second, sees no need to arrive at fresh forms of organisation. Newman seems always to know where his argument is heading, especially in *The Grammar of Assent,* and is content for the reasoning process as such not to take the reader every step of the way to the affirmation of belief — which is what he deeply responds to in the Athanasian Creed:

> For myself, I have ever felt it as the most simple and sublime, the most devotional formulary to which Christianity has given birth, more so even than the *Veni Creator* and the *Te Deum*. Even the antithetical form of its sentences, which is a stumbling block to so many, as seeming to force, and to exult in forcing a mystery upon recalcitrant minds, has to my apprehension, even notionally considered, a very different drift. It is intended as a check upon our reasonings, lest they rush on in one direction beyond the limits of truth, and it turns them back in the opposite direction. Certainly it implies a glorying in the Mystery; but it is not simply a statement of the Mystery for the sake of its mysteriousness.[93]

Theologically, impediments to "the direct course of religious inquiry," concerning for example the nature of evil or the consistency of God's intentions, are similarly averted from the main route pursued:

> — these, and a host of like questions, must arise in every thoughtful mind, and, after the best use of reason, must be deliberately put aside, as beyond reason, as (so to speak) no-thoroughfares, which, having no outlet themselves, have no legitimate power to divert us from the King's highway, and to hinder the direct course of religious inquiry from reaching its destination.[94]

[92] In his essay, "On the Signs of Health and Decay in the Arts," *The Journals and Papers of Gerard Manley Hopkins*, ed. Humphry House and Graham Storey (London: Oxford University Press, 1959) 76.

[93] *Grammar of Assent*, 133.

[94] *Ibid.*, 218.

Culminatingly, the "illative sense" conducts the key underlying process — "the intellectual process by which we pass from conditional inference to unconditional assent,"[95] which occurs when "the practised and experienced mind is able to make a sure divination that a conclusion is inevitable, of which his lines of reasoning do not actually put him in possession."[96] The destination turns out to be an enhanced inscription in propositions of belief which are always "useful in their dogmatic aspect as ascertaining and making clear for us the truths on which the religious imagination has to rest."[97] The language itself remains unaltered, but the subject is able to re-bond with it as a much fuller expression of its accumulated knowledge and experience:

> For myself, it was not logic which carried me on; as well might one say that the quicksilver in the barometer changes the weather. It is the concrete being that reasons; pass a number of years, and I find my mind in a new place; how? The whole man moves; paper logic is but the record of it.[98]

"Paper logic" represents "notional assent," which "is an assent to a large development of predicates, correlative to each other, or at least intimately connected together, drawn out as if on paper, as we might map a country which we had never seen… ".[99] A key passage is from notional to "real assent," when the extended range of the signified has developed in such a way as to re-empower the signifier, putting life — indeed, the reader's whole life — into his response:

> Let us consider, too, how differently young and old are affected by the words of some classic author, such as Homer or Horace.

[95] *Ibid.*, 329.

[96] *Ibid.*, 321.

[97] *Ibid.*, 120.

[98] *Apologia pro Vita sua*, 285.

[99] *Grammar of Assent*, 102.

> Passages, which to a boy are but rhetorical common-places, neither better nor worse than a hundred others which any clever writer might supply, which he gets by heart and thinks very fine, and imitates, as he thinks, successfully, in his own flowing versification, at length come home to him, when long years have passed, and he has had experience of life, and pierce him, as if he had never before known them, with their sad earnestness and vivid exactness. Then he comes to understand how it is that lines, the birth of some chance morning or evening at an Ionian festival, or among the Sabine hills, have lasted generation after generation, for thousands of years, with a power over the mind, and a charm, which the current literature of his own day, with all its obvious advantages, is utterly unable to rival.[100]

The same change over time is brought to meet *the* Word: "And what the experience of the world effects for the illustration of classical authors, that office the religious sense, carefully cultivated, fulfils towards Holy Scripture. To the devout and spiritual, the Divine Word speaks of things, not merely of notions."[101] Yet individual re-interpretation is helplessly inadequate when it comes to dogmas of the faith:

> Thus I may know London quite well, and find my way from street to street in any part of it without difficulty, yet be quite unable to draw a map of it. Comparison, calculation, cataloguing, arranging, classifying, are intellectual acts subsequent upon, and not necessary for, a real apprehension of the things on which they are exercised. Strictly speaking then, the dogma of the Holy Trinity, as a complex whole, or as a mystery, is not the formal object of religious apprehension and assent; but as it is a number of propositions, taken one by one. That complex whole also is the object of assent, but it is the notional object; and when presented to religious minds, it is received by them notionally; and again implicitly, viz. in the real assent which

[100] *Ibid.*, 78.
[101] *Ibid.*, 79.

> they give to the word of God as conveyed to them through the instrumentality of His Church.[102]

The inscription of "real assent" in the Church's Magisterium, the ultimate and most authoritative representation in the Symbolic Order of the desired condition of belief for "religious minds," was "Rome" as Newman's ultimate destination.

[102] *Ibid.*, 129-130.

NEWMAN AND THE ALEXANDRIAN TRADITION "THE VEIL OF THE LETTER" AND THE PERSON OF CHRIST

Brian E. Daley

> Oh, that there were such an heart in us, to put aside this world, to desire to look at it as a mere screen between us and God, and to think of Him who has entered in beyond the veil, and who is watching us, trying us, yes, and blessing, and influencing, and encouraging us towards good, day by day![1]

Newman's soul was — to twist a hackneyed Latin phrase — an *anima naturaliter Patristica.* It was not simply that "the Fathers made me a Catholic," as he later confessed publicly to Pusey;[2] even in his Anglican years, in many ways, he thought, argued, read and interpreted the Scripture, more like a Greek Christian of the fourth century than like a Westerner of the nineteenth. He was, like

[1] John Henry Newman, *Parochial and Plain Sermons* I, 2: "The Immortality of the Soul" [before 1834] (San Francisco, CA: Ignatius Press, 1087) 20. — I am deeply grateful to Damon McGraw, my doctoral student and assistant at Notre Dame, for his help both in the conception of this article and in the research behind it.

[2] *A Letter to Dr. Pusey* [1864], later published in *Certain Difficulties Felt by Anglicans in Catholic Teaching* 2 (London: Pickering, 1876) 24. See also his often-cited earlier remarks at the end of chapter 2 of the *Essay on the Development of Christian Doctrine* (1878 edition; repr. Notre Dame, IN: University of Notre Dame Press, 1989) 97-98: "On the whole, all parties will agree that, of all existing systems, the present communion of Rome is the nearest approximation in fact to the Church of the Fathers, possible though some may think it, to be nearer still to that church on paper. Did St. Athanasius or St. Ambrose come suddenly to life, it cannot be doubted what communion he would take to be his own."

so many of the Fathers he admired, a passionate preacher, a tireless polemicist, a promoter of the independence and continual reform of the Church, an occasional writer rather than a systematician with a grand plan.[3] Much as he denied it, he was also a theologian: not in the scholastic or nineteenth-century German vein, but still a theologian of comprehensive vision and surprisingly consistent convictions, whose thought always remained concrete and concerned for Christian practice, anchored in Biblical texts, focused on God's primordial reality, and rooted in prayerful contemplation of the Jesus of the New Testament. Newman's description of his aim in discussing the Biblical language of justification, in his Fifth Lecture on that subject in the spring of 1837, can also be read as a programmatic statement about theology as a quest for truth:

> Our business is, if so be, to fix that one real sense [of justification] before our mind's eye, not to loiter or lose our way in the outward text of Scripture, but to get through and beyond the letter into the

[3] See, for instance, his remarks in the introduction to "The Last Years of St. Chrysostom," first published in the *Rambler*, 1859-60: "Now the Ancient Saints have left behind them just that kind of literature which more than any other represents the abundance of the heart, which more than any other approaches to conversation... Instead of writing formal doctrinal treatises, they write controversy; and their controversy, again, is correspondence. They mix up their own persons, natural and supernatural, with the didactic or polemical works which engaged them. Their authoritative declarations are written, not on stone tablets, but on what Scripture calls 'the fleshly tables of the heart'. The line of their discussion traverses a region rich and interesting, and opens on those who follow them in it a succession of instructive views as to the aims, the difficulties, the disappointments, under which they journeyed on heavenward, their care of the brethren, their anxieties about contemporary teachers of error. Dogma and proof are in them at the same time hagiography. They do not write a *summa theologiae*, or draw out a *catena*, or pursue a single thesis through the stages of a scholastic disputation. They wrote for the occasion, and seldom on a carefully-digested plan" (John Henry Newman, *Historical Sketches*, 2 [London: Longmans, 1888] 221, 223).

> spirit. Our duty is to be intent on things, not on names and terms; to associate words with their objects, instead of measuring them by their definitions; to speak as having eyes, and as if to those who have eyes, not as groping our way in the dark by intellectual conceptions, acts of memory, and efforts of reason... Here is the especial use of the Fathers as expositors of Scripture; they do what no examination of the particular context can do satisfactorily, acquaint us with the *things* Scripture speaks of.[4]

Like his hero, St. Gregory Nazianzen, whose first "Theological Oration" (Or. 27) strenuously warns against letting public theological discussion become a theatre for the showmanship of competing egos, and specifies discretion, reverence, and a contemplative attitude as indispensable dispositions for valid theological debate,[5] Newman also suggested, in a Passiontide sermon of the early 1840s, that Lent, the season of self-discipline, rather than the more boisterous celebrations of Christmas, was the best time for reflecting on the Mystery of the Incarnation:

[4] *Lectures on Justification* (New York: Scribner, Welford and Armstrong, [3]1874) 121.

[5] Gregory writes: "Not to everyone, my friends, does it belong to philosophize about God; not to everyone — the subject is not so cheap and low — and, I will add, not before every audience, nor at all times, nor on all points; but on certain occasions, and before certain persons, and within certain limits. Not to all men, because it is permitted only to those who have been examined, and are past masters in meditation, and who have been previously purified in soul and body, or at the very least are being purified... And what is the permitted occasion? It is when we are free from all external defilement or disturbance, and when that which rules within us is not confused with vexatious or erring images... For it is necessary to be truly at leisure to know God... And who are the permitted persons? They to whom the subject is of real concern, and not they who make it a matter of pleasant gossip, like any other thing, after the races, or the theater, or a concert, or a dinner, or still lower employments" (Or. 27.3; trans. Charles Gordon Browne and James Edward Swallow: *Nicene and Post-Nicene Fathers* [NPNF] II, 7 [Peabody, MA: Hendrickson, repr. 1994] 285).

> Let me observe, that we ought not to speak, we ought not to hear, such high truths, without great reverence and awe, and preparation of mind. And this is a reason, perhaps why this is a proper season for dwelling on them... When we are engaged in weaning ourselves from this world, when we are denying ourselves even lawful things, when we have a subdued tone of thought and feeling, then is an allowable time surely to speak of the high mysteries of the faith.[6]

The real place for the language of theology, he seems to say, is neither the classroom nor the market-place, but a setting of quiet, un-self-conscious worship and contemplation.[7]

All of these echoes of the great orthodox Fathers of the fourth and fifth centuries were doubtless due to Newman's increasingly intense study of their writings, from his days as a young don at Oriel. But Newman took as his particular inspiration and model that tradition of early theological writers he, and many other modern scholars, have identified as the "school of Alexandria" — the forebears and heirs of Athanasius, to whom he devoted so much of his own scholarly labors in the crucial years of the early 1840s.

6 "Christ, the Son of God Made Man," sermon for the Fifth Sunday of Lent [before 1842]: *Parochial and Plain Sermons* VI, 5 (1218).

7 Compare also his remarks in an earlier sermon, for Christmas Day, on the devotional and doxological effect of the dogmatic language of the Creeds: "The declarations in them, the distinctions, cautions, and the like, supported and illuminated by Scripture, draw down, as it were, from heaven the image of Him who is on God's right hand, preserve us from an indolent use of words without apprehending them, and rouse in us those mingled feelings of fear and confidence, affection and devotion towards Him, which are implied in the belief of a personal advent of God in our nature, and which were originally derived to the Church from the very sight of him. And we may say further still, these statements — such, for instance, as occur in the Te Deum and Athanasian Creed — are especially suitable in divine worship, inasmuch as they kindle and elevate the religious affections. They are hymns of praise and thanksgiving; they give glory to God as revealed in the Gospel, just as David's Psalms magnify His Attributes as displayed in nature." "The Incarnation" [before 1835], *Parochial and Plain Sermons* II, 3 (244).

Newman reflects on this spiritual and intellectual predilection in a famous passage in the first chapter of his *Apologia*, where he speaks of his early discovery — after being drawn to "Antiquity" by reading Bishop George Bull's *Defensio Fidei Nicaenae* [1685] — of the Alexandrian theological tradition before Athanasius.

> What principally attracted me in the ante-Nicene period was the great Church of Alexandria, the historical centre of teaching in those times. Of Rome for some centuries comparatively little is known. The battle of Arianism was first fought in Alexandria; Athanasius, champion of the truth, was Bishop of Alexandria; and in his writings he refers to the great religious names of an earlier date, to Origen, Dionysius, and others, who were the glory of its see, and of its school. The broad philosophy of Clement and Origen carried me away; the philosophy, not the theological doctrine; and I have drawn out some features of it in my volume [*The Arians of the Fourth Century* (1833)] with the zeal and freshness, but with the partiality of a neophyte. Some portions of their teaching, magnificent in themselves, came like music to my inward ear, as if the response to ideas, which, with little external to encourage them, I had cherished so long. These were based on the mystical or sacramental principle, and spoke of the various Economies or Dispensations of the Eternal. I understood these passages to mean that the exterior world, physical and historical, was but the manifestation to our senses of realities greater than itself. Nature was a parable: Scripture was an allegory: pagan literature, philosophy, and mythology, properly understood, were but a preparation for the Gospel. The Greek poets and sages were in a certain sense prophets… In the fullness of time both Judaism and Paganism had come to nought; the outward framework, which concealed yet suggested the Living Truth, had never been intended to last, and it was dissolving under the beams of the Sun of Justice which shone behind it and through it. The process of change had been slow; it had been done not rashly, but by rule and measure, 'at sundry times and in divers manners', first one disclosure and then another, till the whole evangelical doctrine was brought into full manifestation. And thus room was made for the anticipation of further and deeper disclosures, of truths still under the veil of the letter,

> and in their season to be revealed. The visible world still remains without its divine interpretation; Holy Church in her sacraments and her hierarchical appointments, will remain, even to the end of the world, after all but a symbol of those heavenly facts which fill eternity. Her Mysteries are but the expressions in human language of truths to which the human mind is unequal.[8]

Newman sketches here a compelling, if rather idealized portrait of a strand of early Christian thought that today would doubtless be seen as forming a continuous tradition, but perhaps as less consistent, and less continuously orthodox, than he supposed.[9] Furnished with fewer details than we now have on early Christianity, particularly details of Gnostic and other deviant forms of theology, Newman saw the Alexandria of the second to fifth centuries as the main center of an emerging Christian orthodoxy, later supported by Rome and some of the Western Churches, but more often in theological tension with other, more independent-minded cultural centers of the Greek Christian world, where intellectual acumen seemed to Newman usually to have trumped religious fidelity. In his late essay, "The Causes of the Rise and Success of Arianism" (1872), Newman asserts his conviction that the intellectual inspiration of Arius, a presbyter of the Alexandrian Church, came, like a contagious "spiritual malady," from free-thinking Antioch rather than from his more traditionally-minded home city. The reason, in his view, was one of religious culture:

> Asia, with Antioch as its metropolis, had a culture which the other parts of Christendom had not. Alexandria, which had so firm a tradition and grasp of orthodoxy, was but one city, situated at the extremity of the Empire, commanding only the narrow valley of the Nile,

[8] *Apologia pro Vita Sua* ([2]1865; London: Longmans, Green, 1913) 26-27.

[9] For a portrait of ancient Alexandrian Christianity that brings out its diverse, often conflicted theological voices, see C. Wilfred Griggs, *Early Egyptian Christianity from its Origins to 451 C.E.* (Leiden: Brill, 1990).

> and cut off by deserts and by the broad sea from the rest of the Roman world. Antioch, on the contrary, was but the chief of many flourishing seats of learning, and, by means of the public roads, was in easy communication with the whole of Syria, Palestine, and Asia Minor, not to speak of Thrace and Greece. Moreover, its separate Churches, enjoying an autonomy which the Egyptian Churches had not, exercised a freedom of thought, and had a practice in controversy, peculiar to themselves; and preferring the study of the literal to that of the allegorical sense of scripture, were indisposed to submit either to the authorities or to the proofs on which orthodoxy, such as the Alexandrian, rested the sacred doctrine in dispute.[10]

Today, scholars would be more inclined to see fourth- and fifth-century Antioch, the world of Theodore of Mopsuestia and Theodoret of Cyrus, as the minority voice in the theological culture of early Christianity. But for our understanding of Newman, the point is unimportant. Here, as in *The Arians of the Fourth Century*, one encounters Newman's reading not just of ancient Antioch and the East, but of the Erastian, learned, but spiritually pedestrian Anglican theologians of the 18th and 19th centuries, ranged against the minority voice of Athanasius and the orthodox tradition, for whom Rome — in the early Church as in the modern world — always acted as champion.[11]

[10] "Causes of the Rise and Success of Arianism" [February, 1872], *Tracts Theological and Ecclesiastical* (London: Pickering, 1874) 99. Here and in his essay "On St. Cyril's Formula μία φύσις σεσαρκωμένη," *Atlantis* 1858 (= *Tracts Theological*, 294-296, 306, etc.), Newman assumes that mainstream Alexandrian theologians, from Clement and Origen through Athanasius to Cyril, had their own characteristic terminology for Trinitarian theology and Christology; see also "Rise and Success," 191-196.

[11] See also Newman's appendix on "The Syrian School of Theology" in the third edition of *Arians* [1871] (repr. Leominster/South Bend: Gracewing/Notre Dame, 2001) 403-415. For a brief but penetrating analysis of Newman's influential interpretation of Arius and Alexandria, see Rowan Williams, *Arius: Heresy and Tradition* (London: Darton, Longman & Todd, 1987) 2-6. Williams's own judgment is that Arius was in fact a rather typical follower of the Origenist tradition,

For Newman, the peculiar genius of the Alexandrian tradition was its unified vision of God's mysterious but dynamic presence, God's immediate transcendent reality, in both the events and personalities of Scripture and in the longer trajectory of human history, all reaching its culmination in the person of Christ, the Word made flesh, and in Christ's continuing, mysterious presence, through the Spirit, in the Church and the individual believer. It was the "mystical or sacramental" approach of the great Alexandrian theologians, in other words, to the discovery of truth in Scripture and history — a hermeneutic rooted in a Christology whose terminology evolved, but whose heart was always a clear vision of the divine person of the Son of God, as Truth itself revealed in the midst of human reality — that gave their exegesis and theological polemics both its coherence and its normative theological value. Let us now consider Newman's understanding of the Alexandrian tradition more closely, by looking briefly at his interpretation of three crucial stations in its development.

1. The Second and Third Century: Clement and Origen

It is significant that when Newman, in the *Apologia*, relates his ravished discovery of Clement and Origen, the two most celebrated "mainstream" representatives of early Alexandrian Christian thought, he emphasizes that it was their "philosophy," not their

who exaggerated the conclusions he wanted to draw from what had become the more or less standard way of understanding the relations of Father and Son: "Arius was a committed theological conservative; more specifically, a conservative *Alexandrian*" (175; for his analysis of Arius's theology, see 95-178). For a thoughtful and provocative analysis of Newman's understanding of classical Christian heresies, in the years before 1845, and of his rhetorical use of heretical labels in dealing with Anglican issues of his own day, see Stephen Thomas, *Newman and Heresy: The Anglican Years* (Cambridge: Cambridge University Press, 1991).

"theological doctrine," that most impressed him. In distancing himself from their doctrine, Newman presumably means to disown those aspects of these early writers' theological speculation that seemed questionable in the light of later doctrinal debates: their embrace of universal salvation or *apokatastasis*, perhaps, or Origen's highly spiritualized conception of the resurrection of the body, as well as the clear, if carefully nuanced, subordination of Son to Father that marks Origen's Christology.[12] The Alexandrian Fathers' "philosophy," on the other hand, seems, for Newman, not simply to have included their general affinity to the late Platonic tradition — which was, for all genuinely religious people in late antiquity, the most congenial mode of thought — but more specifically their habitual approach to finding meaning in the things and events of created history. For both Clement and Origen, the salvation of humanity from the destructive cycle of sin and death, idolatry and sensuality, was accomplished by the compassionate God's gradual revelation of his truth to darkened human minds, first through the skills and knowledge gained by human education and culture — especially philosophy — then through God's

[12] For their views of the risen body and universal salvation, see Brian E. Daley, *The Hope of the Early Church: A Handbook of Patristic Eschatology* (Peabody, MA: Hendrickson, rev. ed. 2003) 46-47 (Clement), 51-55, 58-59 (Origen). For Origen's conception of the subordinate, if everlasting relation of Son to Father, see *Commentary on John* 2.75; *On First Principles* 1.1.8; 1.2.6; 1.3.5. Newman, by contrast, follows Athanasius closely in emphasizing the Son's absolute equality with the Father, in all activities and characteristics of the divine Being (see, for instance, *Select Treatises of St. Athanasius* 2 [1881] [London: Longmans, Green, 1900] 289). So in his sermon, "The Humiliation of the Eternal Son," Newman distinguishes between the "accordance, concurrence [and] co-operation" which are characteristic of a son, and which eternally characterize the Son's relationship to the Father, and the obedience which "belongs to a servant" and which Jesus is said to have "learned" when he took on "'the form of a servant', taking on Himself a separate will and a separate work, and the toil and sufferings incident to a creature" (*Parochial and Plain Sermons* II. 12 [582]).

involvement in the history of Israel, and climactically in the person and teaching of Jesus, God's Wisdom made flesh.[13]

For Clement of Alexandria, a Greek layman of the turn of the third century, who seems to have come to Christian faith as the result of a first-rate humanistic and philosophical education, human beings are saved from self-destruction through the enlightenment of the mind by divine Truth and through its integration into action by the acquisition of virtue. Virtue, in turn, prepares the purified person to share in God's eternal life. Christ, the eternal Logos, has come into human history as the revealer of Truth: the new Orpheus, whose "new Song" tames human wildness, frees us from slavery, and guides us to the wholesome, original harmony of the cosmos.[14] For Christians, Christ is the *paidagogos*, the one who instructs us not only in the principles of moral living, but even in good taste and good manners — the final rule of thumb for Christian behavior, even for Clement, was the familiar modern question, "What would Jesus do?"[15] To assimilate the teaching and

[13] For a helpful general comparison between Newman's habits of thought and those of Clement and Origen, see Charles Frederick Harrold, "Newman and the Alexandrian Platonists," *Modern Philology* 37 (1940) 279-291.

[14] See his *Protrepticus* 1, 11, 12.

[15] See, for instance, the conclusion to Clement's long advice on how a Christian should behave at dinner-parties: "In what manner do you think the Lord drank when He became man for our sakes? As shamelessly as we? Was it not with decorum and propriety? Was it not deliberately? For rest assured, he also partook of wine, for He, too, was man. And he blessed the wine, saying, 'Take, drink: this is my blood' — the blood of the vine... And that he who drinks ought to observe moderation, He clearly showed by what He taught at feasts. For he did not teach affected by wine" (*Paid.* 2.2; trans. in Alexander Roberts and James Donaldson [eds.], *The Ante-Nicene Fathers* [ANF], 2 [repr. Peabody, MA: Hendrickson, 1994] 246) — For reflections on parallels in Clement to Newman's ideas on culture and education, see Vincent F. Blehl, "Newman, the Fathers, and Ecucation," *Thought* 45 (1970) 196-212; "The Patristic Humanism of John Henry Newman," *Newman-Studien* 10 (1978) 60-67. For a somewhat rambling, but still useful, list of possible theological parallels between Clement's and Newman's

example of the Logos is to share in the eternal beauty and perfection of God:

> That person with whom the Word dwells does not adorn himself, does not make himself up: he has the form of the Word; he is made like God; he is beautiful. He does not ornament himself: his is beauty, the true beauty, for it is God; and that person becomes divine, since God so wills. Heraclitus, then, was right when he said, "men are gods, and gods are men, for their structure (*logos*) is the same." It is a manifest Mystery: God in man, and man divine.[16]

To benefit fully from the Logos's revelation, Clement insists, one must share the Christian understanding of who the Jesus of the Gospels is, and how he is related to God:

> It is necessary to believe truly in the Son: that He is the Son, and that He came, and how, and why, and concerning His passion; and we must know who the Son of God is. Now there is no knowledge without faith, nor faith without knowledge; for there is also no Father without the Son. The Father is, at the same time, Father of the Son, and the Son is the true teacher respecting the Father. And in order that one may believe in the Son, one must know the Father, in relation to whom the Son also exists. Again, in order for us to know the Father, we must believe in the Son, since the Son of God is our teacher.[17]

Yet since he is divine Wisdom and Lord of all, the Logos must be presumed to reach out to all human beings, whatever their culture and religious background.[18] Even though the full expression of the Word's ῖλανθρωπία is, for Clement, unquestionably "that he scorned not the weakness of human flesh, but clothed himself with

works, see Franz Michael Willam, "Newmans Drei Analysen der Dogmenentwicklung im Anschluss an Klemens von Alexandrien," *Newman-Studien* 9 (1974) 31-63.

16 *Paed.* 3.1.1.5-2.1 (trans. ANF 271 [altered]).

17 *Stromateis* 5.1.2-4, echoing Matt 11:27.

18 See, for example, *Stromateis* 7.6-8.

it,"[19] Clement strongly believes that God has also revealed his redeeming goodness to humanity more widely; so he writes in Book VI of the *Stromateis*:

> For clearly, I think, [the Logos] showed that the one and only God was known by the Greeks in a Gentile way, by the Jews in a Jewish way, and in a new and spiritual way by us. And further, he has made it clear that the same God who furnished both covenants was the giver of Greek philosophy to the Greeks, by which the Almighty is glorified among the Greeks.[20]

For all religious people, however — pagans, Jews and Christians — Clement believes that the saving Truth that comes from God is veiled in particular cultures and traditions, in literary and material symbols, whose interpretation always requires a human guide: someone already purified morally and enlightened intellectually, who is ready to teach others.

> All things that shine through a veil show the truth in a grander, more imposing way, like ripe fruit seen through water, or shapes that are given added visual qualities because they appear through veils... Since, then, it is possible to draw several meanings, as we often do, from what is expressed obscurely, the ignorant and the unlearned person misses this sort of thing — but the knower [literally: the "Gnostic"] apprehends.[21]

For Clement, a central aspect of the role of the Christian teacher, then, is to interpret the Mysteries of human history, especially as they are contained in the Biblical narrative. This became the

[19] *Stromateis* 7.8 (trans. Joseph B. Mayor; in J. L. Oulton and Henry Chadwick [ed.], *Alexandrian Christianity* [Philadelphia, PA: Westminster, 1954] 97).

[20] *Stromateis* 6.5.41.7-42.1 (trans. ANF 2.489 [altered]); see also *Stromateis* 6.8.67.1, where Clement speaks of Greek philosophy as "covenant peculiar to them, the stepping-stone to the philosophy that is according to Christ."

[21] *Stromateis* 5.9.56.5-57.1 (trans. ANF 457-458 [altered]). Book 7 of the *Stromateis* is an extended description of the character of the "Christian Gnostic" and of his service to the community as teacher and moral guide.

life-work of Origen, the great Alexandrian theologian of the following generation, and the first professional Christian exegete. Most of Origen's surviving works illustrate the kind of figural or "allegorical" interpretation of the Christian Bible Newman found to be "music to his inward ear:" an interpretation of human history, narrated normatively for faith in the Jewish and Christian Scriptures, in terms of creation, fall and redemption, in which Christ, the Logos made flesh, is the central core of meaning, the "treasure hidden in the field."[22] In his main reflection on the theological principles of Christian exegesis, Book 4 of his treatise *On First Principles*, Origen makes it clear that it is only in light of the coming of Jesus, as the one who brings fulfillment to what the Hebrew Scriptures offer as promise, that one can see the divine inspiration that has guided the composition of the Bible since the beginning.[23] He draws a telling analogy here with our ability to see the workings of divine providence in human history: sometimes, in retrospect, the pattern of meaning is clear to us, while at other times it remains obscure.[24] So too, he implies, in the light of Christ one knows the overall meaning of the Biblical narrative and texts, but one must still often struggle to find the spiritual or Christian content of particular passages. That central, Christ-centered meaning,

[22] Matt 13:44; see Origen, *Commentary on Matthew* 10:5. For contemporary discussion of ancient figural interpretation of canonical texts by both pagans and Christians in Alexandria, up to Clement, see John David Dawson, *Allegorical Readers and Cultural Revision in Ancient Alexandria* (Berkeley, CA: University of California Press, 1992); and *Christian Figural Reading and the Fashioning of Identity* (Berkeley, CA: University of California Press, 2002), with a chapter on Origen. For introductory surveys of early Christian Biblical interpretation, see Manlio Simonetti, *Biblical Interpretation in the Early Church* (Edinburgh: T. and T. Clark, 1994); and Frances M. Young, *Biblical Exegesis and the Formation of Christian Culture* (Cambridge: Cambridge University Press, 1997).

[23] *On First Principles*, 4.1.6.

[24] *Ibid.*, 4.1.7.

in Origen's view, is summed up in the Church's creedal statements or "rule of piety," though it runs through the whole Bible as well:

> We must point out that the aim of the Spirit, who, by the providence of God, through the Word 'who was in the beginning with God', enlightened the servants of the truth — that is, the prophets and apostles — was pre-eminently concerned with the unspeakable mysteries connected with human affairs... And when we speak of the needs of souls, who cannot otherwise reach perfection except through the rich and wise truth about God, we attach of necessity pre-eminent importance to the doctrines concerning God and his only-begotten Son: of what nature the Son is, and in what manner he can be the Son of God, and what are the causes of his descending to the level of human flesh and completely assuming humanity; and what, also is the nature of his activity, and towards whom and at what times it is exercised...[25]

In the opening section of his *Commentary on the Gospel of John*, Origen offers a stunningly coherent presentation of his view of the Scriptures. A "Gospel', he argues, is any proclamation of future or present good news, or as he puts it, "a discourse containing a promise of things which naturally, and on account of the benefits they bring, rejoice the hearer as soon as the promise is heard and believed."[26] In this sense, all Scripture is a promise — originally an obscure, unfulfilled promise — of the coming of Christ, and all

[25] *Ibid.*, 4.2.7 (trans. G. W. Butterworth; New York: Harper, 1966) 282-283 [altered]. Origen goes on to list other points of doctrine essential to the perfection of the soul: the nature of rational beings, the fall of souls and the reasons for the different conditions of intelligent creatures in the present order, the nature of the material world, and the origin of evil. For an interpretation of the whole structure and purpose of *On First Principles* as guided by this understanding of how to discover the meaning of Scripture, see Brian E. Daley, S.J., "Origen's *De Principiis*: a Guide to the Principles of Christian Scriptural Interpretation," in John Petruccione (ed.), *Nova et Vetera: Patristic Studies in Honor of Thomas Patrick Halton* (Washington, DC: Catholic University of America Press, 1998) 3-21.

[26] *Commentary on John* 1:7 (trans. Allan Menzies; ANF 9.300).

becomes Gospel, to the believer, in the light of his coming.[27] "The good things the Apostles announce in the Gospel are simply Jesus,"[28] he continues, for those who live by this faith, "even our own good actions, and the sins of those who stumble," become part of this same Gospel narrative, this same joyful proclamation of God's victory.

> If the one who preaches the Gospel preaches good things (τὰ ἀγαθά), and if all those who spoke before the coming of Jesus in the flesh preach Christ, who is, as we saw, 'good things', then the words spoken by all of them alike are in a sense a part of the Gospel.[29]

Origen's sense of the unified, Christ-centered meaning of the Biblical canon and the life of the Church, filled with puzzles and challenges to the interpreting mind but radiantly clear when read as a proclamation of Christ, must have been one of the main things that made his "philosophy" so attractive to the young Newman. Along with it, one imagines that the warm devotion expressed by both Clement and Origen for the person of Christ, teacher and redeemer, must have resonated well with Newman's own desire, evident in so many of the *Parochial and Plain Sermons*, to draw his hearers not just to see the truths of faith more clearly, but to feel them more deeply and more reverently. This passage on the Incarnation, for instance, from the second book of Origen's *De Principiis*, could have been penned by Newman himself:

> When we consider those great and marvelous truths about the nature of the Son of God, we are lost in the deepest amazement that such a

[27] *Ibid.*, 1:8: "Before the sojourn of Christ, the law and the prophets — since He had not come who interpreted the mysteries they contained — did not convey such a promise as belongs to our definition of the Gospel; but the Savior, when He sojourned with us and caused the Gospel to appear in bodily form, by the Gospel caused all things to appear as Gospel" (ANF 9.301).

[28] *Ibid.*, 1:10 (ANF 9.302).

[29] *Ibid.*, 1:15 (ANF 9.305 [altered]).

> being, towering high above all, should have 'emptied himself' of his majestic condition and become man and dwelt among men... When, therefore, we see in him some things so human that they appear in no way to differ from the common frailty of mortals, and some things so divine that they are appropriate to nothing else but the primal and ineffable nature of deity, the human understanding with its narrow limits is baffled, and struck with amazement at so mighty a wonder knows not which way to turn, what to hold to, or whither to betake itself. If it thinks of God, it sees a man; if it thinks of a man, it beholds one returning from the dead with spoils after vanquishing the kingdom of death. For this reason we must pursue our contemplation with all fear and reverence, as we seek to prove how the reality of each nature exists in one and the same person...[30]

It is in what Newman would call the "heavenly fact" of Christ that the "mystical or sacramental principle" has its key, and the promise of faith finds its astonishing fulfillment.

2. The Fourth Century: Athanasius

Of all the Fathers, Athanasius clearly stood closest to Newman's heart. Newman's masterful annotated translation of Athanasius's main controversial writings, produced at Littlemore in 1842 and 1843 as he struggled to clarify his own place in the Catholic Church, seems to have established a personal bond, a kind of identification with the great Alexandrian bishop, which eased Newman's movement towards Rome. His thumbnail sketch of Athanasius's character, in the alphabetically rearranged notes on his works published in 1881, brings this out clearly: calling him "the foremost doctor of the Divine Sonship,"[31] Newman singles out as Athanasius's "more prominent traits" his "deep sense of the

[30] *On First Principles*, 2.6.1 (trans. Butterworth 109).

[31] *Select Treatises of St. Athanasius*, 2 (repr. London: Longmans, Green, 1900) 56.

authority of Tradition," precisely as a key to interpreting Scripture;[32] his "fierceness" in combating doctrinal error, but gentleness and civility towards others with whom he disagreed;[33] his compassion shown even towards Arius, when recounting his unreconciled death;[34] his ability to stand firm against the Emperor, when he turned against the orthodox faith;[35] his "prudent, temperate spirit"[36] in explaining controversial aspects of doctrine; his modesty of language,[37] along with his high intellectual accomplishments and graceful writing style.[38] Not every scholar would agree today with Newman's characterization; its importance, perhaps, lies as much in what it shows us of Newman's ideal of ecclesiastical controversy as in its depiction of Athanasius. In the words of Roderick Strange, "Newman absorbed Athanasius's standpoint; the consequent sense of kinship was vital to him."[39]

Athanasius's theological significance for Newman is undoubtedly centered on the Alexandrian bishop's relentless campaign to clarify the Church's understanding of the person of Christ, as literally the "Son of God."[40] In the works of his mid-career, especially in his three *Orations against the Arians* (written probably 340-346) and in the somewhat later *Defense of the Nicene Definition* (*De Decretis*) (351), Athanasius concentrated his literary energies on expounding the orthodox sense of Jesus' title of Son, and on suggesting that this is the primary concept for understanding his

[32] *Ibid.*, 51.
[33] *Ibid.*, 52.
[34] *Ibid.*, 53-54.
[35] *Ibid.*, 54-55.
[36] *Ibid.*, 56.
[37] *Ibid.*, 56-58.
[38] *Ibid.*, 58-59.
[39] *Newman and the Gospel of Christ* (Oxford: Oxford University Press, 1981) 6.
[40] *Ibid.*, 24-31.

relationship to God.[41] Newman's own summary, in one of his notes on Athanasius, puts Athanasius's position accurately, yet also more concisely than the Alexandrian ever managed to do:

> The Son of God must be God, granting that the human word 'Son' is to guide us to the knowledge of what is heavenly; for on earth we understand by a son one who is the successor and heir to a given nature. A continuation of communication of nature enters into the very idea of γέννησις; if there is no participation of nature there is no sonship… The Son then participates in the Divine Nature, and since the Divine Nature is none other than the One individual Living Personal True God, He too is that God, and since that One True God is eternal and never had a beginning of existence, therefore the Son is eternal and without beginning… The Second Person in the Holy Trinity is not a quality, or attribute, or a mere relation, but the One Eternal Essence; not a part of the First Person, but whole or entire God, all that God is; nor does the *gennesis* impair the Father's Essence, which is already whole and entire God. Thus there are two infinite Persons, in Each Other because they are infinite. Each of Them being wholly One and the Same Divine Being, yet not being merely separate aspects of the Same. Each is God as absolutely as if the Other were not.[42]

In Athanasius, too, Newman found a way of speaking about the humanity of Christ that was to prove centrally important for the formation of his own Christology: because Christ is a single person, a single subject or agent, and because that person is literally and uniquely the eternal Son of God, everything that constitutes

[41] See *Oration I*, 10-36; *De Decretis*, 6-17. Athanasius stresses the centrality of the title "Son," for instance, in *De Decretis*, 17: "The Son of God, as may be learnt from the divine oracles themselves, is Himself the Word of God, and the Wisdom, and the Image, and the Hand, and the Power; for God's Offspring is one, and of the generation from the Father these titles are tokens. For if you say 'the Son', you have declared what is from the Father by nature…" (trans. Newman; NPNF II, 4; 160).

[42] *Athanasius*, 2.287-292.

Jesus' humanity is to be thought of as constituting an "instrument" (ὄργανον) or acquired attribute of the Son, through which he makes himself humanly present and active in the world, but not as part of the ontological constitution of his Person in itself. In his notes on Athanasius, Newman cites several passages in the *Orations against the Arians* to make this point: "Thus being without personality of its own, [Christ's] human nature was, relatively to Himself, really what the Arians falsely said that his divinity was relatively to the Father, a περὶ αὐτόν, a περιβολή, a συμβεβηκός, a 'something else besides his substance', e. g., an ὄργανον."[43]

Clearly Newman's interest in Athanasius's approach to understanding the Person of Christ was more than just academic; a number of the *Parochial and Plain Sermons*, for instance, emphasize this same powerful, unified conception of the incarnate Christ as divine Son. In the Passiontide sermon on Christ quoted above, for instance — probably given in 1841 or 1842, while Newman was working on his translation of Athanasius — we encounter it strongly:

> Here we are brought to the second point of doctrine which it is necessary to insist upon, that while our Lord is God He is also the Son of God, or rather, that He is God because He is the Son of God. We are apt, at first hearing, to say that He is God though He is the Son of God, marveling at the mystery. But what to man is a mystery, to God is a cause. He is God, not *though*, but *because* he is Son of God... The great safeguard to the doctrine of our Lord's Divinity is the doctrine of his Sonship; we realize that He is God only when we acknowledge Him to be by nature and from eternity Son.
>
> Nay, our Lord's Sonship is not only the guarantee to us of His Godhead, but also the condition of His incarnation. As the Son was God,

[43] *Ibid.*, 427, citing Athanasius, *Or.* 2.45; cf. *ibid.*, 450, where Newman cites Athanasius, *Or.* 3.31 and 53. For the humanity of Christ as an instrument of the Logos in healing creation, one might also add *On the Incarnation*, 42 and 45.

> so on the other hand was the Son suitably made man; it belonged to Him to have the Father's perfections, it became him to assume a servant's form... He who spoke [about his Father] was one really existing person, and He, that one Living and Almighty Son, both God and man, was the brightness of God's glory and His Power, and wrought what His Father willed, and was in the Father and the Father in Him, not only in heaven but on earth. In heaven He was this, and did this, as God; and on earth He was this, and did this, in that manhood which He assumed, but whether in heaven, or on earth, still as the Son.[44]

Similarly, it seems mainly from his study of Athanasius that Newman drew his own strong sense of salvation as actual transformation in Christ, as "divinization," a participation in the holiness and in

[44] "Christ, the Son of God Made Man," *Parochial and Plain Sermons* VI, 5 (1212-1214) [for the Fifth Sunday of Lent; before 1842]. For the same theme, see also Newman's sermon "The Humiliation of the Eternal Son," from before 1834, on the text of Hebrews 5:7-8: "What, then, is meant by the 'Son of God'? It is meant that our Lord is the very or true Son of God, that is, His Son by nature. We are but *called* the sons of God — we are adopted to be sons — but our Lord and Savior is the Son of God, really and by birth, and He alone is such... Thus when the early Christians used the title, 'The Son of God', they meant, after the manner of the Apostles when they use it in Scripture, all we mean in the Creed, when, by way of explaining ourselves, we confess Him to be 'God from God, Light from Light, Very or True God from True God'. For in that He is the Son of God, He must be whatever God is, all-holy, all-wise, all-powerful, all-good, eternal, infinite; yet since there is only one God, He must be at the same time not separate from God, but ever one with and in Him, one indivisibly; so that it would be as idle language to speak of Him as separated in essence from His Father, as to say that our reason, or intellect, or will, was separate from our minds..."

"The text goes on to say, 'Though He were a Son, yet learned He obedience by the things which He suffered'. Obedience belongs to a servant, but accordance, concurrence, co-operation are the characteristics of a son. In His eternal union with God there was no distinction of will and work between Him and His Father... But in the days of His flesh, when He had humbled Himself to 'the form of a servant', taking on Himself a separate will and a separate work, and the toil and sufferings incident to a creature, then what had been mere concurrence became obedience" (*Parochial and Plain Sermons* II, 12, 581-582).

the very being of God. Although this idea appears as early as Irenaeus,[45] it was Athanasius who first emphasized it clearly as the purpose and result of the Incarnation of the Word. So he writes in the *Second Oration against the Arians:*

> The truth shows us that the Word is not of things originate, but rather is Himself their framer. For therefore did he assume the body originate and human, that having renewed it as its Framer, He might deify it in Himself, and thus might introduce us all into the Kingdom of heaven after his likeness. For we would not have been deified if we were joined to a creature, or if the Son were not true God; nor had man been brought into the Father's presence, unless He had been His natural and true Word who had put on the body.[46]

In his Anglican sermons, even as he rejected the Lutheran idea of a purely extrinsic or forensic justification, Newman also came to stress more and more boldly the real assimilation of the graced Christian, in the Spirit, to Christ, as Christ realized the Mysteries of our redemption in his own humanity.

> What was actually done in Christ in the flesh eighteen hundred years ago, is in type and resemblance really wrought in us one by one even to the end of time. He was born of the Spirit, and we too are born of the Spirit. He was justified by the Spirit, and so are we. He was pronounced the well-beloved Son, when the Holy Ghost descended on him, and we too cry 'Abba, Father', through the Spirit sent into our hearts...[47]

45 See, for example, *Against the Heresies*, 5.praef., 5.36.3; Irenaeus develops his idea of deification from the Biblical creation story, in which the human person is made in the image and likeness of God. For a classic survey of Patristic theology of divinization, now available in an English translation, see Jules Gross, *The Divinization of the Christian according to the Greek Fathers* (trans. Paul A. Onica; Anaheim, CA: A and C Press, 2002).

46 *Or. II Against the Arians*, 70 (trans. Newman: NPNF II, 4.70 [altered]). For further examples, see also *On the Incarnation*, 4; *De Decretis*, 14; *Or. III Against the Arians*, 19, 25, 34, 39. And see Gross, 163-175.

47 "Righteousness, not of Us but in Us." "Epiphany" [before 1840], *Parochial and Plain Sermons* V, 10 (1038).

So, in a Christmas sermon probably from 1842, Newman invites his hearers to contemplate the full meaning of the feast in terms that still more powerfully echo the Greek Fathers:

> Let us steadily contemplate the mystery, and say whether any consequence is too great to follow from so marvelous a dispensation; any mystery so great, any grace so overpowering, as that which is already manifested in the incarnation and death of the Eternal Son... Men we remain, but not mere men, but gifted with a measure of all those perfections which Christ has in fullness, partaking each in his own degree of His Divine Nature so fully, that the only reason (so to speak) why His saints are not really like Him, is that it is impossible — that He is the Creator, and they His creatures; yet still so, that they are all but Divine, all that they can be made without violating the incommunicable majesty of the Most High.[48]

All of these Athanasian strains in Newman's preaching and theological writing center on the person of Christ and his significance for the person in grace. It seems to me that there is also a possible hermeneutical parallel between Newman's thought and that of the Alexandrian bishop — one not remarked on by Newman or, as far as I know, by his modern students — in the way both of them see the role of historically developing dogmatic and creedal language in the articulation of the Church's traditional teaching and Biblical faith. Rowan Williams has perceptively observed that Newman, at least in the early 1830s as he worked on *The Arians of the Fourth Century*, admired the figurative, heterogeneous, imprecise language of ante-Nicene writers precisely because it conveyed something important about the excess of divine meaning beyond the confines of technical terms; for him, Williams suggests,

[48] "Religious Joy." "Christmas" [before 1843], *Parochial and Plain Sermons* VIII, 17 (1698-1699). For similar language, see Maximus the Confessor, *Quaestiones ad Thalassium*, 22 and 60.

> the advance of dogma is something almost tragic, a poignant ideological puberty… Newman comes close to a *Verfallstheorie* of dogmatic language, the notion of formulation itself being a kind of betrayal of some richer truth; but it is a necessary fall, a *felix culpa*, given that the Church lives in a history of change, contingency, and human sinfulness, and that the gospel must be preached in a variety of contexts."[49]

Something close to this same attitude is revealed by Athanasius in his own explanation of the formulation of faith issued by the Council of Nicaea. The two new phrases added by the Council to an otherwise standard confession of baptismal faith were its assertions that the only Son, begotten of the Father, is "of the substance of the Father (ἐκ τῆς οὐσίας τοῦ Πατρός)," and that, as one "begotten, not made," he is "of the same substance as the Father (ὁμοούσιον τῷ Πατρί)."[50] In the context of fourth-century Greek theology, these phrases were to many Church leaders more troubling than Arius's assertions, suggesting a modalist understanding of the relation of Son to Father — that he and the Father are simply "the same thing" — and with it a denial of the distinct divine personal agency of Christ. After almost two decades of diplomatic silence, Athanasius — backed by the Roman bishops but virtually alone in the East, and vigorously, often brutally opposed by the Emperor Constantius — began to campaign actively in favor of the Nicene

[49] "Newman's *Arians* and the Question of Method in Doctrinal History," Ian Ker and Alan G. Hill (eds.), *Newman after a Hundred Years* (Oxford: Clarendon Press, 1990) 270.

[50] For a discussion of the evolution of the Nicene creed from older formulas, and of its significance in the context of the Arian controversy, see J. N. D. Kelly, *Early Christian Creeds* (London: Longmans, [3]1972) 205-262. For a complete collection of Christian creeds and doctrinal definitions, see Jaroslav Pelikan and Valerie Hotchkiss, *Creeds and Confessions of Faith in the Christian Tradition*, 4 vols. (New Haven, CT: Yale, 2003); for the text of the Nicene creed: *ibid.*, 1.158-158; comment, 4.414-415.

formulation, eventually convincing his more moderate contemporaries, who wanted to avoid Arius's position but to remain simply with the language of the Bible, that this new, metaphysical terminology was the only way to safeguard the Church's traditional understanding of the Bible's message that Christ is truly God.

The main scruple in the minds of many moderate Greek theologians of the 340s and 350s seems to have been that the language of the Nicene formula departed from tradition by intruding ontological vocabulary into the Scriptural images of a liturgical creed; like Newman, they seem to have suspected that philosophical terminology always introduces into religious language the risk of distortion by over-definition.[51] Athanasius, in his *De Decretis*, describes dramatically the theological discussion at the Council, and the frustration felt by the anti-Arian majority at the ability of Arius's sympathizers, knowingly winking at each other, to use Scriptural language for Father and Son in their own sense; he continues:

> on this account the Holy Council declared expressly that He was of the essence of the Father (*homoousion*), that we might believe the Word to be other than the nature of things originate, being alone truly from God, and that no subterfuge should be left open to the irreligious... Therefore if they, as the others, make an excuse that the terms are strange, let them consider the sense in which the Council so wrote, and anathematize what the Council anathematized... [And] if a person is interested in the question, let him know that even if the expressions are not in so many words in the Scriptures, yet, as was said before, they contain the sense of the Scriptures, and expressing it, they convey it to those who have their hearing unimpaired for religious doctrine.[52]

[51] See Ian Ker's discussion of Newman's own hesitations about the role of definition and dogma in the language of religion: *Newman and the Fullness of Christianity* (Edinburgh: T. and T. Clark, 1993) 86-87.

[52] *De Decretis*, 19, 21 (trans. Newman: NPNF II, 4.163-164 [altered]).

Athanasius's argument here and in other works of the 350s, addressed to his contemporaries who wanted to oppose Arius's position but hesitated at the ontological boldness of the Nicene formula, was that there was no alternative, no *via media*, no other way than this to insure the Church against interpretations of Christ's Sonship that made him into a super-creature, a delegated mediator, divine by participation but not by right of his own being. At this point in the Church's history, Athanasius argued, one was either a Nicene — with all the new dogmatic language that that entails — or one was some form of Arian.

It was precisely as he worked at translating this and other polemical treatises of Athanasius, at Littlemore in the summer and autumn of 1841, Newman tells us in the *Apologia*, that his conviction of the rightness of the Anglican doctrinal tradition, as a "middle path" between the excesses of Protestantism and Catholicism, was finally shaken.

> I was reading and writing in my own line of study, far from the controversies of the day, on what is called a 'metaphysical' subject; but I saw clearly, that in the history of Arianism, the pure Arians were the Protestants, the semi-Arians were the Anglicans, and that Rome now was what it was then. The truth lay, not with the *Via Media*, but with what was called "the extreme party."[53]

By backing the otherwise isolated position of Athanasius in the mid-fourth century, Newman felt, Rome had proved its providential instinct for following the track of orthodox faith through the thicket of theological controversy. The analogy to the positions of the Churches of his own day was for him unmistakable. More important, perhaps, the implication was clear that the formulation of Christian doctrine has to develop, to be couched in new and

[53] *Apologia*, 139.

sometimes unscriptural language, if error was to be named and resisted, and the truth preached by the Apostles, the Good News of the promise fulfilled in Jesus, was to remain clear. Language is always a shifting veil over the real face of Christ.

3. The Fifth Century: Cyril of Alexandria

In December, 1871, Newman completed one of his last substantial essays on a Patristic subject, a biographical sketch of the fifth-century Antiochene historian and theologian Theodoret of Cyrus, with the title, *The Trials of Theodoret.*[54] It is a readable, lively essay, a sympathetic portrait of one of the most prolific and balanced writers of the early Church. In it, Newman was forced to deal with the embarrassing fact that although Theodoret has generally been regarded, in ancient historiography and modern scholarship, as both a good pastor and an orthodox theologian, much of his career was spent in bitter controversy with another leader of orthodoxy, Cyril of Alexandria, whom Theodoret and others accused both of theological error and of all kinds of high-handed maneuvers in pursuit of his own ends. Newman charitably assumes that if the charges (as is likely) were true, Cyril probably underwent a moral conversion in later life,[55] and observes diplomatically:

> If Cyril was a Saint in spite of his violent acts and his intimacy with Eutyches, Theodoret does not forfeit his claim to be accounted such, by being hot in his resentments and obstinate in his protection of Nestorius.[56]

[54] This appeared in *Historical Sketches*, II (London: Longmans, Green, 1888) 303-362. Unlike the other essays in both volumes of the *Historical Sketches*, it did not appear independently in a periodical.

[55] *Historical Sketches*, 2.354.

[56] *Ibid.*, 352.

Neither sanctity nor orthodoxy is determined by one's choice of friends. Newman's need to make excuses, however, points up a certain tension discernible in his reading of the later phase of the Alexandrian Patristic tradition. The understanding of the single person of Christ that emerged from Athanasius's emphasis on the divine identity of the Savior, and most richly developed in the writings of Athanasius's successor Cyril, half a century after his death, was, in the mid-fifth century, at least, clearly at variance with the more complex and "symmetrical" representation of Christ as one acting person (*prosopon*), one concrete individual (*hypostasis*), in two continuing, real and active substances (*ousiai*) or natures (*physeis*), which was proposed by Pope Leo, supported by theologians like Theodoret, and canonized as ecclesiastical and imperial orthodoxy by the Council of Chalcedon in 451. As an orthodox Christian, Newman was of course committed to affirming the normative value of the Chalcedonian statement of faith, which the Council's decree actually presents not as new doctrine, so much as a hermeneutical lens through which to understand rightly the older creeds of Nicaea and Constantinople. But although Newman is silent on the later councils of the Patristic era, as far as I know, he clearly understood the Chalcedonian Christological formula as the later Greek and (eventually) Latin ecclesial traditions came to understand it, reading it, consciously or unconsciously, through the qualifying lens of the Second Council of Constantinople, of 553.

The Chalcedonian formula, as has often been pointed out, represented the attempt of the Emperor Marcian and the assembled bishops in 451 to forge a consensus statement on the Church's understanding of the person of Christ that would embody terms and concepts central to both the thought of Cyril of Alexandria (who had died seven years earlier, in 444) and to Cyril's Antiochene critics — especially Theodoret, then the intellectual leader of the Antiochene school. To speak in the most general terms, the leading

Antiochene theologians since the late fourth century had struggled to find ways of speaking of the person and work of Christ that would not imply any limitations on God's transcendence: conceptions and terms that would not suggest *God* was born or suffered or died. So they spoke of the joint activity of God the Word and Jesus, the man "assumed" by the Word, as a "conjunction" (*synapheia*) of two complete and operative substances or natures, a unity on the level of "person" or "*persona*," (*prosopon*), a unity of behavior, of self-presentation in a world of active individuals, rather than some denser kind of ontological identity.[57] Cyril of Alexandria, on the other hand — especially after his heated controversy with Nestorius, the Antiochene who became bishop of Constantinople in 428 — drew on Athanasius's treatises to develop a dynamic, highly integrated conception of Christ as a single divine agent, the Son of God, who made a full human reality his own. In one of his classic expressions of his view of Christ, his *First Letter to Succensus*, written between 433 and 438, Cyril writes:

> We have learned from holy Scripture and from the holy fathers to acknowledge one Son, Christ and Lord, I mean the Word from God the Father, begotten of him in a mysterious and divine manner before the ages yet the self-same born in the last days of the world in flesh of the holy Virgin. So we unite the Word from God the Father without merger, alteration or change, to holy flesh that possessed mental life in a way that is inexpressible and past understanding, and we

[57] For a description and analysis of the Christology of the Antiochene "school," see the classic, if somewhat sketchy, account of Aloys Grillmeier, *Christ in Christian Tradition*, I (Oxford: Mowbrays, 1975) 417-439 (John Chrysostom and Theodore of Mopsuestia), 447-463 (Nestorius), 488-495 (Theodoret), and 501-519 (the later Nestorius). See also Frederick G. McLeod, *The Image of God in the Antiochene Tradition* (Washington, DC: Catholic University of America Press, 1999) 116-190. For a discussion of the council of Chalcedon and its formula, see *ibid.*, 541-550; for a fuller narrative, see R. V. Sellers, *The Council of Chalcedon* (London: SPCK, 1953) and P.-T. Camelot, *Ephèse et Chalcédoine* (Paris: L'Orante, 1962).

> confess one Son, Christ and Lord, the self-same God and human, not a diverse pair but one and the same… We see that two natures have met without merger and without alteration in unbreakable mutual union — the point being that flesh is flesh and not Godhead even though it has become God's flesh, and equally the Word is God and not flesh even though in fulfillment of God's plan he made the flesh his own. Whenever we take this point into consideration, therefore, we do not damage the concurrence into unity by declaring it was effected out of two natures; however, after the union we do not divide the natures from each other, and do not sever the one and indivisible into two sons, but say 'one Son', and, as the Fathers have put it, 'one incarnate nature of the Word'.[58]

Although it can (and perhaps should) be read as compatible with this way of speaking of the incarnate Son, the dogmatic formula of Chalcedon — strongly influenced by language in Pope Leo's letter or "Tome" to bishop Flavian of Antioch of 449 — is clearly designed to emphasize the continuing, complementary duality of the human and the divine in the one Christ, a duality which is "without confusion or change, without division or separation:"

> The distinction between the natures was never abolished by their union, but rather the character proper to each of the two natures was preserved as they came together in one *persona* (*prosopon*) and one concrete individual (*hypostasis*).[59]

In the decades after the Council, a curious but important shift of sympathies began to reveal itself. The bishops of Rome, who had

[58] *To Succensus* 1.4-6 (trans. Lionel Wickham, *Cyril of Alexandria: Select Letters*; Oxford: Clarendon Pres, 1983) 73-77 [altered]. For detailed recent analyses of Cyril's Christology, see Thomas G. Weinandy, "Cyril and the Mystery of the Incarnation," *The Theology of St. Cyril of Alexandria: a Critical Appreciation*, ed. Thomas G. Weinandy and Daniel A. Keating (London: T. and T. Clark, 2003) 23-54; John McGuckin, *Saint Cyril of Alexandria and the Christological Controversy* (Crestwood, NY: St. Vladimir's, 2004).

[59] Council of Chalcedon, "Definition of Faith," *The Christian Faith*, ed. and trans. J. Neuner and J. Dupuis (New York: Alba House, 1982) 154-155.

earlier supported Athanasius and Cyril in their doctrinal struggles, became, from Pope Leo on, staunch defenders of the two-nature Christology of Chalcedon, on which Leo's *Tome* had been such a formative influence. Most of the other bishops of the Latin West followed suit, and through the sixth century resisted any attempts of the Greek Church or the Emperors to question the orthodoxy of Chalcedon, or of Theodoret and his Antiochene colleagues, in matters Christological. A large majority of Christians in the Eastern provinces of the Empire, on the other hand — bishops, monks, theologians, and ordinary believers — immediately rejected the Chalcedonian formulation of the faith of Nicaea, despite its echoes of Cyril and Athanasius, as little more than a thinly whitewashed version of Nestorian dualism. In a determined, but largely unsuccessful attempt to provide a new basis for the reconciliation of these alienated Eastern Christians, the Emperor Justinian called together another Council, at Constantinople in 553, which was to be received eventually by East and West as the Sixth Ecumenical Council of the Church. The canons of faith which it produced — hermeneutical rules, now, for the right interpretation of Chalcedon as well as of the earlier creeds — make it clear that although the two natures or substances recognized in Christ, the divine and the human, were never confused into a single hybrid,[60] still the Savior

[60] See, for instance, canon 8: "If anyone, while confessing that the union was made out of two natures, the divinity and the humanity, or while speaking of 'one incarnate nature (*physis*) of God the Word', does not understand these expressions according to the teaching of the holy Fathers, but if by these expressions he attempts to introduce one nature or essence (*ousia*) of divinity and the flesh of Christ, *anathema sit*. For when we say that the only-begotten Word was united according to the hypostasis, we do not say that there took place any confusion between natures; rather we think that God the Word was united to the flesh, each of the two natures remaining what it is. This is why Christ is one, God and man; the same, one in being (*homoousios*) with the Father as to the divinity, and one in being with us as to the humanity" (*The Christian Faith*, ed. Neuner-Dupuis, 161).

who acts in the Gospel narrative, the subject of all the things, human and divine, that are predicated of Christ, is none other than the eternal Word, God the Son.[61] The dogmatic statement of the Sixth Ecumenical Council — less well-known, perhaps, in modern times than the formula of Chalcedon but equally normative for the Churches of East and West as an expression of Christian orthodoxy — was, in fact, an unambiguous reinterpretation of Chalcedon's portrait of Christ in unitive, clearly Cyrillian terms, a purging of whatever hints of Antiochene dualism (or its Roman equivalent!) might still cling to the wording of the definition of 451.

Newman's reading of the doctrinal discussion of the person of Christ in the fifth and sixth centuries reveals the complex and subtle, but undoubtedly tendentious, way in which he tended to see Patristic controversies, as parallels to the theological and ecclesial issues with which he himself struggled. His long narrative of the "Monophysite controversy" — the fifth and sixth century struggle over whether one must confess in Christ one nature or two — in the *Essay on Development*,[62] presents the main body of

[61] So canon 2: "If anyone does not confess two births of the Word of God, one from the Father before the ages, which is timeless and incorporeal, the other [which took place] in the latter days when the same [Word], descending from heaven, was made flesh from Mary, the holy and glorious Mother of God ever Virgin, and was born of her, *anathema sit*" (*ibid.*, 159). And canon 3: "If anyone says that the Word of God who performed miracles was someone other than the Christ who suffered, or that God the Word was with the Christ born of a woman or was in him as one in another, but [does] not [confess] one and the same our Lord Jesus Christ the Word of God incarnate and made man, to whom belong the miracles and the sufferings which He has voluntarily endured in the flesh, *anathema sit*" (*ibid.*). And canon 10: "If anyone does not confess that He who was crucified in the flesh, our Lord Jesus Christ, is true God, Lord of glory and one of the Holy Trinity, *anathema sit*" (*ibid.* 162).

[62] *An Essay on the Development of Christian Doctrine*, Part II, chapter VI, section III,3 ([3]1878; in *Conscience, Consensus, and the Development of Doctrine: Revolutionary Texts by Cardinal Newman*, ed. James Gaffney [New York/London: Doubleday, 1992] 269-288).

Chalcedon's opponents as again attempting to find a "middle position" between the two Christological extremes of contemporary debate: the separation of Christ into two subjects implied by the theological language and exegesis of the Antiochene school, and the extreme unitive position promoted in Constantinople by the hyper-Cyrillian monk Eutyches in the late 440s, which saw the one person of Christ as a kind of ontological blend of the divine and the human. Under the leadership of able, philosophically sophisticated thinkers like the sixth-century "monophysite" bishop Severus of Antioch, Newman argued, the later critics of Chalcedon sought in the pre-Chalcedonian terms and phrases of Cyril of Alexandria a Christology that was mainstream, traditional, and free from innovation; but their motive for rejecting Chalcedon, he suggests, was not so much theological — the Chalcedonian formula, after all, "is in simple accordance with the faith of St. Athanasius, St. Gregory Nazianzen, and all the other Fathers," as "will be evident to the theological student in proportion as he becomes familiar with their works"[63] — as it was ecclesiastical and political: the Chalcedonian formula had been

> forced on the Council by the resolution of the Pope of the day, acting through his legates and supported by the civil power. It cannot be supposed that such a transaction would approve itself to the Churches of Egypt... For here was the West tyrannizing over the East, forcing it into agreement with itself, resolved to have one and one only form of words...[64]

The real reason the Monophysite party, led by the able and moderate Severus, opposed the Chalcedonian formula in the late fifth and early sixth centuries, Newman argued in 1845, was less the substance of its portrait of Christ than opposition to Pope Leo, who had promoted it, and to his successors, who insisted on its binding

[63] *Ibid.*, 280.
[64] *Ibid.*, 281.

character.[65] The ancient monophysites' quest for a sixth-century *via media* between Eutychianism and Nestorianism, in Newman's eyes, was in fact a screen for simple anti-papal resentment, "pure Protestantism." Almost twenty years later, in the *Apologia*, Newman describes his conclusions about the Monophysites as a stunning discovery of his own actual position:

> Down had come the *Via Media* as a definite theory or scheme, under the blows of St. Leo… I had no longer a distinctive plea for Anglicanism, unless I would be a Monophysite. I had, most painfully, to fall back upon my three original points of belief, which I have spoken so much of in a former passage — the principle of dogma, the sacramental system, and anti-Romanism. Of these three the first two were better secured in Rome than in the Anglican Church… In consequence, my main argument for the Anglican claims lay in the positive and special charges, which I could bring against Rome. I had no positive Anglican theory. I was very nearly a pure Protestant.[66]

What is interesting in Newman's reading of these fifth and sixth century controversies over Chalcedon is that his attention is focused almost exclusively on the questions they raised about teaching authority in the Church.[67] As far as his own understanding of the

[65] The classic exposition of the "verbal monophysitism" of Severus and his followers remains Joseph Lebon, "La christologie du monophysisme syrien," in Aloys Grillmeier and Heinrich Bacht, *Das Konzil von Chalkedon: Geschichte und Gegenwart* (Wurzburg: Echter, 1951) 425-580. For a more recent treatment of the political and theological issues behind the post-Chalcedonian schisms of the fifth and sixth centuries, see W. H. C. Frend, *The Rise of the Monophysite Movement* (Cambridge: Cambridge University Press, 1972), esp. 143-148, 193-199, 231-236.

[66] *Apologia*, 120.

[67] See Heinrich Fries, "Die Dogmengeschichte des fünften Jahrhunderts im theologischen Werdegang von John Henry Newman," in A. Grillmeier and H. Bacht (eds.), *Das Konzil von Chalkedon*, 3 (Würzburg: Echter, 1954) 420-454. Fries concludes: "So ist also das Konzil von Chalkedon für Newman theologisch und religiös entscheidend geworden nicht so sehr wegen seines dogmatischen Gehalts und Ertrags — dieser stand für Newman zu keiner Zeit seines Denkens

person of Christ was concerned, Newman's theological sympathies were not with Antioch, nor even, to be frank, with Leo; rather, they lay clearly with Cyril, and implicitly with all those (such as the "monophysite" Severus) who shrank from language that would downplay the personal unity and identity of Christ, even in his full humanity, as the eternal Son of God. In the summer of 1858, Newman published a long and detailed essay in the Irish journal *Atlantis*, in defense of Cyril's favorite way of formulating the identity of Christ in his later letters, a phrase which was to become the rallying cry of Chalcedon's "monophysite" critics: "one nature of the Word, made flesh."[68] Though he professes to be writing "a purely historical investigation into the use and fortunes of certain scientific terms," and carefully insists he is not questioning conciliar dogma or (by implication) papal teaching, Newman's argument, worked out in abundant detail, is that Cyril's controversial formula, properly understood in its linguistic and intellectual context, is in fact an indispensable expression of the longer orthodox tradition of faith behind Chalcedonian Christology.

For the Alexandrians, such as Athanasius, Newman rightly observes, the terms "substance" (*ousia*) and "individual" (*hypostasis*) referred essentially to the same reality: what a thing is. In the case of God, Newman argues, these terms are even less easily

in Frage — sondern infolge der mit diesem Konzil verbundenen theologischen, kirchlichen, geschichtlichen und politischen Situation… Nicht die zu Chalkedon definierte Offenbarungswahrheit als solche, sondern das damals und dort sich manifestierende Verhalten der verschiedenen Gemeinschaften und Gruppen zur dogmatischen Wahrheit über das Wesen und die Natur Christi, sowie das dort realisierte theologische Prinzip des kirchlichen Lehramts, der Unfehlbarkeit und die Stellung des Papstes wurde zum Spiegel und zum Kriterium für Newmans bisherige anglikanische Position und zugleich zu deren Korrektur" (453-454).

[68] "On St. Cyril's Formula, μία φύσις τοῦ Θεοῦ Λόγου σεσαρκωμένη," *Atlantis*, July 1858; later published in *Tracts Theological and Ecclesiastical* (London: Pickering, 1874) 287-336.

distinguished than they are for creatures, since the substance of God is always personal and concrete, and the three "hypostases" or individuals of the Trinity each possess and realize the divine substance completely, if in distinctive ways.

> I suppose this means that each Divine Person is to be received as the one God as entirely and absolutely as He would be held to be, if we had never heard of the other Two, and that He is not in any respect less than the one and only God, because they are each that same one God also...[69]

"Nature" (*physis*), Newman argues (probably incorrectly), is a peculiarly Alexandrian term when used in the discussion of God and Christ, and suggests not simply "substance" but the particular condition in which a substance is found: it "may be said to be a predicate of which *ousia* may be made the subject."[70] Newman's conclusion is that in the context of Alexandrian discussion of Christ, it is permissible and even necessary to speak of Christ as both one "substance" (*ousia*) and one "hypostasis," because he is himself the one infinite, personal, substantial Word of God, who has taken on a full humanity as his own instrument of self-revelation and saving grace;[71] in the same linguistic setting, he insists, it would be

[69] *Ibid.*, 298-299.

[70] *Ibid.*, 326; for the peculiarly Alexandrian venue of the term, see also 306, 318.

[71] This notion of the Word's complete human nature as an "instrument" (ὄργανον) used by the Word, rather than being a distinct agent and center of attribution in itself, has its roots in Athanasius: see, for example, *Or. 3 Against the Arians*, 31, 53; *De Decretis*, 23. Newman comments on it in *Athanasius*, 2.450-451. Although the term was later used in an unorthodox sense by Apollinarius of Laodicaea and his followers, to suggest that the humanity of Jesus lacked a human mind, Newman himself stresses its importance, when properly understood, and uses it in a number of his Anglican sermons on the person of Christ: e.g., "The Humiliation of the Eternal Son," [before 1835], *Parochial and Plain Sermons* II, 12 (583); "Christ, the Son of God Made Man," [before 1842], *ibid.* VI, 5 (1215, 1217). See Strange, 63-65.

impermissible to speak of Christ as having a full human "nature" at all, since that would imply that his divine personal being had undergone "a contamination with human passions and excesses,"[72] so as to behave in a way "natural" to fallen humanity.

> In matter of fact, the humanity of the Word was *not* left in its natural state, but as the Council of Antioch [268] had said, τεθεοποίηται ["it has been divinized"]; since then it was beyond all doubt in a state *above* nature or *super*natural, why... should it be any longer called a nature? It was that which *would have been* a nature, had it not been destined to be united from the first to the Word.[73]

Newman's real concern, throughout his analysis of Cyril's Christological formula, is to stress the central dogmatic importance of the personal identity of Christ as eternal Son of God, as Word with his flesh, and to emphasize that the unity of divinity and humanity in him must never be taken in a "symmetrical" or purely complementary way, as the coming-together of two autonomous, ontologically commensurate realities to form a single composite. In such a composite — the kind of composite talked about freely by the Antiochene theologians, and even conceivable within the framework of the Chalcedonian formula — the divine and the human in Christ would always be competitors, and his personal unity would always remain extrinsic, a matter of the collaboration of God and a human agent in a purely functional way. But the Mystery of Christ is something much more astounding: "God with us," the Word and his flesh.

In one of his notes on Athanasius, Newman sums up the classical doctrine thus:

> The One Self-existing Personal God created, moulded, assumed, a manhood truly such. He, being from eternity, was in possession and

[72] "St. Cyril's Formula," 327.

[73] *Ibid.*, 328.

> in the fullness of his Godhead before mankind had being. Much more was He already in existence, and in all his attributes, when He became man, and He lost nothing by becoming. All that He ever had continued to be His; what He took on Himself was only an addition. There was no change; in His Incarnation, He did but put on a garment… His manhood had no Personality of its own; it was a second φύσις [nature], but not a second Person; it never existed till it was His; for its integrity and completeness it depended on Him, the Divine Word… Such was His human nature; it might be called an additional attribute; the Word was 'made man', not was made a man.[74]

This understanding of the personal identity of Christ as Son of God in his own flesh clearly takes its inspiration from the Alexandrian tradition, as represented by Athanasius and Cyril,[75] not from the more ontologically "symmetrical" portrait suggested, if not fully elaborated, by Leo's *Tome* and the Chalcedonian definition. Newman's Christology, in other words, is not simply, or even primarily, dependent for its content on the Christology of Chalcedon, even though he stoutly professes Chalcedon to be part of orthodox dogma. Nor does it sit easily with the divine-human balance rhetorically promoted by Leo's *Tome*, despite Newman's acknowledgement of the Pope's prophetic originality.[76] It is, in fact, really

74 *Athanasius*, 2.426-427.

75 A typical, brief example is the second "anathema" contained in Cyril's programmatic Third Letter to Nestorius, of autumn, 430: "If anyone does not confess that the Word of God the Father was united in his own individuality (καθ' ὑπόστασιν) to flesh, and is one Christ with his own flesh — in other words, the same one at once God and human — let him be anathema." (ed. L. Wickham, *Select Letters*, 28; my translation).

76 Towards the end of his article on Cyril's Christological formula, Newman insists that "after we have done our utmost, we shall be unable to discover more than a few instances in the early Fathers, compared with the multitude of opportunities which the subject-matter of their works admits, of dogmatic statements verbally contrary to Cyril's Formula, while, on the other hand, that formula

the Alexandrian, Cyrillian understanding of Christ, which only later was acknowledged as a central element in Christian Orthodoxy, by being overlaid on the Chalcedonian formula: first in the work of sixth-century theologians sponsored by Justinian, and eventually the official standard for interpreting Chalcedon proclaimed in the canons of Constantinople II. This Cyrillian way of reading Chalcedon was given its full theological expression by later Greek Fathers such as Maximus the Confessor and John of Damascus[77] — theologians whom Newman echoes but, curiously, rarely mentions, and whom he seems not to have studied as fully as he did the earlier Alexandrians. Yet this is the portrait of Christ that Newman himself develops, with great poignancy and religious intensity, not just in later scholarly articles but in a number of his sermons from the 1830s and 1840s. A good example is this passage

admits, or even requires by its very wording, an explanation absolutely consistent with the Catholic dogma..." Only Papal authority, he suggests, working in the interest of Church unity, could have won acceptance for Chalcedon's language as equally orthodox: "No wonder that... it remained for a Pope, who saw with a Pope's instinctive sagacity the need of the times, to explain the old truth, in which all parts of Christendom agreed, under the comparatively new formula of the ἐν δυσὶ φύσεσι [= '*in* two natures', rather than Cyril's formula '*from* two natures']" ("St. Cyril's Formula" 328-329).

[77] See, for instance, John of Damascus's discussion of the natures united in the personal or individual being (*hypostasis*) of the Word: "He took on Himself the elements of our compound nature, and these not as having an independent existence or as being originally an individual, and in this way assumed by Him, but as existing in his own subsistence (*hypostasis*) [i.e., as Word]. For the subsistence of God the Word in itself became the subsistence of the flesh, and accordingly 'the Word became flesh', clearly without any change, and likewise the flesh became Word without alteration, and God became human. For the Word is God, and a man is God, through having one and the same subsistence. And so it is possible to speak of the same thing as being the nature of the Word and the nature of this individual." (*Exposition of the Orthodox Faith*, 55.14-21 (ed. B. Kotter, *Die Schriften des Johannes von Damaskos* 2 [Berlin: de Gruyter, 1973] 131) [= III, 11; trans. S. D. F. Salmond, NPNF II, 9.2.55].

from his Lenten sermon of the early 1840s, "Christ, the Son of God Made Man":

> He took upon Him our nature, as an instrument of His purposes, not as an agent in the work. What is one thing cannot become another; His manhood remained human, and his Godhead remained divine. God became man, yet was still God, having His manhood as an adjunct, perfect in its kind, but dependent upon His Godhead. So much so, that unless Scripture had expressly called Him man, we might well have scrupled to do so. Left to ourselves, we might have felt it more reverential to have spoken of Him, as *incarnate* indeed, come in human flesh, human and the like, but not simply as man. But St. Paul speaks in plain terms of our one Mediator as 'the man Christ Jesus', not to speak of our Lord's own words on the subject. Still, we must ever remember, that though He was in nature perfect man, He was not man in exactly the same sense in which any one of us is a man. Though man, He was not, strictly speaking, in the English sense of the word, *a* man; He was not such as one of us, and one out of a number... We may not speak of Him as we speak of any individual man, acting from and governed by a human intelligence within Him, but He was God, acting not only as God, but now through the flesh also, when He would. He was not a man made God, but God made man.[78]

What Newman struggles to express here, in non-technical, non-metaphysical terms, is what Clement and Origen, Athanasius and Cyril also struggled to express: the central insight of faith that the real subject of the deeds told of Jesus — the one who taught the crowds, healed lepers, raised the dead, and died in agony and obedience on the cross — was fully human, but not simply or autonomously so; he was fully human, in body and mind, but was, as a personal, active subject, the eternal Son of the Father, the giver of the Spirit, the Wisdom who orders creation and brings about its renewal. The person whom Jesus humanly "personifies" is the Son

[78] *Parochial and Plain Sermons* VI, 5 (1215) [before 1842]

of God; this is what allows him to be our priest, mediator and healer.[79] Only if we can see and hear God in Jesus, with all the reverence an encounter with God must summon within us, will we be able to see the truth behind the veil of Scripture and history, and to find in it salvation and transformation.

It is here, it seems to me, in the fully developed "Alexandrian" view of the divine person of Jesus, articulated by Athanasius and Cyril and developed in the work of the later Greek Fathers, that Newman discovered the theological reason why "the Alexandrian philosophy" of their forebears Clement and Origen had been "music" to his "inward ear." He had found in this strand of Patristic thought the recognition that created history, the world of human reasoning and action, is not, for faith, an autonomous realm, any

[79] *Ibid.*, 1216-1217. In a still earlier sermon, "The Humiliation of the Eternal Son" [before 1834], Newman meditates on the rich challenges posed to faith by the recognition that the one who died on the cross really is, as person and subject, God the Son. Towards the end, he connects this central doctrine with the controversies of the Patristic age, perceptively pointing out that in modern theology, as well, a *de facto* Sabellianism, or modalist conception of God, seems to go hand in hand with a *de facto* Nestorianism, or separation of the human Jesus from the divine Word: "In consequence we are too often led, as a matter of necessity, in discoursing of His words and works, to distinguish between the Christ who lived on earth and the Son of God Most High, speaking of His human nature and His Divine nature so separately as not to feel or understand that God is man and man is God. I am speaking of those of us who have learned to reflect, reason, and dispute, to inquire and pursue their thoughts, not of the incurious or illiterate, who are not exposed to the temptation in question; and of the former I fear I must say (to use the language of ancient theology), that they begin by being Sabellians, that they go on to be Nestorians, and that they tend to become Ebionites and to deny Christ's Divinity altogether" (*Parochial and Plain Sermons* III, 12 [587]). For further reflection on the connection of Trinitarian theology and Christology in the Patristic controversies, see Brian E. Daley, "The Persons in God and the Person of Christ in Patristic Christology: an Argument for Parallel Development of Doctrine," in Lewis Ayres and Vincent Twomey (eds.), volume on Patristic theology of the Trinity (Dublin: Four Courts, forthcoming).

more than Christ's humanity is an autonomous natural unit. The human world, like the humanity of Jesus and the human words of Scripture, have been taken up, by God's grace, to be the ὄργανον for incomparably deeper personal encounters between the transcendent God and the created mind: encounters that lie at the root of faith, that shape the Church, that lead not just to enlightenment but to transformation, divinization, participation in God's very life.

In an article reflecting on Keble's defense of Patristic exegesis in Tract 89,[80] Ephraim Radner suggests, as an implication of Tractarian thought, that only a Church that learns to read Scripture figurally will be able to find saving meaning in a world of constantly fractured significance, and "embrace the coherent character of nature's divinely transparent sheaths."[81] Although not himself a Scripture scholar, Newman had learned, like Keble, that a merely historical approach to the Bible must end in a rationalistic flattening of its message; his preaching represented a continuing effort to contemplate the central mysteries of faith through a reverent, imaginative reading of the persons and events the Scriptures portray, as representing not merely the "facts" of a past age but the truth about ourselves. What he learned from the Alexandrian Fathers was "the mystical or sacramental principle" of Christian Biblical hermeneutics and a unified, Word-centered understanding of the person of Christ. It was an approach to the saving meaning of God's revelation that opened up a new vision of truth to him, but which also, as he discovered, needed to be embedded in a continuing ecclesial tradition of faith and worship, and guided by the Church's authoritative voice of interpretation, if it was not to dissolve

[80] [John Keble,] "Tracts for the Times, No. 89: On the Mysticism attributed to the Early Fathers of the Church" (London: Rivington, 1841).

[81] "The Discrepancies of Two Ages: Thoughts on Keble's 'Mysticism of the Fathers'," *The Anglican* (April, 2000) 10-15.

into self-serving, arbitrary speculation. Figural interpretation of Scripture is essential, if the Bible is to speak God's abiding word freshly to each succeeding age; but it requires, in turn, a Church in continuity with Christian origins, if it is to be true to its own inspiration. And the heart of such interpretation, as Origen knew — the "treasure hidden in the field" of God's Word — is Christ himself, the Truth always waiting to be found under "the veil of the letter," the Word always becoming human in Scripture and history.

"SAYING THE THING THAT IS NOT" NEWMAN ON THE LIE

Paul J. GRIFFITHS

1. The Question of the Lie[1]

There are two fundamental questions about the lie: What is it to lie? When, if ever, is it permissible to do so? These questions are very intimate with one another: defining what it is to lie will ordinarily proceed in part by looking at clear cases of speech understood to be forbidden under that description; and offering an argument about when the lie is permitted will always require at least one eye on the definitional question. Adjustments in the answers given to one question will, too, usually require adjustments in the answers given to the other. If, for instance, you are quite sure that the lie is something never defensibly to be done, and if you discover a speech-act that you are quite sure is not only defensible but required, then you are likely to exclude that act from the category

[1] Recent theoretical work of interest on lying includes: Alasdair MacIntyre, "Truthfulness, Lies, and Moral Philosophers: What Can We Learn from Mill and Kant?," *The Tanner Lectures on Human Values*, vol. 16, ed. Grethe B. Peterson (Salt Lake City, UT: The University of Utah Press, 1995) 307-361; Eberhard Schockenhoff, *Zur Lüge Verdammt? Politik, Medien, Justiz, Wissenschaft und die Ethik der Wahrheit* (Freiburg: Herder, 2000); Jacques Derrida, "History of the Lie: Prolegomena," trans. Peggy Kamuf, *Futures: Of Jacques Derrida*, ed. Richard Rand (Stanford, CA: Stanford University Press, 2001) 65-98; Jonathan E. Adler, "Lying, Deceiving, or Falsely Implicating," *Journal of Philosophy* 94 (1997) 435-452; Mary Mothersill, "Some Questions About Truthfulness and Lying," *Social Research* 63 (1996) 913-929.

of the lie no matter what ordinary usage suggests. There is a symbiotic relation between the two questions.

This is so, anyway, in the order of discovery. In the order of exposition, however, things can be simpler and more linear. There, it is usual to begin with a definition and proceed to consider whether there are defensible occasions for the performance of the act so defined. The appearance of clarity and step-wise order is specious but useful. I will adopt it here.

What then is it to lie? The English verb and noun are used with many overlapping senses and connotations. The two most common, perhaps, have to do with falsehood and the desire to deceive. But neither of these two ideas is anything less than muddy. Does 'falsehood' mean a statement actually false — 'Trollope wrote *Vanity Fair*' — or rather one that seems false to its proposer — I say 'Thackeray wrote *Vanity Fair*' while thinking, wrongly, that Trollope did — or must it denote only statements that fulfil both qualifications? What is a statement intended to deceive intended to deceive about — what is the case, what the speaker takes to be the case, sometimes one and sometimes the other — or what? Ordinary English usage covers all this and more, as does the ordinary usage, for example, of *mentiri*, *mendacium*, *mendax*, and cognate and derived terms in Latin. In such a situation, stipulative definition is in order so that a particular kind of speech can be isolated with sufficient precision to make productive conceptual analysis possible. I stipulatively define the lie as any utterance that seems to the one uttering it at the time of its utterance to contradict what he takes to be the case.[2] The hallmark of such utterance is intentional duplicity: according to this definition, the liar is someone who has deliberately introduced a fissure between his thought and

[2] I follow Augustine in this definition, which can be found, with variations, in (inter alia), *De mendacio* 3.3; *Enchiridion* 6.18; *Contra mendacium* 12.26; *Enarrationes in Psalmos* 5.7.

his speech, someone with a *duplex cor* who has, as Homer's Achilles says of Odysseus, or as Sallust laments of the populace during the Catiline War, one thing hidden in his heart and another ready on his tongue.[3]

To speech of this kind, truth and falsehood are irrelevant. What matters is only the relation between what the speaker says and what he thinks. If I think that Newman wrote *The Water-Babies* and yet say that Kingsley did, I shall have lied even though what I say is true. And if I both think and say that Newman wrote *The Water-Babies* I shall not have lied, even though what I say is false. To duplicitous speech, too, motive, intent (other than the intent to divide thought from speech), and result are all entirely irrelevant. I may, by my lie, intend to deceive, to comfort the dying, to avert the shedding of innocent blood, to defame the just, to besmirch the pure, or to praise the praiseworthy. But nothing of this will affect whether I am speaking duplicitously, which is to say, lying.

The Augustinian stipulative definition offered here will not neatly separate all utterances into lies and non-lies. There will be many about which it is unclear whether they fall under the definition. But there will also be many — or at least some — about which it is abundantly clear. Rahab says that she does not know where the spies are while at the same time thinking that they are on the roof (Joshua 2:5); Jacob claims to be the elder son while thinking himself the younger (Genesis 27:19); the Egyptian midwives say that Hebrew women give birth unusually quickly, while thinking that this is not so (Exodus 1:19); and so on. All that is needed to give the definition bite and purchase is that there be some clear cases, and there are.

[3] Homer's Achilles: *Iliad* 9.413 & passim. Sallust: *Bellum Catilinae* 10.

2. Christian Interest in and Response to the Question of the Lie

With this definition, the first fundamental question about the lie is answered and the second becomes: When is it permissible to use one's speech to contradict one's thought? This is a question of some considerable interest to Christians, and for several reasons.

First, there is the bulk and ambiguity of scriptural material that speaks to it. Some parts of scripture may be read as placing the lie under a ban, or at the very least restraining severely the circumstances under which it is proper to lie. In this category may be placed the commandment against false witness, the fulminations of the Psalms against the lying tongue, and much else.[4] Here too may be placed the New Testament claim that Jesus is truth — truth incarnate, that is, as well as truth's speaker; that the Holy Spirit leads us into truth; that truth belongs to God; and so on.[5] If truth is taken as the lie's antonym, then this places considerable pressure upon Christians to state and defend a consistently negative view of the lie, perhaps even to the extremity of claiming that it is never defensible.

But there is also scriptural matter warm in the lie's defense. I have already mentioned Jacob, Rahab, and the Egyptian midwives: all these, it may reasonably be argued, reap rewards for lying, and scripture says nothing critical about the lies for which they are rewarded. To these examples might be added, more controversially, Paul's harsh criticisms of Peter in the second chapter of his letter to the Galatians. Some commentators on this letter, most notably Jerome,[6] have interpreted Paul's words here as benevolent

4 Exodus 20:16; Deuteronomy 5:20; Psalm 5:7; Wisdom of Solomon 1:11.

5 Romans 1:25; Galatians 2:5, 14; John 1:14, 17; 8:32, 40; etc.

6 Jerome's commentary on Galatians, the *Commentarius in Epistolam S. Pauli ad Galatas*, in Migne, vol. 26, cols. 331-468. His comments on Galatians 2:11-14 are at cols. 363-367.

and well-intentioned lies, claiming that Paul could not really have judged Peter as harshly as his words suggest, and concluding that his words must have been intended as pedagogical devices of a broadly duplicitous sort.

This last example brings to the fore a broader question about scripture and the lie: is it possible to say that some parts of scripture not only depict lies but are themselves lies, that their human authors wrote or spoke duplicitously, and that their duplicitous words are preserved for us as God's word in the text of scripture? This was a vexed question in the fourth century, especially, and it provided yet another reason for Christians to be interested in the question of the lie's acceptability.[7] If scripture itself could be thought to contain (not just to depict) lying speech, what effects would this have upon how it was to be interpreted?

In addition to these particular questions about scripture's content and nature, we Christians are also pressed toward analysis of the lie's acceptability by our interest in speech's nature. All treatment of the lie will inevitably entail discussion of the nature and purposes of speech, for the lie as defined is a particular kind of speech, and if there is something wrong with it (or indeed if there is something right with it), saying what this is will most naturally involve appeal to speech's nature and purposes. And in this we Christians have always had special interests, for our preferred technical vocabulary for God's triune nature consists in part in words for speech. God the Father utters the divine Logos eternally, and it is by means of this uttered Son that the created order is brought into being. Serious Christian thought about human speech's nature and purposes is not likely to go far without paying attention to this essential trinitarian trope.

[7] This debate can be seen with great clarity in the letters exchanged between Jerome and Augustine. See, especially, Augustine's *Epistula* 82. Cf. *De mendacio* 5.5; *Contra mendacium* 15.32.

Even this is not all. Christian interest in speech, and in the possible propriety of some duplicitous speech, is intertwined with the fact that we are constrained by scripture and liturgy to say of God that not only is he eternally both speaker and speech in the economy of the Holy Trinity, but also that he is in some sense speaker of scripture's words. But what kind of speech is this? Can it be partial, deliberately obscure, reserved, economized with, parcelled out and held back, deliberately duplicitous? Does God dispense and withhold the truth by not fully speaking his mind, or even by contradicting it? If so (or if not) this will have its effects upon Christian thought about the acceptability of humanly duplicitous speech.

All this, and more, has motivated Christian interest in the lie. But no standard Christian position on the question has developed. Of course, Christian moral theologians and preachers generally treat the lie negatively. It is hard to imagine any Christian thinker arguing, for example, that intentional duplicity ought to be maximized. However, within this very broad agreement — which really amounts to no more than the claim that lying, left undefined, is on the whole not a good thing — the tradition has generated and preserved two incompatible families of thought about lying.[8] Each deploys a particular understanding of speech and its purposes; each draws upon explicitly Christian claims in doing so; each offers arguments and conclusions about the nature and acceptability of lying speech; and each perforce offers exegesis of the same scriptural

[8] On the kinds of Christian thought about the lie see: Boniface Ramsey, "Two Traditions on Lying and Deception in the Ancient Church," *The Thomist* 49 (1985) 504-533; Julia Fleming, *The Helpful Lie: The Moral Reasoning of Augustine and John Cassian*, Ph.D dissertation, Catholic University of America, 1993. Essential background may be had from Marcia Colish, "The Stoic Theory of Verbal Signification and the Problem of Lies and False Statements from Antiquity to St. Anselm," *Archéologie du signe*, ed. Lucie Brind'Amour and Eugene Vance (Toronto: Institut Pontifical d'Études Médiévales, 1982) 17-43.

texts and discussion of at least some of the same theological topics. Augustine may serve as representative of the first family of thought, and Newman of the second. The two views are incompatible in almost every respect, as we shall see.

The fact that there are such deeply divergent Christian understandings of the acceptability of lying speech shows that no single account of the matter is clearly required or perhaps even strongly suggested by the grammar and syntax of orthodoxy. If there is a correct Christian view on the question of the lie, it is found at some interpretive and argumentative distance from orthodoxy's explicit content, which is to say at least that decisions about where to begin, theologically speaking, in considering the lie can reasonably be (and have reasonably been) made differently by those who acknowledge approximately the same constraints on what constitutes orthodoxy. It may seem that this means that any judgment about the lie's nature and acceptability has, for Christian thinkers, the status of a theologoumenon, which is to say an expression of private and always disputable theological opinion rather than a position that ought to be binding upon the orthodox. But it does not follow from the fact that orthodoxy's explicit content — its first-order grammar, we might say — contains no clear position on the lie that any position on those questions must necessarily be a private and speculative judgment. It is entirely possible that in cases such as this, where a historical study of the tradition's data shows there to be no dominant position, and a conceptual analysis of orthodoxy's explicit content shows that incompatible positions can be derived from it, there is nonetheless a preferable position. It may be that one among the possible positions is able to explain and account for the substance and difficulties of the others while not itself being so accountable; or it may be that one among the possible positions stands in less tension with some fundamental and explicit deliverances of the tradition, than do the others; or it may be that one among the possible positions poses desiderata for itself that it lacks the resources to meet, while these self-same desiderata can be met by another. In any case, instances of apparently theologoumenal difference within the tradition are always of particular interest because exploration of them will usually be powerfully illuminative of the tradition's deeper grammar. In order to see whether any of these scenarios in fact obtains we need before us a sketch of Augustine's and Newman's thought on the lie as representative of the two families of Christian thought about the matter, so to that I now turn.

3. The Lie and the Imago Dei: Augustine

The ideal-typical representative of the first family is Augustine.[9] He derives a position on the lie from an understanding of human speech and thought rooted in the relations between the first and second persons of the Trinity as imaged in the human. Those who think about the lie in these terms tend to think about the nature and purposes of human speech in terms of the divine Logos: that Logos, eternally begotten (spoken) by the Father, becomes enfleshed as Jesus of Nazareth, Jesus the Christ; so also human thoughts, *verba interna* or *verba mentis* as Augustine likes to call them, are stored in the memory as *arcana notitia*, hidden notions or concepts.[10] The gaze of thought may become conformed to these hidden or stored notions, and thus reproduce them in active mode.

[9] Augustine gave his most concentrated attention to the question of the lie in *De mendacio* and *Contra mendacium*. An edition of the Latin text (together with a facing-page Italian translation) of these treatises is in *Sant'Agostino: Morale e Ascetismo Cristiano*, ed. Carlo Carena et al. (Rome: Città Nuova Editrice, 2001) 293-488. An English version is in *Saint Augustine: Treatises on Various Subjects*, ed. Roy J. Deferrari, Fathers of the Church, 16 (Washington, DC: Catholic University of America Press, 1952) 145-179.

[10] On *arcana notitia* see, e.g., *De trinitate* 4.6.10.

When this happens, the intelligence is at work. And the force that joins the active intelligence to the memory is the will, which Augustine also often calls love. This set of relations provides an inner trinity: memory as store for the concept seen; intelligence as active reproducer of this concept; will as the loving act of intention that makes possible the joining of memory and intellect, and thus also of concept stored and concept activated.[11]

Augustine often uses sexual imagery for the relations among these three: memory is the begetter (*gignens*), intelligence the begotten (*genitum*), and will the love by which the two are joined (*copulantur*). This sexual imagery is, for Augustine, more fundamentally to be understood as trinitarian imagery. The archetypal begetter is the Father, the archetypal begotten is the Son, and (more obscurely) the archetypal act of loving intent that proceeds from and connects both begetter and begotten is the Spirit. The inner mental trinity of memory-intelligence-will, then, is the mirror in which we see enigmatically the divine trinity of which it is a created image. Augustine likes to appeal to a text from Paul on this point: "*Videmus tunc per speculum in aenigmate*" (1 Corinthians 13:12), which may be nicely rendered as the King James Version does in one of its notes, "Now we see through a glass in a riddle." The enigma or riddle within which we cannot help seeing is classed by Augustine as a kind of allegory — an especially obscure analogy. It, like all allegories when understood as such, displaces the gaze of those who read it from its surface detail to what it allegorizes. And in the instance of interest here, it is the surface detail of the birth of the inner word (the concept) from the memory into the active intelligence, and the clothing of that inner word with sound so that it can be voiced, that points those who can understand it to,

[11] This paragraph summarizes elements from *De trinitate* 11-15, and *De civitate Dei* 11.

first, the eternal begetting of the Son from the Father, and, second, the Son's taking of flesh in the incarnation. The voicing of the concept is formally analogous to the enfleshing of the Logos: the concept invoked is like (participatorily like) the Logos incarnate.[12]

The analogy works in two stages. First, there is the production of the inner word from the memory. This is the trace of the eternal begetting of the Son by the Father, and Augustine uses language for it that intentionally echoes Christian credal affirmations about the relation of the Son to the Father. Just as Jesus Christ is true God from true God, so the inner word is true word from true thing:

> Everything, therefore, that human consciousness knows, whether by perceiving through itself, or through its physical senses, or by way of the testimony of others, it holds stored away in the treasure-house of memory. From these [stored] things is begotten a true word when we speak what we know, a word prior to all sound and to all thought of sound. For it is then that the word is most like the things known, begotten from them and in their image. This is because [in such a case] the vision of thought proceeds directly from the vision of knowledge; it is a word that belongs to no language, true word from true thing; it has nothing of its own, but everything from that knowledge from which it is born.[13]

[12] This paragraph relies principally upon *De trinitate* 15.

[13] Translating "Haec igitur omnia, et quae per se ipsum, et quae per sensus sui corporis, et quae testimoniis aliorum percepta scit animus humanus, thesauro memoriae condita tenet, ex quibus gignitur verbum verum, quando quod scimus loquimur, sed verbum ante omnem sonum, ante omnem cogitationem soni. Tunc enim est verbum simillimum rei notae, de qua gignitur et imago eius, quoniam de visione scientiae visio cogitationis exoritur, quod est verbum linguae nullius, verbum verum de re vera, nihil de suo habens, sed totum de illa scientia de qua nascitur," from *De trinitate* 15.12.22, in *La Trinité, livres VIII-XV*, ed. Paul Agaësse, Œuvres de Saint Augustin, 16 (Paris: Institut d'Études Augustiniennes, [2]1997) 484.

In this first stage of the analogy, we remain in the place of thought. The memory is the treasure-filled storehouse, the *thesaurus* in which all inputs (whether via thought or sensation or testimony) are stored. The active concept is then born directly, as perfect image, from the memory, just as the eternal word is born from the Father. The image contributes nothing of its own: it is begotten, rather, which is to say that it participates in the nature of its begetter. Lying, of course, cannot yet occur because lying requires vocalized speech and nothing has yet been vocalized. (Augustine does use the vocabulary of speech in the passage just quoted, but in an extended or metaphorical sense which does not imply vocalization.) But already it is possible to see that anything less than a perfect imaging of memory by intelligence would be a break, a fissure, in the image of God. It would be a misbegetting: intelligence is supposed to image memory by participating in its nature. When it fails to do so, this is because the divine image has been broken by sin — a point that will be applied, too, to the act of lying.

The second stage of the analogy moves to the incarnation, to the taking of flesh by the divine word as the inner word takes on voice. Augustine understands the second person of the divine trinity's incarnation through the category of 'assumption', which he typically contrasts with both 'transmutation' and 'consumption'. For you to assume some new state or condition is for you to take it on without losing the properties which make you who you are independently of the new condition. In this sense I can assume the state of being married or the office of president, for in doing either I remain the person I was before. But if I am transmuted into or consumed by something new, I cease to have any distinctive properties of my own: to lose myself in (be consumed by) the presidential office would be to have no identity other than that provided by the office — and this, it seems reasonable to say, would not be a good thing.

When the second person of the divine trinity assumes the flesh of a human being, then, he is not transmuted into or consumed by that condition. Similarly, for Augustine my inner word, my thought, can assume voice without being transmuted into voice. It can be invoked without ceasing to be thought. This is how he puts it:

> And so the word vocalized externally is a sign of the word that illuminates internally; this latter more properly deserves the name 'word' because what is uttered with the bodily mouth is the voiced word, and this is called 'word' in virtue of the one [viz. the inner word] that assumes it so that it may appear outwardly. It is in this way that our word becomes — after a fashion — a bodily word, by assuming that by which it is manifest to the senses of men. In the same way, the Word of God became flesh, by assuming that by which it is manifest to the senses of men. Furthermore, just as our word became voice without being transmuted into voice, so the Word of God became flesh; but it should not be thought that it was transmuted into the physical.[14]

The application of the second stage of the analogy to vocalized speech is straightforward enough:

> When the [inner] word is vocalized or given by way of some other sign, it is not spoken just as it is, but rather as it can be seen or heard with the body.[15]

[14] Translating "Proinde verbum quod foris sonat, signum est verbi quod intus lucet, cui magis verbi competit nomen. Nam illud quod profertur carnis ore, vox verbi est: verbumque et ipsum dicitur, propter illud a quo ut foris appareret assumptum est. Ita enim verbum nostrum vox quodam modo corporis fit, assumendo eam in qua manifestetur sensibus hominum; sicut Verbum Dei caro factum est, assumendo eam in qua et ipsum manifestaretur sensibus hominum. Et sicut verbum nostra fit vox, nec mutatur in vocem; ita Verbum Dei caro quidem factum es, sed absit ut mutaretur in carnem," from *De trinitate* 15.11.20, in *La Trinité*, ed. Agaësse, 470-472.

[15] Translating "Nam quando per sonum dicitur, vel per aliquod corporale signum, non dicitur sicuti est, sed sicut potest videri audirive per corpus," from *De trinitate* 15.11.20, in *La Trinité*, ed. Agaësse, 474.

There can be no exact replication of the inner word by the vocalized outer word because the former is nonlinguistic and the latter necessarily in some language or other. The same is true of the relation between the second person of the trinity and the incarnate Son: the latter does not replicate the former in every respect because (among other things) the latter is physical and the former is not. The relationship is no longer one of simple substantive identity. However, Augustine continues,

> But when that which is found in the judgement is also in the [vocalized] word, it is a true word, possessing the kind of truth expected by men. What is in the concept is also in the vocalized word, and what is lacking in the concept is also lacking in the vocalized word. Here one recognizes 'Yes, yes; no, no'.[16]

A vocalized word is true, on this view, when there is in what it says just and only what is in the concept to which it gives voice. Nothing is to be subtracted and nothing added. This is how Augustine understands Matthew 5:37, which he quotes in part in the passage just translated. Jesus there said, to give the verse more fully in the form in which Augustine would probably have known it: "Let your speech consist of 'yes, yes' and 'no, no'. Anything more than this comes from the Evil One." The 'yes, yes' indicates the positive relation between inner and vocalized word: the latter says yes to the former by giving in vocalized form what was already provided in concept. And the 'no, no' indicates the negative relation: what was not present in the concept is not added in the vocalization. This view of what it is for an utterance to be true is derived from Augustine's view of the relation between the eternal divine word and the incarnate word. This relation is participated in by the

[16] Translating "Quando ergo quod in notitia est, hoc est in verbo, tunc est verum verbum, et veritas, qualis exspecta ab homine, ut quod est in ista, hoc sit et in illo; quod non est in ista, non sit et in illo: hic agnoscitur, 'Est, est; Non, non'," from *De trinitate* 15.11.20, in *La Trinité*, ed. Agaësse, 474

relation between concept and vocalized word in us. Any change in this relation is therefore a rupture of the divine image in us.

Not every such rupture will occur by way of the lie, but every lie, every act of deliberately duplicitous speech, will intentionally and knowingly produce such a rupture, and will thereby be a sin. The fact that duplicitous speech produces this rupture is the evil proper to the lie; Augustine takes this conclusion to entail (or even to be identical with) the claim that the lie can never defensibly be performed.

So much, in excessively brief compass, for the Augustinian view. It is a view defended by him with uncompromising vigor. It has an afterlife in the Christian tradition, but most often as a position honored by being affirmed while simultaneously being sufficiently modified to be effectively rejected.[17]

4. The Lie and Divine Pedagogy: Newman

Newman's thought about the lie has his understanding of reserve and economy in speech as its fertile soil. Both these ideas have deep roots in the tradition, most especially (though by no means exclusively) in the writings of the Greek Fathers, of which Newman had extensive knowledge; both, too, are important threads in the fabric of his thought in general, from his earliest published work as an Anglican priest to the end of his life as a Cardinal of the Catholic Church. Indeed, his analysis of reserve and economy is among the strongest continuities between his work as an Anglican and as a Catholic. The ideas denoted by these terms are already complex in the thought of Clement, Origen, Chrysostom, and Cassian; they become even more so in Newman's subtle mind, and

[17] Aquinas, for example, says that he accepts Augustine's view, but in fact rejects enough of it that what he argues becomes in important respects a quite different position. See *Summa Theologiae* IIaIIae, q. 110.

sometimes the convolutions of his elegant prose make it difficult to determine how best to understand him. In what follows, I shall not attempt anything like a complete study of Newman on reserve and economy, for these ideas embrace much more than the lie; I'll focus instead on the direct relevance of Newman's treatment of these ideas for his understanding of duplicitous speech's defensibility.[18]

Neither will I essay a full historical treatment of the development of these ideas in Newman's thought, but I will look briefly at his discussion of them at four key moments in his career: 1831-1833, when as a young Anglican priest he was preparing *The Arians of the Fourth Century*;[19] 1843, when, approaching ever more closely the tender embraces of Rome, he preached a sermon, 'The Theory of Developments in Religious Doctrine', at Oxford, in which there is matter of direct relevance to the question;[20]

[18] I have found Robin C. Selby, *The Principle of Reserve in the Writings of John Henry Cardinal Newman* (Oxford: Oxford University Press, 1975), of considerable help in thinking through what Newman means by reserve and economy. There appears, however, to be rather little by way of secondary scholarship on Newman's treatment of lying.

[19] The book was first published in 1833. I have used the photographic reproduction of the fourth (1895) edition in *The Arians of the Fourth Century*, ed. James Tollhurst, with an introduction and notes by Rowan Williams (Notre Dame, IN: University of Notre Dame Press, 2001). Useful comments on the composition of this work include: those given by Williams in the edition cited (pp. xix-xlviii); Ian Ker, *John Henry Newman: A Biography* (New York: Oxford University Press, 1995) 48-53; Maurice Wiles, *Archetypal Heresy: Arianism Through the Centuries* (Oxford: Clarendon Press, 1996) 165-173; Frank M. Turner, *John Henry Newman: The Challenge to Evangelical Religion* (New Haven, CT/London: Yale University Press, 2002) 142-161.

[20] The sermon was preached on the Feast of the Purification in 1843, and was published in *Fifteen Sermons Preached Before the University of Oxford Between 1826 and 1843*. I have used the photographic reprint of the 1872 edition, edited by Mary Katherine Tillman (Notre Dame, IN: University of Notre Dame Press, 1997). The sermon is found at pp. 312-351. I must acknowledge Professor Tillman's kind help to this novice in Newman studies, as well as the very useful

1864-1865, when, two decades after his conversion, in response to Charles Kingsley's accusation of having an excessively relaxed attitude to the truth, he composed and revised the *Apologia*, in which, necessarily, he addressed head-on the question of the lie;[21] and 1877, when, just before being made Cardinal by Leo XIII and as a man now approaching old age, he wrote a long preface to the republication of his *Lectures on the Prophetical Office of the Church*[22] in which, in part as a means of explaining (what he had as an Anglican criticized) why it is that the Catholic Church appears sometimes to countenance or even encourage a prima facie difference or contradiction between its formal teaching and its "popular and political manifestations,"[23] he had to address the question of duplicity. These four occasions do not exhaust the material relevant to the question of Newman's thought about the lie, but they do provide matter of paradigmatic importance to its understanding.

Arians began as a doctrinal history intended as prolegomenon to a high-churchly study of the Thirty-Nine Articles. As Newman worked on it, however, it turned into something considerably more ambitious and methodologically sophisticated: a study of the Arian controversy from its beginnings until the end of the fourth century, in which fundamental questions are addressed about the nature of

introduction she provides to her edition of these sermons. Stimulating, though inflammatory and I think misguided, comments on the sermon may also be found in Turner, *Newman*, 501-505.

[21] I rely principally upon Notes F and G to the 1865 edition (the *Apologia* was first published in pamphlet form in 1864) of Newman's *Apologia Pro Vita Sua, Being a History of his Religious Opinions*, ed. Martin J. Svaglic (Oxford: Clarendon Press, 1967) 299-311.

[22] I have used John Henry Newman, *The Via Media of the Anglican Church*, ed. H. D. Weidner (Oxford: Clarendon Press, 1990). Weidner's edition reproduces the text of the 1889 Uniform Edition of Newman's works, which for the *Via Media* is identical to the text of the 1877 edition. The *Lectures on the Prophetical Office* were first published in 1837.

[23] *Via Media*, ed. Weidner, 23.

doctrine, of orthodoxy, of heresy, and of the problem of writing doctrinal history. In the first chapter of the book, Newman provides a detailed study of the institutional form and characteristic doctrinal and exegetical emphases of the Alexandrian Church, and as part of this study he gives his first detailed statement of the economy's grammar.

He begins with the *disciplina arcani*, which he understands as the practice of reserving the explicit teaching of the Church's doctrine to the initiate, the baptized, and concealing it from those outside, which is to say from the Jews, the pagans, and even from catechumens until they had almost arrived at baptism.[24] This required a distinction between exoteric and esoteric teaching, the chief difference between which was that the exoteric teaching lacked some matter present in the esoteric. Whence the term 'reserve': the fuller truth is simply reserved, kept back. This discipline of keeping secret what is not to be revealed inappropriately is what Newman takes to be intimately linked (as he sees it) with the Alexandrian interest in allegorical methods of interpreting scripture. Allegory, he says, is what thought and language turn to when faced with a topic too vast and too complex for literal or everyday speech; it is among the principal means of observing the *disciplina arcani*, for once it is realized that the full meaning of scripture is vastly richer and more extensive than any literalist or superficial exegesis could suggest, it is easy to say that the esoteric (allegorical) interpretation of scripture is to be reserved to the baptized (or perhaps even to some sub-group of the baptized), while the exoteric (literal) interpretation is what can be offered to the unregenerate world.

Allegory provides the bridge between reserve and the economy, the other main doctrine of the Alexandrian Church as depicted by

[24] *Arians*, ed. Tollhurst, 51-52.

Newman. If the *disciplina arcani* withholds the truth, the economy sets it out to best advantage.[25] The economical method in speech is one of accommodation: the speaker's words and tropes are chosen so as to be most effective in leading some particular hearer or group of hearers to "the reception of a novel or unacceptable doctrine,"[26] and so those who economize with speech are driven by the pragmatical necessities of their situation to choose their words, their diction, and their idiom in such a way as to be most effective in persuasion and instruction. This is a necessity well understood by all who have to teach, and many of Newman's examples are drawn from pedagogical situations. But economizing speech in this way can easily lead to the use of deliberately duplicitous speech, which is to say the lie; and Newman is very well aware of this possibility too. Indeed, he quotes Clement to the effect that the economy may sometimes permit or even require the lie (though Newman explains neither just what Clement means by *pseudos* nor what he himself means by lying), as when a physician speaks duplicitously to his patient in order to cure him.[27] But Newman also says, without rejecting Clement's claim (also, of course, a fundamentally Platonic one) about the propriety of the useful lie, that the economy must not be overdone, that "substantial truth"[28] must at all costs be maintained. But here too Newman does not say just what 'substantial truth' means.

The upshot for the question of the lie's permissibility is very unclear. Economy and reserve are both strongly affirmed; it is shown that the former may lead to duplicity (the most natural interpretation of Clement); and yet Newman also says that substantial truth must be preserved. It is impossible, then, to tell from the first

[25] *Ibid.*, 65.
[26] *Ibid.*, 72.
[27] *Ibid.*, 74.
[28] *Ibid.*, 72 & passim.

chapter of *Arians* whether Newman does in fact wish to stop economizing speech short of duplicity. It is, however, clear that his emphasis on the importance of reserve and economy in our speech is grounded upon the claim that God's utterances and actions are all understood as instances of the economy: God, in creating the heavens and the earth, taking flesh, being crucified, rising, ascending into heaven, and descending upon the faithful at Pentecost is displaying "His character in action"[29] under the sign of the economy. This must be so, thinks Newman, because the full meaning of all these actions, and a full account of this God's character, is quite beyond human cognitive capacity, and so we must be satisfied with "the best practical communication… which our minds in their present state will admit."[30] We must make do with God's economies or dispensations (Newman uses these words interchangeably: *dispensatio* was the standard Latin rendering of *oikonomia*) because of our cognitive limitations, and God must so act and speak for the same reason. A high view of God's transcendence coupled with a skepticism about human cognitive capacity leads Newman to endorse this view of God as necessarily and always a dispenser of speech and action. Newman does not mean by this that God is duplicitous in the sense that he sometimes chooses to have his speech and action fully represent what he takes to be the case about the matter at hand, and sometimes chooses to be duplicitous. He means instead that the inadequacies of human language and human cognitive capacity make 'representation' the wrong category to capture the relation between what God does and says, on the one hand, and what he is and knows, on the other. A better category would be effectiveness in persuasion and exhortation: speech about God, whether ours or his (in scripture), cannot

[29] *Ibid.*, 75.
[30] *Ibid.*, 75.

capture or represent or image God's nature. It should not, then, be judged by the extent to which it does or fails to do those things, but rather by the extent to which it persuades people to conform themselves to God's will. There is in *Arians*, as in so much of Newman's work, a deep skepticism about the descriptive capacities of thought and language.

The same is true in "The Theory of Developments in Religious Doctrine," a sermonic first draft of material later to be worked up into the *Essay on Development*. Here Newman treats the economy in connection with the ordinary pedagogical situation of parents and teachers of the young, which he thinks is in essentials like that of God with respect to us:

> [W]e [adults] must dispense and 'divide' the word of truth, if we would not have it changed, as far as they [our juvenile hearers] are concerned, into a word of falsehood; for what is short of truth in the letter may be to them the most perfect truth, that is the nearest approach to truth compatible with their condition.[31]

It is to this passage that Newman appends the famous note (perhaps absent from the sermon as delivered) that "it is not more than a hyperbole to say that, in certain cases, a lie is the nearest approach to the truth." It is worth paying some attention to this, for it raises in pointed form the question of whether Newman does take the necessity of dispensing speech to extend so far as to require or permit the lie. It seems reasonable to think that what Newman means by "a lie" here is exactly duplicitous speech, for he is expounding the technique of the economizer, and the economizer must, in order to be one, know what he does. If this is right, then Newman may be paraphrased as saying that it is not false (for this is a minimal meaning of "not more than a hyperbole" — if it were more than a hyperbole it would be false) to say of a lie that it

[31] *Fifteen Sermons*, ed. Tillman, 351.

permits a closer approach to the truth on the part of its hearer than would any other speech. He may also mean (I think he does) that it is not even an exaggeration to say so; but the form in which he casts his sentence, full of art as it is, makes it impossible to tell whether he does mean that additional thing. Whatever is the case about that, however, it is fairly clear that he does, in this place at least, say that the principle of the economy permits (and may require) duplicity on the part of speakers.

But for the most part in this sermon he does not go so far. His examples of the economy at work in God's speech and ours are of verbal formulae inadequate to their topic, as in the case of a mathematical formula which is "an expedient for practical purposes, not a true analysis or adequate image of those recondite laws which are investigated by means of it."[32] These examples do not involve duplicity: they are simply the best we can do, "the nearest approximation to the truth which our condition permits."[33] Newman can throw off the possibility that the laws of physics might be "generalizations of economical exhibitions,"[34] — which is to say that they might be propositions false of the true order of things and known by their propounders so to be. But this need not be so, of course. The Newtonian laws of motion do not apply to all phenomena, and so they are false if stated as though they did. But if not so stated — if framed with an appropriate disclaimer — then they are not false, and one who so states them is not duplicitous if he so understands them.

The materials treated to this point show that Newman understands language (God's and ours) to be an expedient, incapable, certainly, of imaging the order of thought or of things, and not in any case designed principally for that purpose. It is, rather, a tool

[32] *Ibid.*, 345.
[33] *Ibid.*, 346.
[34] *Ibid.*, 347.

to be honed and polished by careful choices as to what is not said, and how what is said is said. This is reserve and economy, and when they are well practised language performs its principal function, which is to move its hearers toward active obedience, and thus closer to God. But, so far, it is not clear that these doctrines require or permit the lie, which is to say, deliberately duplicitous speech. There are hints that they might; but there are also suggestions that they need not. The doctrine of the economy, however, moves naturally in the direction of permitting or encouraging duplicity (it certainly moved many of its patristic defenders in that direction), and so if Newman does wish to restrain or ban the lie, this doctrine does not give him the resources to do so. Can he draw such resources from elsewhere? Some comment on the *Apologia* might help to answer this question, for it is there that Newman offers his fullest treatment of the lie.

Newman rhapsodizes about the rule of the economy in the body of the *Apologia*, in terms sufficiently close to those of *Arians* that I am tempted to think he had that book open in front of him as he was writing.[35] He also treats the economy in one of the extensive notes to the book. There, he says that economizing speech amounts to a "cautious dispensation of the truth, after the manner of a discreet and vigilant steward."[36] The principle governing this cautious dispensation is that you ought to choose from among licit utterances whichever is "most expedient and most suitable at the time for the object in hand."[37] Newman provides scriptural examples of the application of this principle, including: Jesus' pretense of going further on the road past Emmaus when in fact he intended to stop and break bread with those he had been accompanying (Luke 24:28); Jesus' harsh words to the Syro-Phoenician woman whose

[35] *Apologia*, ed. Svaglic, 36, inter alia.

[36] *Ibid.*, 299.

[37] *Ibid.*, 299.

daughter he was about to heal (Mark 7:24-30); and Paul's circumcision of Timothy performed at a time when Paul had come to think circumcision useless (Acts 16:3; Galatians 5:6, 6:15).

These illustrative scriptural examples are not all of the same sort. Each seems meant to illustrate some division or dissonance between what is thought and what is done or said; but in the case of the Syro-Phoenician woman, at least, it is not obvious that there is any such dissonance. The most natural reading of that story is that Jesus changes his mind about his willingness to help the woman and her daughter, not that what he thinks is at odds with what he does and says. It seems, however, that Newman did cite the story to illustrate a disharmony between Jesus' thought and action, like that between Paul's circumcision of Timothy and his view (or at least his claim) that circumcision is never necessary or efficacious, and like that between Jesus' gesture of continuing to walk and his intention not to do so. Other interpretations of these scriptural texts are possible, too; but since Newman takes them to be illustrative of the economy as applied to speech and action, I assume that he understands them all to depict instances of intentional dissonance between thought and speech or action.

Newman emphasizes that these scriptural instances show the principle of the economy applied to speech (and action) because none of them involves intrinsically illicit or sinful speech. If they did, he acknowledges, then economizing speech would be an example of doing evil in order that good might come, and this is neither what the economy advocates nor what Newman accepts. The economy advocates only finding and using the most appropriate and effective words for the situation in which you find yourself, and this is a "rule which nature suggests to everyone."[38] But the rule as it stands gives no guidance as to what makes an utterance licit;

[38] *Ibid.*, 300.

those criteria are, and must be if Newman's formulation is to be accepted, extrinsic to the rule of the economy.

In the *Apology*, Newman speaks more directly to the question of intentional duplicity than anywhere else in his work — though still not very directly. He is slippery on the question of the lie's definition. He notes, forcefully and repeatedly, that the definitional question is difficult, no less so for Protestants than for Catholics; and that even vigorous proponents of muscular Christian virtue like Milton have been troubled by it and have often ended by defining it in such a way as to make particular lies defensible or required. But in the end, Newman forces himself to the sticking point, and makes some necessary distinctions.

The fundamental question, he thinks, is whether "some kind or other of verbal misleading"[39] is licit for just cause. Newman's answer to this question is yes, and he thinks that everyone will agree that it should be yes. What, then, are the kinds of verbal misleading, and what are the just causes that do (or might) permit them? This way of posing the question shows clearly that Newman's thought on the lie is framed by the question of justice.[40] This predisposes him toward the use of a consequentialist calculus to decide particular disputed cases: if what is wrong with the lie is that it offends against duty to others, then it will not be difficult to justify particular lies when they seem likely to prevent more damaging transgressions of duty to others, such as murder or rape. The phrase "verbal misleading," too, as a portmanteau-word for kinds of lie, suggests that Newman's interest is in the lie's effects, actual or intended, upon its hearers rather than upon its speakers.

[39] *Ibid.*, 300.

[40] This is true of Aquinas' treatment, as well as for most of Liguori's. It is emphatically not true of Augustine.

Newman distinguishes four kinds of verbal misleading that might be justifiably performed under some circumstances (*ex iusta causa* as he likes to put it).

The first[41] is silence, which he thinks poses no particular moral problems and which cannot properly be characterized as a kind of verbal misleading. Misleading silences — for example, Abraham's about the fact that Sarah is his wife[42] — may be morally problematic in many ways, but they clearly do not fall under the definition of the lie: since they are not utterances they cannot be duplicitous utterances.

Second, there is evasion. To evade, on Newman's understanding, is for someone to "state some truth, from which he is quite sure his hearer will draw an illogical and untrue conclusion."[43] 'Illogical' here means a conclusion that does not strictly follow from what has explicitly been said; and 'untrue' means that the conclusion drawn by the hearer will be one not taken as true by the speaker. Evasion, so understood, is not a lie just because its practitioners claim verbally only what seems to them to be the case. They are of course doing so with intent to mislead or deceive, but since the definition of the lie in play here rules out such intentions as relevant to whether one is lying, it follows that evasions are not lies — which is not to say that there may not be other things wrong with them.

Third, there is equivocation, which Newman also calls a play upon words. This he understands to occur when a speaker, knowing that a particular word has two or more acceptable senses, uses it in one of them (according to which he takes what he says to be true) while intending that it be taken in one of its other senses,

41 I alter Newman's order here.

42 Genesis 12:10-20, 20:1-8, 26:6-11.

43 *Apologia*, ed. Svaglic, 308.

according to which it will be understood to mean what is false. Newman provides no examples, but the idea is clear enough. For example, the verb 'to let' has still in English at least two different and almost diametrically opposed senses: it may mean 'permit' or 'prevent' (the latter more common in legal usage) — British passports used to include the request from Her Britannic Majesty that the bearer be permitted to pass "without let or hindrance." If I know this, I may say "I'll let you borrow my car," while thinking that I intend to prevent you from borrowing my car and at the same time intending you to think that I will permit you to do so. This is equivocation, and the speaker who equivocates in this way says something he takes to be true while knowing (and intending) that his words might be taken in such a way as to convince his listeners that he thinks the opposite of what he thinks.

Equivocation and evasion, on Newman's understanding of them, are identical in intention and effect. But while Newman allows the latter, with regret and reservation, he rejects the former completely, because, he says, he has "the English habit" of directness and straightforwardness. Newman does not further expound his reasons for rejecting equivocation. This silence is interesting, and is partly explicable by the context that prompted this particular discussion of the lie. Newman had been accused by Kingsley of not thinking truth a virtue; and a prominent thread in the fabric of Kingsley's accusations and Newman's responses is precisely the question of Englishness: English habits, and English virtues.[44] For Kingsley,

[44] In Kingsley's accusations of Newman, masculinity is to femininity as Englishness is to foreignness. This is quite pervasive, and is not challenged by Newman; he simply denies that Catholic priests need be foreign or effeminate, not that being foreign is connected with effeminacy. Connected with this pattern of thought in Kingsley, of course, is a polemic against priestly celibacy: for Kingsley, Catholic priests are always and necessarily effeminate foreign liars, and this is among the reasons why they are not married and attempt to persuade others to celibacy.

and for many other Anglican (especially evangelical Anglican) writers of the time, being Roman Catholic was already enough to make you un-English, which also meant (if you were of the right social class to begin with) that you could not properly be called a gentleman. Among the evidences of loss of Englishness was abandonment of the ideal-typical English gentleman's virtue of bluff, hearty frankness, and the substitution for it of the effeminate (and of course Catholic) habits of equivocation and reserve. Newman accepts this equation to an astonishing extent, and it is because he does that he offers only an appeal to the English habit as a defense against equivocation.[45] Newman is simply (he says) revolted by equivocation's calculating deviousness, by its incompatibility with the mid-Victorian ethic of the gentleman, and by its general inelegance. He rejects it on that ground alone.

This leads him to the remarkable claim that he can more easily imagine himself thinking it permissible for him to lie materially than to perform or advocate equivocation. In saying this he mentions his fourth kind of verbal misleading and at the same time shows how very far he is in thinking about the lie from the Augustinian position. The material lie as Newman understands it is "saying the thing that is not,"[46] by which he means (though does not

[45] It is worth making his words more fully available: "[A]s to playing upon words, or equivocation, I suppose it is from the English habit, but, without meaning any disrespect to a great Saint [he means Alphonsus Liguori], or wishing to set myself up, or taking my conscience for more than it is worth, I can only say as a fact, that I admit it as little as the rest of my countrymen: and, without any reference to the right and the wrong of the matter, of this I am sure, that, if there is one thing more than another which prejudices Englishmen against the Catholic Church, it is the doctrine of great authorities on the subject of equivocation." *Apologia*, ed. Svaglic, 309-310.

[46] This phrase is used at *Apologia*, ed. Svaglic, 307 & passim. It is (almost) Jonathan Swift's phrase: when the Houhyhnhm who is teaching Gulliver to speak the Houhyhnhm language doubts something Gulliver tells him, the Houhyhnhm says, "That I must needs be mistaken, or that I *said the thing which was not*. (For

quite say) speaking against the mind, uttering what one takes to be false (he usually calls this just 'falsehood', with some evidence of the usual confusions this leads to). "Saying the thing that is not," then, just is the lie. To lie formally, as distinct from materially, is then to say the thing that is not — to speak duplicitously — without just cause. The presence of just cause is what distinguishes the material lie from the formal lie. The latter is always and without exception forbidden, says Newman; but the former may be allowed precisely because there is just cause for it.

Newman draws upon analogies with murder and theft for this position. Materially, he says, murder is killing: killing another human being is its matter, the action in which it essentially consists. But formally, murder is killing in the absence of just cause: this is the full form of the act. And clearly, he thinks, there are material murders (killings) that are not formal murders precisely because there is just cause for them: killing in self-defense, killing done by the state of those guilty of capital crimes, and so on. Similarly with theft: its matter is taking what you do not own without permission; but just cause (imminent starvation, perhaps) can exempt some acts of this sort from the formal category of theft.

These analogies show as clearly as anything could that Newman thinks of the lie's matter — saying the thing that is not, simple

they have no Word in their language to express Lying or Falsehood.)," Jonathan Swift, *Gulliver's Travels*, ed. John Hayward (London: Cresset Press, 1949; first published 1726), pt. 4, ch. 3, p. 326 and passim. Newman may have drawn the phrase from Swift, and perhaps assumes knowledge of Swift on the part of his readers — though the change of pronoun from 'which' to 'that' is interesting, and may indicate that the words are a half-remembered and unattributed echo in Newman's mind. There may also be an Aristotelian echo: when Aristotle discusses the falsity of claims or statements (*logoi*) in the *Metaphysics* (1024b17-1025a13) he says that the most fundamental characteristic of false statements is that they are misapplied — applied, that is, to "things that are not" (*tōn mē ontōn*). It would be interesting to excavate the history of the English phrase more thoroughly.

duplicity — as capable of exemption from the category of things that should never be done. This exemption can be given only by something external to the matter of the act itself: by the agent's intention, the intended result, the pressures upon the agent, or even, interestingly, the clarity with which norms about the acceptable untruth have been communicated by élites. On this last Newman writes:

> I would oblige society, that is, its great men, its lawyers, its divines, its literature, publicly to acknowledge as such, those instances of untruth which are not lies, as for instance untruths in war.[47]

Why is it important for élites to provide clear and systematic guidance as to when an untruth (an Augustinian lie) is not a lie? Because without it our consciences will be confused and our habits ill-formed. We know (thinks Newman) that when a soldier on the right side kills another in a just war no murder has happened, even though, materially speaking, killing has occurred. We know this because the messages we are sent about it from our élites are unambiguous and frequent. We are not generally confused about the difference between killing-for-just-cause and simple murder. But we have no such clarity about the situations in which duplicitous utterances are not lies; and because Newman is sure that there are such situations, he thinks it possible and desirable that there be such clarity, or at least that we approach more closely to it.

I turn finally and briefly to Newman's 1877 preface to the first volume of the *Via Media*. Here again, there is very strong evidence of the continuity of Newman's thought on reserve and economy across the Anglican/Catholic divide. The central issue with which he is concerned in this preface is the perceived dissonance — even contradiction — between what the Catholic Church teaches (her prophetical office, as he calls it) and what she prescribes or permits

[47] *Apologia*, ed. Svaglic, 309.

by way of popular piety (her priestly office).[48] There may appear to be, he says, a deep difference between the two, even a difference that amount to a contradiction: what the "poor Neapolitan crone who chatters to the crucifix"[49] does and believes may be significantly at odds with the Church's teachings; but this is inevitable: in a "religion which embraces large and separate classes of adherents, there is always of necessity to a certain extent an exoteric and an esoteric doctrine."[50] The distinction between an exoteric and an esoteric teaching here re-emerges essentially unchanged, forty-five years after Newman first distinguished them in *Arians*. It is connected here, as it was there, with the doctrines of reserve and the economy. The only difference is that in 1877 Newman's understanding of the church's nature has changed significantly from what it was in 1832, and so the "duty of concealment, or what may be called evasion, not in religious matters only, but universally,"[51] is connected to a subtle treatment of the church's threefold office: the agent who economizes and reserves her speech is not the individual or God, but instead the church.

It is, says Newman, properly economical of the church to permit popular pieties that might not stand the test of strict theological judgment; and it is properly reserved of her to withhold a critique of them in certain circumstances — specifically, when it is better for some to continue the practices than to be forbidden them. This

[48] Newman treats also discordances produced by tensions between the demands of the royal or kingly ministry of the church and those of the prophetic and priestly ministries. But I pass those by here.

[49] *Via Media*, ed. Weidner, 41. The language here is one example among many of Newman's acute uneasiness about some Catholic popular pieties — especially those widely evident outside England. Here he remains enough of an Englishman to be embarrassed: he wouldn't, I'm sure, have wanted to dine with that Neapolitan crone, defend her faith as he might.

[50] *Via Media*, ed. Weidner, 32.

[51] *Ibid.*, 35.

begins to sound like an unchecked economy of speech for the teaching church, one that would permit it tacitly (or even explicitly) to approve of practices which theologically it knows to be flawed in some important way. Newman gives two interesting examples that make clearer what he means. If a Catholic is ministering to a dying Protestant whom he knows to be sincere and faithful in his Protestantism, it is, says Newman, better to "assist his devotions as far as he will let us carry him" rather than urge upon him the deathbed acceptance of Catholicism. Doing this latter would "unsettle such measure of faith as he has" and would be unlikely to yield good results. This is a pragmatical decision, one that Newman acknowledges might be seen as "theory saying one thing, and practice sanctioning another." The second example supposes that French ecclesiastics early in the nineteenth century were to be ordered by Napoleon to sing a Te Deum for his victory at Trafalgar — "they might have shrewd suspicions about the fact, but they would not see their way not to take part in a national festival." The underlying point is that "errors of fact may do no harm, and their removal may do much." Here too there is a decision according to probabilistic judgment about consequence.[52]

In the 1877 work, too, Newman approaches the brink of approving the Augustinian lie, and then draws back: "An ecclesiastical superior certainly cannot sanction alleged miracles or prophecies which he knows to be false."[53] Clear cases of duplicity, then, are rejected (recall the emphasis in *Arians* on the importance of maintaining "substantial truth"), but, as usual, no reason is given. The possible use of the Augustinian lie is justified by Newman's version of the doctrines of reserve and economy; its ban, though asserted as desirable, is given no such justification. Quite the opposite, in fact: its ban is located in a contingent ethos, that of the English gentleman.

[52] The quotations in this paragraph are from *Via Media*, ed. Weidner, 38-40.
[53] *Ibid.*, 40.

5. Augustine and Newman: A Tentative Adjudication

The Augustinian position on the lie, much too briefly set forth in this paper, derives the conclusion that deliberately duplicitous speech is a sin from a trinitarian understanding of human thought and speech coupled with an ontology of participation. This in turn means that there are no circumstances in which such speech is properly performed. No consequence that might follow from performing it — not the saving of innocent life, not the preserving of the innocent from rape or other torture, not the prevention of apostasy — can justify it because, first, there are no circumstances in which sin is unavoidable; and, second, there are therefore no circumstances in which one may or should sin in order to prevent sin (one's own or someone else's). Sinning to prevent nonsinful harms is, from an Augustinian point of view, ruled out as even more obviously indefensible than sinning to prevent sin. Augustine's position on the lie is at every point referred to and derived from his fundamental understanding of being, speech, and thought.

Newman's understanding of the same question is in almost every interesting respect different.[54] He has a fundamental understanding of speech and thought, too, but it is not a distinctively Christian one. It is constituted, instead, by the rules of reserve and economy, and these are principles, as he says himself, that it is entirely natural to accede to whether you are Christian or not. Who doubts that we should not always say all we think, and that we ought choose the words best suited to our audience when we do speak? This theoretical understanding of the nature and purposes of speech and

[54] As he is himself aware: "St. Augustine took another view, though with great misgiving; and, whether he is rightly interpreted or not, is the doctor of the great and common view that all untruths are lies, and that there can be *no* just cause of untruth. In these later times, this doctrine has been found difficult to work...," *Apologia*, ed. Svaglic, 303.

thought is fundamentally instrumentalist and consequentialist — or, as Newman would say, pragmatical. Speech is understood as an instrument principally of exhortation and persuasion, and is judged according to how well it does those things. It is always profoundly inadequate to the task of imaging, representing, or (as Augustine would say) invoking — giving voice to — thought; and speech's inadequacy to that task is like that of thought's to the imaging or representing of reality. Speech should not, then, thinks Newman, be held accountable principally to that task, but instead to the task of bringing about appropriate transformations in those who hear it. For him, the most important transformation would be in the direction of obedience.

These are deep differences. Their adjudication is not easy or obvious. Both views are subject to criticism (though it is probably already clear where my own sympathies lie), and I will conclude by mentioning and briefly commenting upon the principal criticisms that can be (and have been) brought against both kinds of view about the lie. My goal here is not to resolve these criticisms, but rather briefly to indicate where they point, to show what would need to be done were they to be resolved.

Three criticisms are most often brought against an Augustinian view of the lie, and of the understanding of thought and speech that informs it.

The first is that an Augustinian exceptionless ban upon the lie is unrealistically rigorist and, perhaps, subject to properly moral objections for requiring (inter alia) the sacrifice of innocent life that could be saved by lying. If, however, Augustine is right that to lie is sinful, and if he is also right that no situation requires sin (i.e., there are no strict moral dilemmas), then it must also be the case that the decision to lie is a decision to sin that need not be taken: it is a decision, that is, required by no situation. If we add the claim that it is never defensible to decide to sin, no matter what harms we think might be avoided by so deciding,[55] then the conclusion follows. If Augustine is wrong about the lie, therefore, it must be because he is also wrong about one or another of the claims just mentioned. The rigorist objection also assumes the falsehood of one or another among these claims.[56] Further exploration of these objections would, then, require exploration of these more fundamental claims.[57]

The second objection has to do with what force his fundamental trinitarian analogy should be thought to have. Why should we think about human speech and thought by an analogy derived from our thought about God's inner-trinitarian life? An Augustinian answer here begins by appeal to Genesis 1:26, whose claim is that we are made in God's image and likeness. If that is so, and if also God's image and likeness is triune, anthropology (understood as reasoned discourse about the nature of human beings and not as the degenerate academic discipline by that name) should proceed, wherever possible, by way of the categories given to us for understanding God's triune nature. This might be stated as a procedural rule for Christian thought, and so stating it provides the beginnings of an answer to the theoretical questions about resolving disputed questions raised above: when two incompatible understandings of a topic in anthropology develop within the Christian tradition — as

[55] The modifier "we think" in this sentence is important: it indicates that among the Augustinian reasons for being dubious about the success of consequentialist arguments in favor of lying is the epistemological point that we are unlikely to be able effectively to judge the effects of our lies, and that attempts to do so are on more shaky ground than the judgment that lying is a sin.

[56] Augustine is not interested (not, at least, when discussing whether the lie is defensible) in discussing whether it is possible to cease lying (he has no unrealistic anticipations of the end of sin short of the eschaton), but only in the question of what the right thing is to say about the lie.

[57] I should register my opinion that Augustine is right about these fundamental matters.

is the case with Newman and Augustine on the lie — then other things being equal the one to be preferred is the one more intimately and explicitly linked to the axioms of orthodoxy (what Newman likes to call "the first elements of Revelation").[58] Much hard going is obscured by the phrase 'other things being equal', of course; but the principle, if good, though it would not exactly answer the question about the force of the fundamental trinitarian analogy, would require that question to be considered in the context of other possible answers to the disputed question. The principle also provides Augustine's position with a significant prima facie advantage over Newman's just because Augustine begins from the axioms of orthodoxy and refers his entire exposition to them, while Newman does not.

The third pressing criticism of Augustine's views is the strictly philosophical point that he appears committed to an indefensible form of the view that (human) thought is essentially nonlinguistic. The way in which he applies the trinitarian analogy to human thought and speech, discussed already above, makes it pretty clear that he does think this (and it is a conviction shared by some among those from whom he drew, notably Plotinus and Porphyry): the *verbum internum* is related to the word spoken, the invoked word, just as the eternally begotten Logos is related to the word incarnated as Jesus, from which it (probably) follows that the *verbum internum* can be understood as *verbum* independently of reference to any natural language, and (almost certainly) that the *verbum internum* has among its essential properties none relating it to any natural language. This appears to me the most difficult criticism to meet. Pursuing it would require address to delicate trinitarian questions,[59] and to equally delicate questions in philosophy of

[58] *Via Media*, ed. Weidner, 38.

[59] E.g.: What can be known about the eternally-begotten Logos (the *logos asarkos*) independently of knowledge of the incarnate one (an epistemological

mind and philosophy of language.[60] All I can do here is note the fact.

Further analysis of these criticisms of the Augustinian view of the lie would likely be productive. It seems to me that such analysis is unlikely to yield the conclusion that the view cannot be defended. The same is not true, though (or so I think), of Newman's view — and, of course, of its many precursors. The criticisms to be offered of this view are more damaging.

The first criticism is an internal one. It is clear from Newman's treatment of the principle of reserve, the *disciplina arcani*, the rule of the economy, and the saying of the thing that is not — the Augustinian lie he is uneasy about and usually at the point of explicitly rejecting — to treating human thought and speech primarily under the rule of the economy, and that requires the defensibility of deliberately duplicitous speech. The materials discussed above show this uneasiness again and again. But they show also, with great clarity, that Newman's understanding of thought and speech provide him with no theoretical resources whatever to explain why deliberately duplicitous speech is wrong. His predecessors in treating speech and thought in this way saw clearly that such an approach does permit — or at least possesses no resources to forbid — deliberately duplicitous speech, and some of them were happy to embrace the conclusion that such speech is sometimes permissible and (even) sometimes required.[61] Newman will

question)? What is the exact nature of the relation between the *logos asarkos* and the incarnate one (an ontological question)?

[60] E.g.: Is the idea of an entirely nonlinguistic concept coherent? If it is, what account can be offered of the relations between such entities and natural-language sentences?

[61] Chrysostom, Cassian and Jerome all argue that the lie is sometimes required. See, for example, the first book of Chrysostom's *Peri hierōsunēs* (often referred to by its Latin title, *De sacerdotio*, in *Jean Chrysostome: sur le sacerdoce*, ed. Anne-Marie Malingrey, Sources Chrétiennes, 272 (Paris: Éditions du Cerf, 1980)

not usually embrace this conclusion (though I remind you again of the "it is not more than a hyperbole" claim in the sermon on development as a possible counter-example), but when he refuses it, as he usually does, he has no arguments to offer except the egregious appeal to Englishness. The trajectory of Newman's thought about the lie is, throughout, toward its occasional acceptance: this is the direction in which his fundamental vocabulary and concepts for discussing the matter point him. But he resists that trajectory, and this accounts for the tensions in his writing about the matter that I have noted.[62]

This is a criticism of a different kind than those brought against Augustine. It is a criticism of the internal logic of Newman's position, claiming that his understanding of thought and speech creates a desideratum (banning the lie) which its fundamental commitments provide it no resources to meet. An Augustinian view has the same desideratum, but does have the resources to meet it. Augustinianism is, therefore, at least in this limited case, superior to Newman's thought, for it can do what he needs done, and in so doing show that the tools he has at hand cannot do the same thing.

None of this yields the conclusion that Newman is wrong about the lie (though I think he is). Instead, it begins a line of thought that needs more exploration before anything more than a very

60-98, which is best described as a hymn of praise to the lie. For Cassian, see the seventeenth of his *Collationes*, in *Jean Cassien: Conférences VIII-XVII*, ed. E. Pichery, Sources Chrétiennes, 54 (Paris: Éditions du Cerf, 1958) 248-284. For Jerome, see the correspondence with Augustine, in Migne, vol. 33, usefully collected and translated by Caroline White, *The Correspondence (394-419) Between Jerome and Augustine of Hippo*, Studies in Bible and Early Christianity, 23 (Lewiston-Queenston-Lampeter: Edwin Mellen, 1990).

62 It may also account for the fact that Kingsley's accusation that Newman sits lightly to truth, though ineptly made and defended, and made, as well, by a man with a much inferior mind to Newman's, nonetheless bears some plausibility.

tentative conclusion can be offered. But it does suggest that Newman was led astray, as before him was a goodly portion of the tradition, by doing his anthropology with insufficient attention to theology. The love of God, Augustine often suggests, has as one of its proper modes the love of the triune *imago* that constitutes us; it is then in part a self-reflexive love. And such love requires in turn loving what it is about us that makes it possible for us to know and to speak. A close and loving eye upon that matter will show that any self-created rupture between thought and speech diminishes the one who brings it about, thereby removing him from the *ipsum esse* in which he participates and giving him, as utterly inadequate recompense, the only kind of speech we can own without remainder, which is to say the lie.[63]

[63] Augustine likes to refer to John 8:44, where Diabolus is said (in Latin) to speak *ex propriis*: speech expropriated becomes, inevitably, lying speech, speech spoken as if it were our own. See, inter alia, *De civitate Dei* 14.3-4. Truthful speech is speech disowned; lying speech is speech *sibi tribuere*, made subject to the speaker.

NEWMAN, "CATHOLIC FACT," AND HIGHER EDUCATION

Colin BARR

To posterity, John Henry Newman's Dublin lectures on the nature of University education have gone down as a great success. They form the core of the *Idea of a University*,[1] a classic of educational philosophy that is, as Owen Chadwick put it, "a classic of Victorian literature."[2] And, despite the intense effort the discourses cost him, Newman himself was largely pleased with their reception. He was not sure, however, that he had made himself entirely clear to his hearers; that they understood exactly what he was driving at and, more importantly, what was specifically *Catholic* about his proposed University.

In the summer of 1852, in an effort to clarify his meaning, Newman thought to draw up an introduction, to be published with his sixth discourse. This introduction, although it was never actually published in any of its versions, was Newman's attempt to sum up what he meant by a Catholic University education. We will return to the context in which Newman wrote in due course, but I would like to begin by setting out the most important elements of that proposed introduction:

[1] All references to *The Idea of a University* in this essay will be drawn from Ian Ker's edition *The Idea of a University: Defined and Illustrated. I: In nine discourses delivered to the Catholics of Dublin. II: In occasional lectures and essays addressed to the members of the Catholic University* (Oxford: Oxford University Press, 1976).

[2] Owen Chadwick, *The Sprit of the Oxford Movement: Tractarian Essays* (Cambridge: Cambridge University Press, 1990) 99.

1. The direct object of a University *as such*, is to teach *all* knowledge.
2. The subject-matter of *faith* comes into the idea of "all knowledge."
3. Therefore a University *must*, cannot help, as such teaching the faith, and nothing else.
4. Therefore it does *directly*, virtute Universitateitatis suae, teach and inculcate Catholic expression, feeling, fact, etc etc., and leaven, all instruction with Catholicism.[3]

The phrase "Catholic fact" is particularly interesting. To Newman, truth — fact — was inextricably tied up with religious faith. By positing the existence of Catholic fact, Newman appears to assume the existence of Protestant fact, atheist fact, and, presumably, other "facts" held by members of other faiths. Did then, to Newman, truth vary with one's perspective, with one's "view?"

To be sure, Newman did not always appear to follow-out the apparent implications of this argument, either in his own writings or during his tenure as Rector of the Catholic University of Ireland. A serious tension seems to exist between theory and practice. It is this apparent tension that I intend to explore. To do this, I will focus on Newman's effort to build a University from the ground up. It is often forgotten that Newman actually attempted to put his ideas — so classically spelled out in *The Idea of a University* — into practice. Of this attempt, a great deal of evidence survives, giving us a useful insight into how Newman understood truth, at least in the context of higher education. As, in Newman's own

[3] See Newman to Dalgairns 23 July 1852, *Letters and Diaries of John Henry Newman*, ed. Stephen Dessain et al. (London/Oxford: Nelson/Oxford University Press, 1962) XV (hereafter '*LD*'). Letters from Newman are organised chronologically and can be found thus; letters to Newman, published in whole or in part are inserted to illuminate Newman's own letters. Letters from Newman will simply be noted by correspondent, date, and volume number. Letters to Newman will also have the page number(s).

words, a University's task is to "teach all knowledge," the question of truth is central to its function. And, since Newman had almost total control over the day-to-day running of the Catholic University of Ireland, a close study of his time in Dublin can help illumine his conception of truth, and any tensions that might be inherent in it.

To understand Newman's time in Dublin, it will first be necessary to briefly review the background of the proposed University. As Newman himself noted, "A University is not founded every day; and seldom indeed has it been founded under the peculiar circumstances which will now attend its establishment in Catholic Ireland."[4] The Catholic University of Ireland was first proposed to the Irish Catholic hierarchy by the Holy See in 1846. It was to be a response to the creation the year before of three "Queen's Colleges," to be established in Cork, Belfast, and Galway. In keeping both with the fashion of the time, and the particular realities of Ireland, the colleges were to be secular in nature; their opponents (not just Catholics) quickly christened them the "Godless colleges," a charge that was harsh, but reasonably accurate.[5]

The Irish hierarchy was peculiarly unsuited, in the mid-1840s, to cope either with the government's proposed Colleges, or with the Holy See's alternative. Since at least 1838, the Irish bishops had descended into interminably squabbling factions, with defeated bishops forever appealing the decisions of a temporary majority to Rome. From 1846 to 1850 precious little was done to create the proposed Catholic University. There were, to be sure, good reasons beyond the bishops' own divisions; if for no other reason, the

4 John Henry Newman, *Historical Sketches* (London: Basil Montagu Pickering, 1872) 3: 1-2.

5 The best single volume account of the period is Donal Kerr, *Peel, Priests, and Politics* (Oxford: Oxford University Press, 1992).

Great Famine would have rendered the task beyond even a united hierarchy.

Matters changed in April 1849, when William Crolly,[6] the Archbishop of Armagh and Primate of All Ireland died. Crolly had been, with Archbishop Daniel Murray of Dublin,[7] a qualified supporter of the Queen's Colleges, and thus, in the tangled world of Irish ecclesiastical politics, a passive opponent of a Catholic University. After much confusion, occasioned both by the inability of the hierarchy to settle on a replacement and the presence of Mazzini in Rome, a new Archbishop of Armagh was selected: Paul Cullen of the Irish College in Rome.[8]

Cullen was a Roman to the core of his being. He had been educated there, and was a great star at the Propaganda Fidei, the papal congregation with responsibility for Ireland. In 1832 he was appointed Rector at the recently re-established Irish College, and he rebuilt that College in the face of great obstacles. Cullen served as the agent of the Irish bishops at Rome, and the Roman expert on the Irish bishops; it was a dual role that gave him tremendous power. Since the mid-1840s Cullen had come to be associated with the anti-Government, anti-Queen's Colleges, pro-Catholic University faction in the hierarchy led by Archbishop John MacHale of Tuam.[9] By appointing Cullen to Armagh, Rome was ensuring that a Catholic University would be attempted, if only to block the Godless Colleges.

I have dealt in detail elsewhere with the steps Cullen took to secure episcopal support (partial and grudging) for the University,

[6] 1780-1849. Appointed bishop of Down and Connor 1825, Archbishop of Armagh 1835.

[7] 1768-1852. Appointed coadjutor archbishop of Dublin, 1809, succeeded 1823.

[8] 1803-1878. Appointed archbishop of Armagh 1849, translated to Dublin 1852.

[9] 1791-1881. Appointed coadjutor bishop of Killala 1825, archbishop of Tuam 1834.

and to lay the groundwork for its financial health.[10] By the spring of 1851 he was ready to appoint a head to his new University. His attention fell from the beginning on John Henry Newman, and we must take at least a brief glance at the circumstances of Newman's appointment in order to assess to what extent Newman's later actions can be attributed to Cullen's direction, or to Newman's perception of what Cullen desired in a University.

There can be no question that Cullen chose Newman of his own free will. Although the first suggestion of Newman's name in connection with the University may very probably have come from Robert Whitty, a friend of Newman's and Cardinal Wiseman's vicar-general, Cullen nonetheless made it clear to friends in Rome that Newman was the man he wanted, long before he spoke to Newman himself on the subject.

In fact, Cullen's campaign to gain Newman to his University was a master-class in Roman subtlety. Cullen began by soliciting Newman's own opinion on who might make a suitable head (and faculty) of the new institution. He then arranged, in London, a meeting of Newman's friends — Henry Edward Manning included — to "discuss" the shape and nature of the University. Cullen arranged the meeting to invite Newman to London to discuss matters further, and when Newman declined, visited him in Birmingham to put the offer in person. When Newman demurred, Cullen turned on the charm. He gave money to the Oratory, flattered Newman by continuing to seek his advice, and got him to commit, if he was not yet ready to accept the Rectorship, to at least head a committee specially created to draw up the first plans of the new University. All the while Cullen was ensuring that Rome would not only allow Newman to take up the post — without leaving his

[10] See Colin Barr, *Paul Cullen, John Henry Newman, and the Catholic University of Ireland, 1845-1865* (Notre Dame, IN: University of Notre Dame Press, 2003).

position as Superior of the Oratory in Birmingham — but also exploring the possibility of arranging for Rome to order Newman to Dublin in the event he refused the invitation.

Although Newman, both at the time and later, was unaware of the extent of Cullen's machinations to secure his services (he thought his friends had suggested his name to Cullen at the London meeting), he would nevertheless have been in no doubt as to who, exactly, his primary Irish patron was. This is important to the extent that we must assess, in due course, to what extent Newman's actions in Dublin as University Rector can be attributed to his own settled convictions, or to a desire either to please Cullen or obey his orders.

Newman's first important contact with the nascent University came with his participation in the committee that Cullen had asked him to head. Its membership was, except for Newman himself, Irish.[11] Of the other members, one was Patrick Leahy,[12] the President of St Patrick's College Thurles, and a rising man in the Irish Church. He would in due course become vice-rector of the Catholic University and, in 1857, Archbishop of Cashel. Although a Cullen ally, he was not Cullen's creature. The other member was Myles O'Reilly of Longford.[13] O'Reilly was a prominent Catholic layman, and would in due course go on to figure as an officer in the papal army and as a Member of Parliament.[14] He was a close

[11] Barring the presence of T. W. Allies as secretary — another clever stratagem on Cullen's part, as Allies, a recently converted Church of England clergyman, was a close friend of Newman's and desperately short of money. Cullen knew that Newman would welcome any help for his friend, and suggested that he be secretary to the committee, for which of course he would be paid.

[12] 1806-1875.

[13] 1825-1880.

[14] Although Cullen's clericalism was always real, and became more pronounced over time, it is nonetheless instructive that he chose a layman to be his representative on such an important committee.

ally of Cullen's, and the Archbishop's man on the committee. Although both men, and Leahy especially, were substantial figures in their own right, the clear head and driving force of the committee was Newman himself.

Certainly we have no evidence of dissension amongst the men. They did their work — at Thurles, Co. Tipperary — over only three days in October 1851.[15] The decision was taken that the University would be, on the model of Louvain in Belgium,[16] under the authority of the bishops of Ireland. Further, all University "Officers and Professors" would be required to take a profession of faith, undertaking not to teach anything "contrary to Religion" and also promising to use their office to "point out that Religion is the basis of Science, and to inculcate the love of Religion and its duties."[17] From the beginning, then, Newman was anxious to ensure the catholicity of his University.

Newman informally accepted the Rectorship of the Catholic University of Ireland early in October 1851. His appointment was confirmed by the University Committee on 12 November 1851. During the course of his campaign to secure Newman's services, Cullen had asked his prospective Rector to give a series of lectures, in Dublin, on the nature of University education. These lectures — discourses — were to be aimed at the educated Catholic middle classes of the city, and would, Cullen hoped, serve to set out why a Catholic University, which would cost them money, should be supported over Queen's Colleges that would not.

15 They had earlier (August 1851) met informally in Birmingham to discuss matters, but the primary work was done at Thurles.

16 Louvain had been recently re-founded with the tacit approval of the Belgian government.

17 Report of the subcommittee on the Organization of the Catholic University of Ireland, printed in John Henry Newman, *My Campaign in Ireland, Catholic University Reports and Other Papers*, ed. William Neville (Aberdeen: A. King, 1896) 80.

These discourses, of course, became the core of *The Idea of a University* and have thus secured a form of immortality. It will be necessary, if only briefly, to consider to what extent Newman was writing, in the words of Ian Ker, to "episcopal order,"[18] if only to see how much of what he said can be taken as his own settled conviction.

Although the delivery (and to an extent the composition) of the discourses was delayed by the Achilli affair,[19] Newman nevertheless had from the beginning a clear idea of what Cullen wanted. Writing in mid-September 1851, Cullen set out what it was, in his view, Newman's lectures were to achieve. "What we want," Cullen wrote, "is to persuade the people that education should be religious." "The whole tendency of our new system is to make it believed that education may be conducted as to have nothing at all to do with religion."[20]

That Newman would need little persuading of the truth of Cullen's statement seems clear. His entire history, going back well into his Anglican days, demonstrates that he clearly believed that a University — charged as it was with teaching "all knowledge" — could only safely do so in a religious and moreover a denominational context. Whether he was opposing the relaxation of religious tests at Oxford, or attacking Sir Robert Peel's ideal of secular learning in his *Tamworth Reading Room* (1841),[21] Newman was

[18] Ian Ker, 'The Idea of a Catholic University', paper delivered to the Newman conference 'The Idea of a Catholic University in Mayo' (Ballina: n.p., 1996) 8.

[19] Giacinto Achilli, an apostate Italian Dominican, served Newman with a writ of criminal libel on 27 October 1851. The case, which consumed much of Newman's attention, was not finally resolved until 31 January 1853.

[20] Cullen to Newman, 20 September 1851, Newman papers, Birmingham Oratory Archives, Cullen file.

[21] *The Tamworth Reading Room* was originally published as a letter to the *Times* under the signature of 'Catholicus'.

consistently opposed to education being separated from religious commitment and religious knowledge. This basic assumption underlies the entire course of lectures that Newman delivered in Dublin. To be sure, Newman hoped, as he told Robert Ornsby,[22] to please the "high authority" who had suggested some of his topics, but both the topics and his treatment of them were essentially his own.

It is not the purpose of this essay to re-hash the Dublin discourses: that has been done by other and better scholars. To a great extent — as Dwight Culler noticed — the discourses "deliberately omit any consideration of means and concentrate exclusively on ends."[23] Newman went out of his way to show the purpose of a University, but paid relatively little attention to what part religion (as opposed to theology) should play in it.

To a degree, this was an accurate reflection of some of Newman's own beliefs. As he told his fellow Oratorian J. D. Dalgairns, "A University has no direct call to make men Catholic or religious, for that is the previous and contemporaneous office of the Church."[24] This is not to say, however, that Newman was indifferent to the religious mission of the University, or that he thought truth — after all, the University's product — could in any way be separated from religion. Rather, he was assuming a Catholic ethos, a Catholic "view," that would permeate the University and its teaching. It was more a case of a division of labour between the University and other, subordinate or dependant, bodies: both would be Catholic, but would assume different responsibilities as regards the students.

[22] Robert Ornsby (1820-1889) was appointed professor of Greek in the Catholic University of Ireland in 1854.

[23] A. Dwight Culler, *The Imperial Intellect: A Study of Newman's Educational Ideal* (New Haven, CT: Yale University Press, 1955) 189.

[24] Newman to Dalgairns, *LD* XV.

Newman was not unaware, even as he was delivering his Dublin lectures, that some in his audience might not be clear as to what was Catholic about the proposed University as he was describing it. As Dalgairns told a worried Newman, "Your whole line has been to treat the question of mixed education on general principles without reference to a *Catholic* University. You have not contemplated the question morally but intellectually."[25] It was the ambiguity of that remark which forced Newman to consider preparing a special introduction or summary of his thoughts before delivering the next lecture — the sixth — in his series.

He made his attempt at such an introduction in July 1852. Part of it was quoted at the beginning of this essay. Newman thought it necessary to publicly declare that a University, by virtue of being a University, "does *directly*... teach and inculcate Catholic expression, feeling, fact." This had nothing, or rather little, to do with morals, which a University "contemplates only *indirectly* — and in a general way — i.e. the Church does not use it for morals except in a general way." Morals — which, Newman hastened to add, could be taught as knowledge — were to be inculcated by the Church by means of smaller units on the model of the Oxbridge Colleges. The "Catholic fact," the Catholic view, that Newman thought so crucial to the University was thus distinct from the Catholic morality that Newman thought equally true, but largely beyond the scope of the University per se.

Others besides Dalgairns were invited to comment on the proposed introduction. David Moriarty, the president of All Hallows College and soon to be bishop of Kerry,[26] and Newman's closest Irish friend, picked up immediately on the notion of Catholic fact,

[25] Dalgarins to Newman, 22 July 1852, *LD* XV, 152.

[26] Moriarty (1814-1877) was appointed coadjutor bishop of Kerry in 1854, and succeeded to that see in 1856.

telling Newman that in his view the Queen's Colleges had been condemned in Rome because "being systematically mixed, Catholic expression, Catholic feeling, Catholic fact, should all be suppressed." Whereas, according to Moriarty, "in a University such as the Church would wish, all instruction should be leavened with Catholicism."[27] In the end, Moriarty advised Newman that there was no need to publish an introduction to discourse six, as Newman's meaning was already perfectly clear, and in fact no introduction was published.

Despite this, the issue of an introduction to discourse six raises an interesting question that will be central to the rest of this essay. In it, Newman clearly established, in line with his own past history, his belief in the necessity for a University both to teach all knowledge and by so doing to teach a specifically *Catholic* knowledge. Yet he also moved the University itself as far away as he dared from the business of ensuring the catholicity and morality of its own students. How, then, was "Catholic fact" to be taught? What, indeed, did Newman mean by the term? And how would he attempt in his role as Rector to put his idea into practice?

This last point is key: Newman necessarily had to put abstract ideas and ideals into practice in a real, and in the end unsuccessful, institution. As he himself put it in his report to the Irish bishops on the academic year 1854-55, "While thus endeavouring to illustrate on paper [in the discourses, and in essays published in the *Catholic University Gazette*] the true character and principles of a University, I was also anxiously engaged in reducing those general views to practice in the Institution itself which I had to form."[28] Reality was never too far away.

[27] Moriarty to Newman, 21 July 1852, *LD* XV, 135.

[28] Newman, *My Campaign in Ireland*, 6.

One of the first questions with which Newman had to deal was who was to staff the new University. As we have seen, it was decided at Thurles in 1851 that all officers and professors of the University would need to make a profession of Catholic faith. Of course, there was no chance that the Irish hierarchy in general and Cullen in particular would tolerate non-Catholic faculty.[29] That being as it may, it is clear that Newman himself saw the religion of a University's professors as central to its mission. This can be seen in an answer he gave to William Monsell,[30] the MP for Limerick and a prominent lay Catholic, in early 1853. Monsell, who had recently been appointed a junior member of Lord Aberdeen's coalition government, had written to ask whether there was any chance of the Roman ban on the Queen's Colleges being lifted. In his reply, Newman rather doubted that it would, and went on to say for himself that "while you have professors of different religions [as was the case at the Queen's Colleges], you never can have a genius loci — and the place is no longer a genuine University."[31]

He went even further in his essay "English Catholic Literature" (eventually published in *The Idea of a University*): If, Newman wrote, "we could have Professors who were mere abstractions and phantoms, marrowless in their bones, and without speculation in their eyes, or if they could only open their mouths on their own special subject, and in their scientific pedantry were dead to the world," then, in that impossible circumstance, "Voltaire himself might be admitted, not without scandal, but without risk, to lecture on astronomy or galvanism in Catholic... colleges."[32] The limitation

[29] On one occasion Cullen had written to Newman on hearing the rumour that an appointee to the medical school was a Protestant. Newman assured him that the man in question was in fact a good Catholic. See Cullen to Newman, 31 July 1855, Newman papers, Birmingham Oratory Archive, file 225.

[30] 1812-1894.

[31] Newman to Monsell, 3 February 1853, *LD* XV.

[32] *The Idea of a University*, 251.

of Voltaire's safety to the physical sciences points to a distinction in Newman's thought to which we will return, but the basic point is clear: whatever the abstract theory, no non-Catholics need apply.

If professors did not need, as part of their duties, to inculcate Catholic morality or oversee the morals of their students, why did they all need to be Catholic? The answer, at least in Newman's opinion, came in two, linked, parts. Firstly, at the heart of Newman's vision of the University experience was the fact that professors do, and should, influence their students. As he put it, as "no book can convey the special spirit and delicate peculiarities of its subject with that rapidity and certainty which attend on the sympathy of mind with mind, through the eyes, the look, the accent, and the manner, in casual expressions thrown off at the moment, and the unstudied turns of familiar conversation… The general principles of any study you may learn by books at home; but the detail, the colour, the tone, the air, the life which makes it live in us, you must catch all these from those in whom it lives already."[33] In a University, truth could only be passed on via human contact; knowledge was mediated through professors.

Because professors necessarily influenced their students, it was therefore necessary that they themselves have a Catholic "view," both to ensure the safety of their teaching and its coherence (or even its truth). View is an important word for Newman in the context of University education, and it is one that comes up again and again in his letters and other writings. Dwight Culler has argued that the term should be taken to mean a sort of bird's-eye perspective. He also notes that Newman was critical of the mere retention of facts, or their exposition, without a "view."[34] Ian Ker has quoted

[33] Newman, *Historical Sketches*, 3: 8-9.

[34] Culler, *Imperial Intellect*, 195-197.

Newman drawing an analogy between a mass of knowledge without a view to being in a strange country or strange city, disoriented and without a map.[35]

To Newman it was necessary to survey knowledge both from above, and from within a particular set of beliefs, in this case religious. The point can be made from an exchange of letters with his friend T. W. Allies.[36] Allies had been asked by Newman to be professor of the philosophy of history, and was not unreasonably unsure as to just what Newman meant by the title:[37] "Have you not set me a science almost new, about the meaning of which even people are not agreed."[38] In an effort to explain his meaning to Allies, Newman chose to give examples of what he did not mean. "The fault of [Friedrich] Schlegel's work," Newman wrote, "… is that it has no *view* — only a number of detached remarks." On the other hand, "Gibbon's is a philosophical history," written not as a collection of facts, "but with reference and subservience to a certain philosophy, and a bad one."[39]

Newman clearly saw two extremes to be avoided — a view-less compendium of facts that is analogous to being lost, and a controlling philosophy that ends up anti-Catholic (or anti-Christian as in Gibbon's case). In Newman's opinion, one was clearly worse than the other. Schlegel's work was flawed, but it remained on the curriculum; Gibbon was excluded. What Newman wanted was a Gibbon-like view, but from a Catholic perspective. Catholic fact, in other words.

[35] Ian Ker, *The Achievement of John Henry Newman* (Notre Dame, IN: University of Notre Dame Press, 1991) 12-13.

[36] 1813-1903.

[37] Despite the phrase 'the philosophy of history', it seems quite unlikely that Newman had Hegel in mind.

[38] T. W. Allies to Newman, 10 November 1854, *LD* XVI, 292.

[39] Newman to Allies, 3 September 1854, *LD* XVI.

The men he chose to teach history in the Catholic University of Ireland agreed, and the fact is not insignificant in that it confirms the emphasis that Newman put on a Catholic "view" in the teaching of history (always the subject most open to competing truths). In his lectures to Catholic University students (later published), J. B. Robertson[40] made it clear that his purpose was "the defence of God and His holy Church against unbelief and misbelief, and of social order and liberty against the principles of Revolution, which are but Impiety in a political form."[41] In his treatment of Spanish history, the subject of many of his lectures, and in his concern to undermine Buckle's prominent work on the subject, Robertson echoed and amplified Newman's criticism of Gibbon by pointing out that Buckle as a non-Catholic could not possibly understand the history of a Catholic country like Spain. His attempt to do so, wrote Robertson, was "portentously absurd," "defective," and of a "kind essentially inadequate." That inadequacy flowed from what Robertson thought was Buckle's "sort of materialistic Pantheism."[42] In other words, while Buckle (like Gibbon) clearly had a "view," he did not have a Catholic one, and that made him both unsafe, and, at least in Robertson's view, inaccurate as an historian. Another of the Professors tasked with the teaching of history, Peter le Page Renouf, made his own sense of Catholic view and mission clear in a private letter shortly after his appointment, telling his parents that he saw in his new position the obligation "to advance the spiritual Kingdom of His Son, with reference to myself and all who come under my influence, that Christ may dwell in our hearts

[40] 1800-1877.

[41] J. B. Robertson, *Lectures on Some Subjects of Modern History and Biography: Delivered at the Catholic University of Ireland, 1860 to 1864* (Dublin, 1864) xvi.

[42] *Ibid.*, 164-165.

by faith and that we may be rooted and grounded in his Love."[43] Clearly Newman's professors took a similar line to the man who had appointed them.

Nevertheless, it was not the case that English literature or history, say, could be retrospectively "Catholicised," or that, if it could not be, it should be ignored in a Catholic University. Newman clearly accepted the reality that, in English at least,[44] much great work that was clearly appropriate to University study had been written from within a Protestant (or worse) view. Taking the examples of Gibbon and Milton — both "great English writers, each breathing hatred to the Catholic Church in his own way, each a proud and rebellious creature of God, each gifted with incomparable gifts" — Newman sought to argue that whatever the numerous objections to the spirit of their works from a Catholic perspective, they could nonetheless not be either ignored or edited: "we cannot extinguish them; we cannot deny their power; we cannot write a new Milton or a new Gibbon, we cannot expurgate what needs to be exorcised." "We must," he concluded, "take things as they are, if we take them at all."[45] The last sentence was clearly a rhetorical flourish: Newman wanted to discuss Milton in the University.

Not only was he happy to accept that Protestant-produced texts (if not their authors) should find a place in the Catholic University, Newman clearly distinguished between the sort of truth that classed

[43] Renouf to his parents, 13[?] April 1854, Renouf papers, Pembroke College (Oxford) Archive, 63/9/1/208. Renouf's letters have recently been edited by K. J. Cathcart, and published in four volumes by the University College Dublin Press. The letter cited was consulted by me in Oxford before the appearance of these volumes.

[44] He wasn't convinced that the national literature of any nation — Catholic ones included — would be any better.

[45] *The Idea of a University*, 255.

as University knowledge, and the devotional or "mythical." Not only was Protestant-derived knowledge acceptable, some of what passed as Catholic knowledge was, to Newman, myth and to be avoided in a University. To take one example, Newman told J. Spencer Northcote that he would like to write a biography of St Philip Neri himself, "for I want to see a life of him written which is *not* devotional, but historical."[46]

He expanded on the point in one of the letters he wrote to the American convert Orestes Brownson,[47] during his long and unsuccessful attempt to lure him to Dublin. Brownson's wide knowledge could be useful, Newman wrote, against the "mythical theory" of Christian evidences. The "mythical theory and its attendant errors" were gaining ground in the British isles, Newman wrote, and moreover, "nor are Catholics secure from the infection." "[A]ny logical or historical attack upon them," Brownson was told, "would be of the greatest service to us."[48] To Newman truth — knowledge — could be arrived at by logic, evidence, and historical study, all tasks of the University, either in the researches of its faculty, its lectures or in the mental habits it inculcated in its students. Of course, this would all happen from within a Catholic "view," which would ensure conclusions consistent with Catholic "expression, feeling, [and] fact."

In practical terms much of the actual work of a University, much of what it studied and its professors taught, could be safely distanced from theology as such. As Newman wrote to the Faculty of Arts in 1856 there were some, not many, but "serious and earnest" who would allow religion "unlimited extension in the province of Letters." Those who held this view, Newman wrote, consider "that Classics should be superseded by the Scriptures and the Fathers,

46 Newman to Northcote, 9 April 1854, *LD* XVI.

47 1803-1876.

48 Newman to Brownson, 6 June 1854, *LD* XVI.

and that Scholastic Theology should be taught to the youthful aspirant for University honours."[49] Newman dealt with these opinions bluntly: "I respect, but cannot follow."[50]

Newman even went so far as to excuse a certain amount of theological unsoundness in professors (or potential professors) who were not themselves theologians. One example of this was the eminent German ecclesiastical historian Johann Joseph Ignaz von Döllinger,[51] whom Newman hoped to lure to Dublin, even if only for a series of lectures. Writing to Archbishop Cullen (not the most sympathetic of audiences for such an argument), Newman agreed that Döllinger's theological ideas could be slightly unsound, "But I have always considered that he was an historian, not a theologian, and only professed to depose to historical testimony; not to doctrines."[52] This is an important distinction, for it shows clearly that in the context of higher education there could be, at least to Newman, truths that were so independent of religion or theology (and not simply unavoidable as were the great works of English literature and history). As he told T. W. Allies in one of his attempts to explain what he meant by "the Philosophy of History," "'Providence' comes into the definition accidentally. In physical nature, an atheist talks of efficient causes, and the theist of final, but the *laws* are the same."[53]

[49] 'Letter of the Rector to the Dean of the Faculty of Philosophy and Letters on the Introduction of Religious Teaching into the Schools of that Faculty', *My Campaign in Ireland*, 157.

[50] *Ibid.*, 158.

[51] 1799-1890.

[52] Newman to Cullen, 1 October 1854, *LD* XVI. Of course, Döllinger turned out to be an unhappy example, as by the mid-1860s, and certainly by the Vatican Council, he had strayed well into doctrine and his ideas, to the orthodox, had gone from the unsound to the heretical.

[53] Newman to Allies, 11 November 1854, *LD* XVI.

As was mentioned earlier, Newman seems to draw a distinction between the physical sciences and the humanities, allowing that the truth of the former could be independent of the faith of the scientist. According to Newman, in "mathematics, chemistry, astronomy, and similar subjects, one man will not, on the score of his religion, treat of them better than another."[54] To Newman, "The object of all science is truth:"

> the pure sciences proceed to their enunciations from principles which the intellect discerns by a natural light, and by a process recognized by natural reason; and the experimental sciences investigate facts by methods of analysis or by ingenious expedients, ultimately resolvable into instruments of thought equally native to the human mind. If then we may assume that there is an objective truth, and that the constitution of the human mind is in correspondence with it, and acts truly when it acts according to its own laws; if we may assume that God made us, and that what He made is good, and that no action from and according to nature can in itself be evil; it will follow that, so long as it is man who is the geometrician, or natural philosopher,[55] or mechanic, or critic, no matter what man he be, Hindoo, Mahometan, or infidel, his conclusions within his own science, according to the laws of that science, are unquestionable, and not to be suspected by Catholics, unless Catholics may legitimately be jealous of fact and truth, of divine principles and divine creations.[56]

According to Newman, then, the scientific works of non-Catholics could be safely placed in the hands of Catholic students. And although in theory the non-Catholic himself could safely be made professor, this, as we have seen, was only if he were the sort of "imaginary bookworm"[57] who never thought of anything beyond his own subject. In his "English Catholic Literature," and indeed

[54] *The Idea of a University*, 248.

[55] The nineteenth century term for the natural sciences.

[56] *The Idea of a University*, 249.

[57] *Ibid.*, 251.

elsewhere, Newman went a very long way, at least seemingly, towards undermining the perceived need to have, in a Catholic University, Catholic students being taught by Catholic professors from Catholic books. If some laws were true regardless of faith, and if students could be trusted to read heretical books if only they were warned that they were so (Newman thought it was the "*surprise* which does the most mischief"[58]), then what was the place of Catholicism within the University; why, indeed, a Catholic University at all? It was this impression, created, he thought, by his first five Dublin discourses, that Newman sought to remove with the proposed introduction to discourse six already quoted.

It might at this point be useful to consider what role, precisely, Newman thought that religion had to play in the University. To be sure, he wanted a Catholic view, but what did that actually entail? As we have seen, he held that the entire professoriate must be Catholic. He further held, indeed insisted, that theology had a place, and an honoured one, in the curriculum; and, of course, that that theology would be, could only be, Catholic. As to morality, he assigned the task — a crucial one in his view — of moral instruction and influence to sub-groupings within the University, such as his proposed colleges. Here, students would both study and pray, and be under clerical supervision. Again, the ethos would be overwhelmingly Catholic. Perhaps remembering his own days at Oxford, Newman placed great importance on University sermons as a method of imparting Catholic truth to the students; for similar reasons he was anxious — perhaps over anxious[59] — to erect a suitable University Church. Whatever the theoretical flexibility (or liberalism) of Newman's approach, there could be no doubt in the

[58] Newman to Ornsby, 19 July 1854, *LD* XVI. Emphasis in original.

[59] To Cullen's not unreasonable annoyance, Newman took an exceedingly short lease on the ground on which the Church was built. The cost of the construction later became a source of disagreement between the two men.

mind of any student of the Catholic University of Ireland that he was indeed in a *Catholic* University.

Beyond theology, which was to be its own faculty,[60] specifically religious subjects could be found throughout the curriculum. An example is the teaching of history: "If the University student is bound to have a knowledge of history generally," Newman wrote, "he is bound to have inclusively a knowledge of sacred history as well as profane."[61] In the history curriculum, a knowledge of "the great primitive divisions of Christianity, its polity, its luminaries, its acts, its fortunes, its great eras, and its course to this day" was expected along with an equivalent understanding of such secular subjects as the fall of republican Rome. Newman's justification was simple, albeit in two parts. Firstly, he argued on prudential grounds that it was both unwise and unbecoming for a Catholic University to leave its students less informed about their own faith and its history then students of a Protestant institution would be about theirs. And, secondly, he of course believed that religious knowledge was both itself knowledge and of a peculiarly important kind, as there was little point to "secular knowledge, without a corresponding acquaintance with those divine truths which alone give to secular knowledge its value and use."[62] It goes without saying that those "divine truths" were truths as understood by the Roman Catholic Church.

Throughout his time at the Catholic University of Ireland, a student would be exposed to lectures on everything from scriptural exegesis to ecclesiastical history to classical literature to natural science. The point is that those subjects that we might deem religious

[60] Appointments were made, and some evening lectures and inaugural lectures were given, but the Faculty of Theology never really took shape during Newman's time in Dublin.

[61] *My Campaign in Ireland*, 160.

[62] *Ibid.*, 135.

were in no way separated or isolated from the rest of the curriculum. (In fact, the curriculum at the Catholic University was markedly similar to that at both the Queen's Colleges and Trinity College Dublin; the difference lay in the ethos of each place: Trinity was Established Church, the Queen's Colleges secular, and the Catholic University Catholic.[63]) Newman, it is true, saw a distinction between the natural sciences and the humanities, a distinction perhaps best summed up in his observation that, if religious knowledge were separated from secular knowledge "pure mathematics will not suffer at all; chemistry will suffer less than politics, politics than history, ethics or metaphysics."[64] In other words, religious knowledge penetrated different subjects to different degrees.

Newman, moreover, drew further distinctions within the humanities, insisting both that theology be allowed its place, and that it keep to that place without intruding on its neighbours. He was anxious both to ensure that the books put in students' hands were written (if possible) from within a Catholic view and, on the other hand, be "not devotional but historical." To be sure, he acknowledged that many works in many subjects — not just in the natural sciences — were both non-Catholic and necessary to a University education. Truth need not appear formally in Catholic dress to still be true.

On the face of it, this apparent tension between an obvious desire to provide a Catholic view — teach "Catholic fact" — and a tolerance for non-Catholic, or even anti-Catholic, works is hard to reconcile. To be sure, Newman trusted his students to an exceptional degree for the time — a fact that often caused consternation in sections of the Irish hierarchy. Moreover his educational aims,

[63] See my *Paul Cullen, John Henry Newman, and the Catholic University of Ireland* (Notre Dame, IN: University of Notre Dame Press, 2003) 217-218.

[64] John Henry Newman, *Discourses on the Scope and Nature of University Education* (Dublin: Duffy, 1852) 104-105.

which might best be summed up as learning to know when the other fellow is talking rot, necessarily entailed a critical engagement with difficult, demanding, and even heretical works.[65]

In the end, however, Newman was comfortable with such an apparently liberal approach to University education because of his fundamentally religious understanding of truth. To Newman everything that can be demonstrated to be true, whether by reason, experiment, or historical inquiry, is necessarily consistent with Catholic faith. Since both truth and our ability to find it come from God, no knowledge, no truth, can be dangerous. And since God's will and revelation is channelled through and mediated by the Catholic Church, nothing that is true can threaten the Church (or its members), nor can anything the Church authoritatively teaches ever be shown to be untrue by mere human inquiry. Moreover, Newman was prepared to wait patiently while apparently inconsistent truths were examined more closely. He was confident in the necessary compatibility of all truths with the Catholic faith, even if the process of finding that harmony might take years. A University, Newman wrote, "is the place to which a thousand schools make contributions; in which the intellect may safely range and speculate, sure to find its equal in some antagonistic activity, and its judge in the tribunal of truth. It is a place where inquiry is pushed forward, and discoveries verified and perfected, and rashness rendered innocuous, and error exposed, by the collision of mind with mind, and knowledge with knowledge."[66]

Catholics had nothing to fear from knowledge: "It is not then that Catholics are afraid of human knowledge, but that they are proud of divine knowledge, and that they think the omission of any kind of knowledge whatever, human or divine, to be as far as it

[65] See Ker, *Achievement of John Henry Newman*, 12-13.

[66] Newman, *Historical Sketches*, 3: 16.

goes, not knowledge but ignorance."[67] It was therefore the case that any fact, if it be a fact (i.e. if it be true) must, cannot help but be, a "Catholic fact." There can be no other kind, even if the teachings of the Church enter in to it (as in the case of, say, pure mathematics) hardly at all.

This fundamental belief lies at the heart of what Newman meant by a Catholic view. That is why all the professors had to be Catholic; that is why non-Catholic or heretical books could be tolerated, so long as their heresies or errors were pointed out (although in practice such authors as Gibbon remained outside the pale); this is why the University could be described in a way as to lead both contemporaries and later commentators to wonder at the extent of its catholicity, or, on the other hand, to imagine that the Irish bishops sought to impose a sort of "lay seminary" on Newman. To Newman, all truth was Catholic, whether or not it came advertised as such, or even disclaimed the distinction.

What Newman sought to create in Dublin was an institution that could both find truth and disseminate it (as well as teaching its students how to think). Since truth was necessarily Catholic, so was the University. Its professors could teach various subjects, more or less influenced by formal Catholic teachings; its students could pursue studies in the arts, in theology, in medicine, or in engineering, safe if they needed to consult non-Catholic books. The atmosphere of the University was pervasively Catholic, and despite the division of function between University and the (hoped for) colleges, and the natural diversity of academic disciplines, "The Unity of the University, thus locally divided in its departments, will consist in the unity of the Catholic dogma and spirit."[68] If anything, Newman's University was so self-confidently Catholic that it could afford to appear, at times, to be less than Catholic.

[67] Newman, *Discourses*, 55.

[68] *My Campaign in Ireland*, 97.

NEWMAN AND THE CHARISMATIC DIMENSION OF THE CHURCH

Ian KER

1. Vatican II and the Charisms

In St John's gospel, Jesus tells the apostles, "when the Spirit of truth comes he will lead you to the complete truth" (16:13). The Second Vatican Council's constitution on the Church, *Lumen Gentium*, asserts that conciliar and papal *ex cathedra* definitions of faith and morals are "irreformable" inasmuch as they are "made with the assistance of the Holy Spirit." (art. 25) But "the complete truth" about Christ includes more than propositional truths of faith and morals. The Holy Spirit leads Christians in various ways into the fullness of truth in its different aspects.

Lumen Gentium speaks specifically of the charismatic dimension of the Church three times in the first two chapters. First, it says that the Holy Spirit bestows upon the Church 'varied hierarchic and charismatic gifts' (art. 4). Secondly, it makes a distinction of priority between these different gifts: 'Among these gifts the primacy belongs to the grace of the apostles to whose authority the Spirit Himself subjects even those who are endowed with charisms' (art. 7). But thirdly, at greater length, the constitution affirms the importance of the charisms:

> It is not only through the sacraments and the ministrations of the Church that the Holy Spirit makes holy the people, leads them and enriches them with his virtues. Allotting his gifts according as he wills (cf. 1 Cor. 12:11), he also distributes special graces among the faithful of every rank. By these gifts he makes them fit and ready to

> undertake various tasks and offices for the renewal and building up of the Church, as it is written, 'the manifestation of the Spirit is given to everyone for profit' (1. Cor. 12:7). Whether these charisms be very remarkable or more simple and widely diffused, they are to be received with thanksgiving and consolation since they are fitting and useful for the needs of the Church. (art. 12)

Commenting on this latter text, Pope John Paul II has said that it was under the guidance of the Holy Spirit that the Council "rediscovered the charismatic dimension as one of [the Church's] constitutive elements," and that the "institutional and charismatic aspects are co-essential as it were to the Church's constitution."[1] In his commentary on this text, published two years after the end of the Council, Aloys Grillmeier also notes that, as well as speaking of the work of the Spirit in sacraments and ministries, "it is equally important that the Council says a special word about the 'charisms', the special gifts of grace in the Church." And he proceeds to quote from an article by Hans Küng on "The Charismatic Structure of the Church," published in the journal *Concilium* in 1965, the same year the Council ended:

> The charismata are not primarily extraordinary but common; they are not of one kind, but manifold; they are not limited to a special group of persons, but truly universal in the Church. All this implies also that they are not a thing of the past (possible and real only in the early Church), but eminently contemporary and actual; they do not hover on the periphery of the Church but are eminently central and essential to it. In this sense one should speak of a *charismatic structure of the Church* which embraces and goes beyond the structure of its government.[2]

[1] *Movements in the Church: Proceedings of the World Congress of the Ecclesial Movements, Rome, 27-29 May 1998* (Vatican City: Pontificium Consilium pro Laicis, 1999) 221.

[2] *Commentary on the Documents of Vatican II*, vol. 2, ed. Herbert Vorgrimler (London: Burns & Oates, 1967) 165.

However, writing twenty-five years after the Council, in his article "The Biblical Question of 'Charisms' after Vatican II," Albert Vanhoye is sharply critical of what was taken in the immediate aftermath of the Council to be the authoritative explanation of what *Lumen Gentium* meant by charisms. He begins by pointing out that, while "The concept of charisms has its starting point in certain New Testament texts that speak of *charisma,*" nevertheless in Western theology "the generalized use of the technical term 'charism' is of relatively recent date," in view of the fact that the "word is found only once in the Vulgate," whereas elsewhere the word is translated by several different words. When Latin theologians following St Thomas Aquinas want to speak of charism they use the phrase "gratia gratis data." With Vatican II, the vocabulary changes, since the official conciliar texts, written in Latin, use the Latin transliteration of the Greek word, except in quotations from the New Testament where the Vulgate is used. At the Council itself, there was a debate between the traditionalist view that charisms are extraordinary, miraculous gifts and that of the reformers who successfully pressed for charisms to be seen as much more ordinary gifts belonging to baptized Christians, such as the gifts of catechesis and evangelization. It was this position that prevailed in *Lumen Gentium.*

However, Vanhoye regards the interpretation of charisms by Küng, which he reproduced in his book *The Church* (1967), as unfaithful to the concilar texts on charisms and overdependent on an influential study of "Ministry and Community" (1964) by the Protestant theologian E. Käsemann. Thus Küng uncritically accepts the concept of charism as describing all ecclesial services and functions. Vanhoye argues that Küng so broadens the notion of charism as to rob it of any "identifying characteristic." For example, Küng sees Christian love as the highest as well as the most ordinary of the charisms. But Vanhoye points out that this is only possible if we take charism to mean simply a gift as opposed to "a special grace granted to one Christian and not to another." But it is manifest that when Vatican II rediscovered the charismatic dimension, to use the Pope's words, it was doing something more significant than saying that all the Christian virtues are gifts. If that was all that *Lumen Gentium* intended in those three texts in the first two chapters, then the dispute between the reformers led by Cardinal Suenens and the conservatives led by Cardinal Ruffini was pointless, as both sides would have agreed that the Christian virtues are gifts. But the issue was whether or not ordinary Christians can possess special charisms which help to build up the Church, or whether the Church is to be seen as sustained primarily and for the most part (except in extraordinary and miraculous instances) by the ministry and sacraments of the ordained priesthood. But, as Vanhoye sarcastically puts it, "meekly" following the Protestant Käsemann, Küng sees charisms everywhere, and so evacuates the term of any special meaning that "it loses any substance and it becomes difficult to see how the charisms could then provide the Church with a 'structure'."

Of course, Küng has a very definite agenda in extending the sense of charism, and that is, to quote Vanhoye again, his anxiety "to limit the sphere of responsibility of the pastors of the Church as much as possible." Insistent that charisms are not the preserve of the hierarchy, "he describes everything as a charism, from theological charity to the actions of eating and drinking. In this way, the authorities of the Church are, so to speak, drowned in an ocean of charisms possessed by all the members of the faithful." But then Küng introduces another concept of charisms as the personal gifts belonging to individuals called to a particular ministry within the Church. This is the basis for his idea of a "charismatic structure" of the Church, which is very different from saying that the Church has a charismatic dimension. But the Church also has a hierarchical dimension, indeed structure, which, according to *Lumen Gentium*, discerns and regulates the charismatic dimension: "Those who have charge over the Church should judge the genuineness and proper use of these gifts, through their office not indeed to extinguish the Spirit, but to test all things and hold fast to what is good." (art. 12) This specific teaching of the Council is ignored by Küng, unsurprisingly. To the question as to how unity is to be preserved in the kind of charismatic Church that Küng envisages, he replies that the same Spirit who gives the charisms also creates unity and order. This is certainly true, but the Spirit acts through the hierarchical dimension, as St Paul says in 1 Corinthians: "In the Church, God has given the first place to apostles, the second to prophets, the third to teachers; after them, miracles, and after them the gift of healing; helpers, good leaders, those with many languages." (12:28)

These are precisely the "varied hierarchic and charismatic gifts" of *Lumen Gentium*, where the hierarchical also takes precedence. Paul himself gives concrete examples of ways in which apostolic authority is to be exercised with regard to the charisms, and adds that what he writes "is a command from the Lord." (14: 27-9, 37) As an exegete himself, Vanhoye concludes that, while in the New Testament the Greek word *charisma* often has only too general or too specific meaning of gift to be translated by the word charism, nevertheless there are clear instances of *charisma* being used to describe a special gift given to an individual for the good of the Church, and it is this usage which the Council employs, "following a theological tradition."[3]

[3] Albert Vanhoye SJ, "The Biblical Question of 'Charisms' after Vatican II," in *Vatican II: Assessment and Perspectives: Twenty-Five Years After (1962-1987)*, vol. 1, ed. René Latourelle (Mahwah, NJ: Paulist Press, 1988) 439-468.

2. Newman and Hierarchy

Turning now to Newman, we can certainly say that he, unlike Küng, is faithful to Scripture and Tradition and in agreement with the Council that there is a charismatic dimension to the Church which involves more than just ordinary spiritual gifts and which is regulated by the hierarchical dimension. Naturally, Newman does not use the word charism because as we have seen the usage was not normal before the Council. Attentive as he was to both dimensions, nevertheless it has to be said that he was more at home with the charismatic than with the hierarchical dimension both as an Anglican and as a Catholic. In both halves of his life Newman was frequently at odds with hierarchical authority, although his obedience was unquestionable, even in the face of policies and views during the Catholic years on which history has vindicated his position.

His disappointment with Anglican bishops was evident from the very beginning of the Tractarian Movement: the first of the *Tracts for the Times* which he himself wrote was on the Apostolic succession and challenged bishops to be bishops in the Catholic sense. In his *Apologia pro Vita Sua* he tells how the second of the "three blows which broke" him as an Anglican was the bishops' condemnation of Tract 90. Newman's "understanding" was that the bishops, apart perhaps for a very few, would not condemn or insist on his withdrawing the tract if he agreed to certain conditions. But in the event —

> The bishops one after another began to charge against me. It was a formal, determinate movement. This was the real "understanding"; that, on which I had acted on the first appearance of Tract 90, had come to nought.... They went on in this way, directing charges at me, for three whole years.[4]

[4] *Apologia pro Vita Sua*, ed. Martin J. Svaglic (Oxford: Clarendon Press, 1967) 130.

In other words, one of the final events that destroyed Newman's Tractarian belief in the catholicity of the Church of England was the failure of the hierarchy both to share this belief and to keep what he understood to be a gentleman's agreement. His experiences of the Catholic hierarchy were hardly happier, although it was not of course their failure to appreciate their apostolic authority that upset him, but rather the opposite. His disillusion began when he went to Ireland to found the new Catholic university. He was upset at the outset by Archbishop Cullen's autocratic attitude and his refusal to delegate the power for Newman to appoint his own Vice-Rector. But he thought the principal cause of friction was his "desire… to make the laity a substantive power in the University." He considered it proper that the management of the finances be in the hands of the laity for whom the university was intended, but clericalism demanded that the laity should be "treated like good little boys" and "told to shut their eyes and open their mouths." Much worse, however, than his abortive desire to have a lay finance committee was Newman's attitude to the "young Ireland" or nationalist party, some of whose leading members were appointed by the English rector to chairs in spite of Cullen's stiff opposition. Newman wanted all but the theology chairs to be filled with the ablest laymen available (whatever their politics) rather than by academically inferior priests. So deep-seated was the clericalism that even a proposal by Newman to draw up a "list of honorary members of the University, principally laymen from Ireland or elsewhere" was viewed with suspicion by Cullen.[5] On his return to England Newman became involved with the liberal Catholic periodical the *Rambler*. Now while it has to be said that he had distinct reservations about its liberal and anti-hierarchical tone,

[5] *John Henry Newman: Autobiographical Writings*, ed. Henry Tristram (New York: Sheed and Ward, 1957) 326-328.

nevertheless he had every sympathy with its complaint that the bishops ignored the laity. His association with the magazine led to his writing in 1859 his famous article "On Consulting the Faithful in Matters of Doctrine," for which he was denounced to Rome by one of the bishops. Although it is usually assumed to be a classic text on the place of the laity in the Church, I have argued in a revisionist study that the article is indeed, as the title indicates, about the *faithful* rather than the laity.[6] For a closer look at the historical examples that Newman gives from the fourth century shows that, while the episcopate as a body was unfaithful in upholding the orthodox faith, the faithful who were faithful included as well as the laity also "holy virgins and brethren" and "monks." In other words, the faithful with charisms are seen as more faithful than the bishops. As a Catholic, Newman had two chief complaints about the way in which hierarchical authority was exercised in the Church. Apart from the question of the rights of the laity, there was also the question of freedom in the Church. He deplored the authoritarian way in which hierarchical, especially Roman, power was exercised in the Ultramontane nineteenth-century Church. As always, Newman never minimized the rights of authority, much to the annoyance of liberals like Lord Acton, but he was no less adamant that theologians too have rights and responsibilities. The classic text for his position is the last chapter of the *Apologia* where he sets out a remarkably balanced and nuanced view of the relationship between authority and freedom. Finally, it is worth noting Newman's own personal attitude to the possibility of hierarchical responsibility. He had no difficulty at all about Wiseman's abortive proposal that he should be made a titular bishop so as to give him

[6] Ian Ker, "Newman on the *Consensus Fidelium* as 'The Voice of the Infallible Church'," in *Newman and the Word*, ed. Terrence Merrigan & Ian T. Ker (Louvain/Sterling, VA/Grand Rapids, MI: Peeters/ Eerdmans, 2000) 69-89.

more authority as rector of the Catholic university. But when earlier he had heard a report that Wiseman had sent in his name to Rome for one of the new dioceses, he exclaimed, "The very thought of it makes me ill." He dreaded "a load of anxiety which would break" him and the "responsibility," and pleaded "the absolute contrariety of all my habits to the duties and life of a Bishop."[7] Again, when at the end of his life he was offered the red hat, he wrote that "it would be a most piercing trial to have to accept it — perhaps the greatest I have had in my life." He dreaded "the dignity, publicity, and ceremonial state" which would be involved in "such a new life."[8] The idea of his becoming a distinguished ecclesiastic struck him as absurd as Caligula's horse being appointed consul! However, his chief objection was the prospect of having to leave the Oratory and go and live in Rome, as was then normal for cardinals who were not diocesan bishops. Only when he was given an assurance that this would not be required did he accept the offer. His only reason for accepting, but it was an important one, was that it would be the "end" of "all those stories which have gone about of my being a half Catholic, a liberal Catholic, under a cloud, not to be trusted."[9] However, the significant point to note here is that for Newman being an Oratorian, a follower of the charism of St Philip Neri, was more important than promotion to the hierarchy of the Church. He felt at home in the charismatic, not the hierarchical part of the Church. It is time, then, to turn to the subject of this paper, Newman and the charisms.

[7] *The Letters and Diaries of John Henry Newman*, ed. Charles Stephen Dessain et al. (London: Nelson, 1961-1972; Oxford: Clarendon Press, 1973-) 15: 310-311. Hereafter abbreviated to *LD*.

[8] *LD*, 29: 29, 160.

[9] *LD*, 29: 72.

3. The Anglican Newman and Charisms

In the *Apologia* Newman describes how as a boy of fifteen he became enamoured with the extracts from the Fathers which he read in Joseph Milner's *History of the Church of Christ* (1794-1809).[10] I suspect that one element in his lifelong devotion to the Fathers was that in these saints and theologians who were also bishops the charismatic and hierarchical dimensions came together as for the most part they were not to do in succeeding centuries. It is worth noting that, although the first of the *Tracts for the Times* on apostolic authority was published first, his first written contribution to the Movement in 1833 was a paper which he intended to be "one of a series" for the *British Magazine*, "called the 'Church of the Fathers'... on the principle of popularity as an element of Church power, as exemplified in the history of St Ambrose." Far from being clerical, the early Church, in Newman's vivid phrase, "threw itself on the *people*."[11] And indeed this is very much a charismatic Church, in which there is a distinct place for prophets, for example: "a child's voice, as is reported, was heard in the midst of the crowd to say, 'Ambrose is bishop.'" At the time Ambrose was governor of the province and had been called to quell a disturbance in the cathedral in Milan, where the people had met to elect a new bishop. But Ambrose was not only not in holy orders but he was still only a catechumen awaiting baptism. However, on the prophetic word of a child he was unanimously elected bishop. So here we have a remarkable instance of charism, preceding, so to speak, hierarchy. The point of writing these sketches of the Church of the Fathers was to show how different the religion of the first centuries was from both Protestantism and the established Church of England. And one point Newman especially

[10] *Apologia*, 20.

[11] *LD,* 4: 14, 18.

enjoys making is that if, as Protestants say, monasticism is a corruption of Christianity, then certainly Protestantism is a very different religion from early Christianity, for "Could" a Protestant's

> *present* system... by any possibility be corrupted... into monasticism? Is there any sort of tendency in it towards — rather, are not all its tendencies from — such a result? If so, it is plain that the religious temper of these times is not like that of the primitive Church...

In other words, Newman is arguing that the monastic charism — monasticism being the first great charismatic movement in the life of the Church — is the fruit of Catholic Christianity. It is not, however, as though non-Catholic Christians do not need or cannot be given charisms by the Spirit. They too can find themselves in a similar situation to the early Christians. "One great purpose answered by Monasticism in the early ages was the maintenance of the Truth in times and places in which great masses of Catholics had let it slip from them." Monasteries, Newman maintains,

> were intended as the refuge of piety and holiness, when the increasing spread of religion made Christians more secular. And we may confidently pronounce that such provisions, in one shape or other, will always be attempted by the more serious and anxious part of the community, whenever Christianity is generally professed. In Protestant countries, where monastic orders are unknown, men run into separatism with this object. Methodism has carried off many a man who was sincerely attached to the Established Church, merely because that Church will admit nothing but what it considers "rational" and "sensible" in religion.

If we may put it in a different way, where Christianity ceases to have a charismatic dimension, then what Newman would have called "enthusiasm" finds no outlet within the apostolic Church (a part of which Newman then conceived the Church of England to be). Because the charism of Wesley could find no place in the

Church of England, he was led into schism and separation from the hierarchical Church. Interestingly, Newman then goes on to point out, with remarkable vehemence, that the charism of religious life can provide much-needed community and support, especially for women in a society where they were denied opportunities:

> Convents are as much demanded, in the model of a perfect Church, by Christian charity, as monastic bodies can be by Christian zeal. I know not any more distressing development of the cruel temper of Protestantism than the determined, bitter, and scoffing spirit in which it has set itself against institutions which give dignity and independence to the position of women in society. As matters stand, marriage is almost the only shelter which a defenceless portion of the community has against the rude world; — a maiden life, that holy estate is not only left in desolateness, but oppressed with heartless ridicule and insult; — whereas, foundations for single women, under proper precautions, at once hold out protection to those who avail themselves of them and give dignity to the single state itself, and thus save numbers from the temptation of throwing themselves rashly away upon unworthy objects, thereby transgressing their own sense of propriety, and embittering their future life.[12]

This may sound rather quaint and dated to our ears, but *mutatis mutandis* I think Newman's point can easily be applied to our own situation where an increasingly atomized and individualistic society, afflicted by the breakdown of marriage and family life, leads to much isolation and loneliness and loss of faith among Catholics whose needs the parish structure cannot meet but which can be met by the new ecclesial communities and movements. Newman's condemnation of those, not least in the hierarchical part of the Church, who dismiss or even forbid the new charisms which the Holy Spirit has provided for our situation and our times, and not

[12] *Historical Sketches* 2: 164-65. Hereafter abbreviated to *HS*. References here as elsewhere, unless otherwise stated, are to the uniform edition of Newman's works of 1868-1881 (36 Vols.) published by Longmans, Green and Co. of London.

least for the marginalized, would, I suspect, be no less severe than his strictures here on the Protestants of his day who rejected religious life out of hand. Those in the post-Vatican II Catholic Church who think that diocese and parish are quite sufficient for the needs of the people and any new movements of the Spirit are at best unnecessary and at worst divisive might reflect on what Newman as an Anglican has to say at the beginning of his biographical sketch of St Antony, where he castigates "the tyranny of those who will not let a man do anything out of the way without stamping him with the name of fanatic." This, Newman insists, the early Church did not do. Rather, it "deals softly with the ardent and impetuous, saying, in effect — '...You wish to live above the common course of a Christian; — I can teach you to do this, yet without arrogance.'"[13] In our own day this is exactly how Pope John Paul II spoke to the new ecclesial movements, whose members are often criticized for their arrogance, at a congress in 1998. Recalling how he had supported them from the beginning of his pontificate, he now recognized a greater maturity in them: "Today I notice, with great joy, that [you] have a more mature self-knowledge." On the other hand, the Pope seemed less sure that other parts of the Church, and of course he would have had in mind particularly the local episcopate and clergy, had grown similarly in knowledge of "something new that is still waiting to be properly accepted and appreciated." Or, as Cardinal Joseph Ratzinger put it more sharply, there is a danger of local bishops and churches turning "their own pastoral plans into the criterion of what the Holy Spirit is allowed to do."[14] Again, just as local Catholic bishops and clergy today are frequently opposed to the new movements entering their dioceses and parishes, so similarly Newman in the same passage deplored "the sensible

[13] *HS*, 2: 96.

[14] *Movements in the Church*, 52-53.

Protestant divine" who "keeps to his point, hammering away on his own ideas, urging every one to be as every one else, and moulding all ideas upon his one small model; and when he has made his ground good to his own admiration, he finds that half his flock have after all turned Wesleyans or Independents, by way of searching for something divine and transcendental."[15] One thinks today of the many Catholics in the United States and Latin America who have turned to Evangelical churches and sects, when their own Church has appeared more preoccupied with issues like social justice than with the divine — that is, when the new movements have not been there to offer an alternative to what often appears a more secular than supernatural agenda.

In the early Church, on the other hand, where charism and hierarchy are in harmony and union with each other, "enthusiasm" can flourish within the Church without getting out of control and without being suppressed. Thus St Antony, the founder of monasticism, would be called an "enthusiast" in the Church of England of the 1830s, and would be

> exposed to a serious temptation of becoming a fanatic. Longing for some higher rule of life... and finding our present lines too rigidly drawn to include any character of mind that is much out of the way... he might possibly have broken what he could not bend. The question is not, whether such impatience is not open to the charge of wilfulness and self-conceit; but... whether there are not minds with ardent feelings, keen imaginations, and undisciplined tempers, who are under a strong irritation prompting them to run wild, — whether it is not our duty... to play with such, carefully letting out line enough lest they snap it, — and whether the Protestant Establishment is as indulgent and wise as might be desired in its treatment of such persons, inasmuch as it provides no occupation for them, does not understand how to turn them to account, lets them run to waste,

[15] *HS*, 2: 96.

> tempts them to dissent, loses them, is weakened by the loss, and then denounces them.

But Antony benefited from a hierarchical Church which accepted his charism but gave it "form… It was not vulgar, bustling, imbecile, unstable, undutiful; it was calm and composed… full of affectionate loyalty to the Church…" Newman makes the point explicitly that the charisms need the hierarchy: "enthusiasm is sobered and refined by being submitted to the discipline of the Church, instead of being allowed to run wild externally to it."[16] The danger, conversely, for the hierarchical Church is that without the charisms it risks losing vitality and becoming atrophied, with organization and routine replacing the Spirit.In the *Essay on the Development of Doctrine*, Newman also writes of the monastic charism, where he is clear about the immense significance of this charism for the history of the Church: "Little did the youth Antony foresee, when he set off to fight the evil one in the wilderness, what a sublime and various history he was opening, a history which had its first developments even in his own lifetime." Antony had simply intended to be a hermit in the desert, "but when others followed his example, he was obliged to give them guidance…" The next stage in the development was when these hermits came together to form a community. There followed further developments with St Pachomius and St Basil. And finally St Benedict consolidated these developments, as well as introducing the vital new element of education that was to be so crucial for the Church in the dark ages when the monasteries became the repositories of learning.[17] As Ratzinger puts it, "apostolic movements appear in ever new forms in history — necessarily so, because they are the Holy Spirit's answer to the ever changing situations in which the Church

16 *HS*, 2: 98-99, 103.

17 *An Essay on the Development of Christian Doctrine*, 395-397.

lives."[18] And this Newman saw quite clearly too. For he proceeds to point out that, while "St. Benedict had come as if to preserve a principle of civilization, and a refuge for learning, at a time when the old framework of society was falling, and new political creations were taking their place... when the young intellect within them began to stir, and a change of another kind discovered itself, then appeared St. Francis and St. Dominic..." Finally, Newman concludes, "in the last era of ecclesiastical revolution" the charism of St. Ignatius made its appearance to meet new needs. "The hermitage, the cloister... and the friar were suited to other states of society; with the Jesuits, as well as with the religious Communities, which are their juniors," the "chief objects of attention" were new kinds of apostolate, such as teaching and the missions.[19] There are half a dozen rhetorical passages in the *Essay on the Development of Christian Doctrine* where Newman sketches a picture of the early Church and asks the reader whether it is not also a likeness of the modern Roman Catholic Church. It is significant that in the first two of these passages it is the charismatic aspect which he singles out as the most characteristic feature in common. The first of these passages, in which Newman appeals to the imagination of the reader, begins with the provocative assertion: "On the whole, all parties will agree that, of all existing systems, the present communion of Rome is the nearest approximation in fact to the Church of the Fathers, possible though some may think it, to be nearer still to that Church on paper." He insists: "Did St. Athanasius or St. Ambrose come suddenly to life, it cannot be doubted what communion he would take to be his own. All surely will agree that these Fathers... would find themselves more at home with such men as St. Bernard or St. Ignatius Loyola... or the holy

[18] *Movements in the Church*, 46.

[19] *Essay on Development*, 398-399.

sisterhood of mercy…" And a couple of pages later he asks whether the faith of the Roman Catholic Church is not "the nearest approach, to say the least, to the religious sentiment, and what is called *ethos*, of the early Church, nay, to that of the Apostles and Prophets; for all will agree so far as this, that Elijah, Jeremiah, the Baptist, and St. Paul are in their history and mode of life… in what is external and meets the eye… these saintly and heroic men, I say, are more like a Dominican preacher, or a Jesuit missionary, or a Carmelite friar, more like St. Toribio, or St. Vincent Ferrer, or St. Francis Xavier, or St. Alphonsus Liguori, than to any individuals, or to any classes of men, that can be found in other communions."[20] The success of the Oxford Movement raised one very serious problem. In 1839 Newman warned that there would be "continual defections to Rome" unless the Church of England would allow the open expression of Catholic devotions and spirituality: "give us monasteries," for example, he demanded. He discussed with Pusey his idea of a "monastic house" out at Littlemore. Community life there began in 1842.[21] It was quasi-monastic, although Newman intended "to master" the "very instructive" *Spiritual Exercises* of St Ignatius Loyola; he admitted to finding the holiness particularly of the Jesuits disconcerting since his complaint that the Roman Church lacked sanctity was one of his last defences for his crumbling Anglicanism.[22] It was thus in the context of both the monastic and Ignatian charisms that three years later he finally decided to become a Roman Catholic. But the charism of St Francis had also played a role earlier in the process of conversion. In 1837 he had read with delight Manzoni's novel *I promesi sposi*. Two years later in September 1839, the year of his first serious doubts about

[20] *Ibid.*, 97-98, 100.

[21] *LD*, 7: 133, 264.

[22] See Ian Ker, *John Henry Newman: A Biography* (Oxford: Clarendon Press, 1988) 271-272.

Anglicanism, he admitted to one of his closest friends: "That Capuchin in the 'Promesi Sposi' has stuck in my heart like a dart. I have never got over him." He was already considering religious life for himself: "if things were to come to the worst, I should turn Brother of Charity in London — an object which, *quite* independently of any such perplexities, is growing on me, and, peradventure, will some day be accomplished..."[23] This remarkable letter was written shortly after the shock he had received from studying the Monophysite controversy during July and August, and a week before he again wrote to the same friend about the new blow he had received on reading an article on the Donatist controversy by Wiseman. In the *Apologia* Newman says nothing about the Capuchin friar in *Promesi sposi*, any more than he speaks of other experiences which contributed to his conversion; the book after all was intended to be about his intellectual not his imaginative history, being simply, in the words of the subtitle, "a history of his religious opinions."[24]

4. The Catholic Newman and Charisms

In 1847 Newman's dream of 1839 came (at least partly) true when he joined not a religious order but the Congregation of the Oratory of St Philip Neri. He was attracted by the charism of Philip, with his mixture of "extreme hatred of humbug, playfulness, nay oddity, tender love for others, and severity."[25] He was characterized by the same kind of Christian humanism as Newman's favourite Father St Athanasius. Philip, too who "lived in an age... when literature and art were receiving their fullest development," was anxious "not to destroy or supersede... but... to sanctify poetry, and

[23] *LD*, 7: 151.

[24] See *Apologia*, ed. Ian Ker (London: Penguin, 1994) xxi-xxiv.

[25] *LD*, 12: 25.

history, and painting, and music."[26] Charisms are for the good of the Church and Newman considered the charism of the Oratory to have been important in the Counter-Reformation for the much-needed reform of the secular clergy. But if Oratorians provided a model for the diocesan priesthood, nevertheless Newman saw them as quasi-religious, and, in spite of the very obvious differences, like the early monks in some respects, who also did not take vows. For Philip's charism was boldly to go back to primitive Christianity in its "plainness and simplicity," not least in the informal "exercises" which consisted of singing, prayer, readings, talks, and discussion, in which, extraordinarily for the time, laymen participated.[27] Newman liked to contrast Philip's charism with that of his contemporary Ignatius Loyola, whose followers were disciplined soldiers as compared with the individualistic, easy-going Oratorian. Naturally, Newman had no illusion about which of the two charisms had been more important for the Church; in terms of influence and numbers there was no comparison between the Society of Jesus and the Oratory. In his 1850 sermon "The Mission of St. Philip" he called Ss Benedict, Dominic, and Ignatius, "the three venerable Patriarchs, whose Orders divide between them the extent of Christian history." Certainly, St Philip was a minor charismatic figure compared to these giants, but nevertheless Newman points out that he "came under the teaching of all three successively." Although he did not have the term "charism" in his theological vocabulary and although he lived at a time when the importance of the hierarchical dimension of the Church was exaggerated, Newman never underestimated the equal significance of the charismatic dimension. For these "masters in the spiritual Israel" had, "in an

[26] *Sermons Preached on Various Occasions*, 118-119.

[27] *Newman the Oratorian: His Unpublished Oratory Papers*, ed. Placid Murray OSB (Dublin: Gill and Macmillan, 1969) 186, 188, 203.

especial way,... committed to them the office of a public ministry in the affairs of the Church one after another, and... are, in some sense, her 'nursing fathers.'" From his youth in Florence at San Marco Philip imbibed the spirit of Dominic, whose vocation was "to form the whole matter of human knowledge into one harmonious system, to secure the alliance between religion and philosophy, and to train men to the use of the gifts of nature in the sunlight of divine grace and revealed truth." This Christian humanism was essential in Philip's age, the age of the renaissance, when "a violent effort was in progress... to break up this sublime unity, and to set human genius, the philosopher and the poet, the artist and the musician, in opposition to religion." Leaving Florence, Philip came to live near Monte Cassino where in turn he imbibed the simpler Benedictine spirit; "and, as from St. Dominic he gained the end he was to pursue, so from St. Benedict he learned how to pursue it." The Oratory resembled those early independent monastic communities without formal vows and not organized in an order, which "were simple in their forms of worship, and... freely admitted laymen into their fellowship." Finally, he met St Ignatius in Rome, with whom "in the care of souls he was one," as "in theological traditions [he] was one with St. Dominic." Newman sums up the influence on Philip of these three great charisms: "As then he learned from Benedict *what to be*, and from Dominic *what to do*, so let me consider that from Ignatius he learned *how he was to do it*." To these he contributed his own special charism: "[he] had the breadth of view of St. Dominic, the poetry of St. Benedict, the wisdom of St. Ignatius, and all recommended by an unassuming grace and a winning tenderness which were his own."[28] In 1855 Newman gave a lecture to the Birmingham Catholic Association entitled "The Three Patriarchs of Christian History, St Benedict,

[28] *Sermons Preached on Various Occasions*, 220-221, 224-225, 228, 240.

St Dominic, and St Ignatius," of which some notes survive.[29] He had had it in mind to write a book, as he put it in 1870, on the "Historical contrast of Benedictines, Dominicans, and Jesuits, which I suppose I shall never finish." In the end, he only managed to write the part on the Benedictines, which was first published in the *Atlantis*, the academic journal he founded at the Catholic University of Ireland, and then republished in the second volume of *Historical Sketches*.[30] It was a source of regret to him, as he explained later, but, when the Abbot of Solesmes criticized what he had written on the Benedictines —

> I felt that if I continued my journey into Dominican, Franciscan, and Jesuit territory, I could not be true unless I mastered a great mass of reading… One question was already asked me, viz. why I confined my review of teaching Orders to Benedictine, Dominican, and Jesuits, omitting Franciscans. I had my reasons. I thought them men of genius rather than systematic teaching or normal authority, viewed as a body; but I ought to have read a great deal to maintain this view; and in consequence I never have been confident in the correctness of my view myself.[31]

One can only regret that Newman was never able to complete this book on these three great charismatic movements in the history of the Church; and perhaps if he could have read more he might have included the Franciscans — but as we have seen the Franciscan charism had played a not unimportant role in the process of his conversion. (Incidentally, the other great loss, also from the period of the 1850s, results from the failure of his tentative plan to go to the United States to raise funds for the Catholic University, since the letters he would have sent home describing his travels would have been a wonderful addition to the wealth of literature on

[29] See *LD*, 16: 378.

[30] *LD*, 25: 228.

[31] *LD*, 28: 130.

America by English writers from Dickens to Chesterton.) "The Mission of the Benedictine Order" was published in the *Atlantis* in 1858 and "The Benedictine Centuries" in 1859; they were republished in *Historical Sketches* in 1873 under the titles of "The Mission of St. Benedict" and "The Benedictine Schools."

Unlike the church of the Fathers this was not a period of history he knew well. His concern was chiefly educational, occupied as he was with the Catholic University; but, even apart from that, as he once wrote, "from first to last, education... has been my line."[32] The history of Christian education could be divided into three periods, ancient, medieval, and modern, dominated by the names of Benedict, Dominic, and Ignatius; clearly Francis could not compete with them in this sphere. The monastic charism was "a reaction from... secular life," a "flight from the world," it offered "retirement and repose... peace." It was a "poetical" charism, unlike the Dominican which was "scientific" and the Ignatian which was "practical." It evoked the "primitive age of the world" and "was a sort of recognized emigration from the old world" ever since St Antony had found "gold... and on the news of it thousands took their departure year after year for the diggings in the desert." It was more devotional than intellectual. But the charism was poetical not because the monks were "dreamy sentimentalists, to fall in love with melancholy winds and purling rills, and waterfalls and nodding groves; but their poetry was the poetry of hard work," since Benedict's "object... was... penance." Still, monasticism was "romantic" in its "adventures" and history. The paradox was that the very monasticism which had been a retreat from a dying world became "in no small measure [the] very life" of the "new order."[33] So far as Newman was concerned it was not the hierarchy

[32] *Autobiographical Writings*, 259.

[33] *HS*, 2: 366, 373, 375, 384-5, 388, 398, 400, 436, 443.

but the charism of one man, who was not even a priest, that saved Christian civilization.

5. Newman and the Contemporary Charismatic Movements

It is something of a truism to say that Newman is the father of the Second Vatican Council. At any rate, if it is true that he anticipated the major themes of the Council, it is likely, or antecedently probable as he would have said, that the late twentieth-century phenomenon of the ecclesial movements and communities would have come as no surprise to him. That is, assuming that they are the charismatic accompaniment, so to speak, of the Council, rather as the Jesuits embodied the spirit of the Council of Trent. I would suggest that there are in fact three ways in which Newman could also be called the father of these new movements of the Spirit.

First, Tractarianism was itself a self-proclaimed "movement" and, like the ecclesial movements, was neither clerical nor lay, but a movement of the baptized. The original initiative was entirely clerical, the idea being to form a society of clergy centred on Oxford, but with branches all over the country. However, Newman wanted a movement not a clerical association, and he was strongly opposed especially to any kind of clerical committee or board supervising the *Tracts for the Times*, which were his idea. Instead, he wanted the *Tracts* to be circulated by personal contact and to be personally written by individuals.[34] As he was to put it in the *Apologia*, "Living Movements do not come of committees."[35] And far from the *Tracts* being exclusively clerical, he was particularly delighted by a contribution from his friend John William Bowden,

[34] See Ker, *Newman: A Biography*, 81, 84-85.

[35] *Apologia*, 46.

precisely because he was a layman. As in the new ecclesial movements, the emphasis was to be upon the personal and charismatic rather than the institutional and structural.

Nor were theological tracts the only form of literature that the Tractarians employed. Newman characteristically saw that the movement must have an imaginative as well as an intellectual appeal. Accordingly, he and his collaborators soon began publishing "Records of the Church" or what he called "little stories of the Apostles, fathers etc., to familiarize the imagination of the reader to an *Apostolical state* of the Church."[36] Clearly this kind of propaganda was intended at least as much for the laity as for the clergy. The same was true of the *Lyra Apostolica*, the verse section in the *British Magazine* which he and Hurrell Froude had conceived of a year before the Movement proper began, hoping to advance their ideas through what Newman called the "rhetoric" and "persuasion" of poetry.[37] When the verses were published in book form in 1836, Newman was amazed by their remarkable success in advancing "Apostolical views, "as he told his friend Maria Giberne, who was herself involved in the movement. He was keen that she should try her hand at writing "some Apostolical stories" for children and hoped that she could collaborate with his sister Jemima and sister-in-law Anne Mozley. What he thought was really needed was "a library on all subjects for the middle classes and the Clergy."[38] In other words, he wanted the movement to be propagated by every possible kind of writing, for the laity as well as the clergy, and for women and children as well as men. Since fiction was becoming a particularly effective medium of communication and since practitioners of the art were often women (including Newman's own sister Harriett, herself a successful author of children's books),

[36] *LD*, 4: 109.

[37] *LD*, 3: 121.

[38] *LD*, 5: 385, 387; 6: 32.

lay women played a significant role in the movement. If the leading Tractarian poet was a clergyman, John Keble, the leading Tractarian novelist was a lay woman, Charlotte M. Yonge. Newman was struck by the fact that prominent precursors of the movement like Alexander Knox, the Irish theologian, and the Romantic philosopher and poet Samuel Taylor Coleridge were both "laymen and that is very remarkable," as was Dr Johnson, "another striking instance."[39] Many of the leading members of the Oxford Movement were laymen, often prominent in public life. It was the absence of this kind of easy collaboration between clergy and laity that impressed Newman so unfavourably when he became a Catholic. On the restoration of the Roman Catholic hierarchy to England in 1850, a storm of anti-Catholicism erupted. Newman's response to the orchestrated campaign against Catholics is interesting. He thought that it could be profitably exploited by making it an excuse for "getting up a great organization, going round the towns giving lectures, or making speeches… starting a paper, a review etc." He recommended gathering laymen to speak at public meetings in the big towns. Young Catholics particularly, he felt, should band together as the Tractarians had. In short, he saw the possibility of another movement, the occasion being again the persecution of the Church, albeit a different one. This time the condemnations of the *Tracts* and the suspensions of preachers by the authorities might be matched by the threatened fining, imprisonment, and even transportation of recalcitrant Catholic bishops. But, as in the past, Newman sadly realized that the bishops would not rise to the occasion. However, now his main complaint was that the Catholic hierarchy had not bothered nor did they intend to consult the laity on the best course of action to take. His own bishop, he was convinced, "has a terror of laymen, and I am sure that they may be made in this day the strength of the Church."[40]

39 *LD*, 5: 27.
40 *LD*, 19: 214, 252.

In the second place, Newman had a clear understanding of the original charism of the Oratory, the character of which is unmistakably similar to the new ecclesial communities particularly. To counter the anti-Catholic agitation, he embarked on a series of public lectures in June 1851. They were published in book form as *Lectures on the Present Position of Catholics in England: Addressed to the Brothers of the Oratory*. These brothers constituted the so-called "Little" or "Secular" Oratory, which was the confraternity of laymen traditionally attached to an Oratory. (Newman got permission from Rome for a separate one for women.) Of all the Oratorian activities and works, Newman, remarkably, considered this as "more important than anything else."[41] What Newman had in mind was that the Oratory, after all, had started in Rome as a lay community. But then, in Newman's words,

> a smaller society was formed in addition to this and by a closer tie. Its members actually lived together, they were priests, or those who were training for the priesthood, and they served the Church. It was this Community which was erected into a Congregation, under the title of the Congregation of the Oratory. The Oratory itself, however, remained as before, with its own rules and members, taking the place of a sort of confraternity dependent on the Congregation, and governed by it, and for distinction [sic] sake being called the Oratorium parvum or the Oratorium externum. It still had possession of the building called the Oratorium, while the place of the Congregation rather was the Church...[42]

This development, in fact, is similar to the way in which out of the new ecclesial communities (and movements) there regularly emerges a smaller more committed group, sometimes consisting of priests, but still closely linked with the larger group which supports it but which in turn is sustained by this inner core of members.

41 *LD*, 14: 274.

42 *Newman the Oratorian*, 164.

By Newman's day, the "little Oratory" had become a shadow of its former self. In reality, the Oratory had undergone the same kind of clericalization as the Benedictines and Franciscans who were invariably ordained, if capable, to the priesthood, even though neither Benedict nor Francis had been priests. Similarly, the original charism of the Oratory had become obscured as the Oratory simply became a congregation of priests, although like other orders and congregations it had lay brothers who did the menial tasks in the community and were seen as second-class members. But Newman knew this was unfaithful to Philip's charism. As he wrote sharply in a letter of rebuke to a priest in the Birmingham Oratory, "The Brothers are our equals… The Father is above the Brother sacerdotally — but in the Oratory they are equal."[43] Third, and most importantly, Newman's fundamental ecclesiology is the same as that of *Lumen Gentium*, an ecclesiology which finds concrete realization in the new ecclesial communities and movements. First, there is his understanding of the importance of the charismatic as well as the hierarchical dimension of the Church, as I have shown. But even more fundamental than that is his conception of the essential nature of the Church which he had learned as an Anglican from the Greek Fathers, namely that the Church is primarily the communion of those who have received the Holy Spirit in baptism. While the Church "is a visible body," and therefore has the character of an institution, it is nevertheless "invested with, or… existing in invisible privileges," for "the Church would cease to be the Church, did the Holy Spirit leave it," since "its outward rites and forms are nourished and animated by the living power which dwells within it." Thus the Church is the Holy Spirit's "especial dwelling-place." For while Christ came "to die for us; the Spirit came to make us one in Him who had died and was alive, that is, to form

[43] *LD*, 16: 267.

the Church." The Church, then, is "the one mystical body of Christ... quickened by the Spirit" — and is "one" by virtue of the Holy Spirit "giving it life."[44] Similarly, *Lumen Gentium*, rejecting the Tridentine model of the Church as first and foremost hierarchical, begins with a chapter on "The Mystery of the Church," in which the Church is conceived of being "in the nature of sacrament." (art. 1) As in Newman, the Church is the Church because of the Holy Spirit: "The Spirit dwells in the Church and in the hearts of the faithful as in a temple." (art. 4) The second chapter called "The People of God" is no more about the laity specifically than the first chapter was concerned with the hierarchy, for this people consists of those "who believe in Christ" and who "are reborn... from water and the Holy Spirit" in baptism. In this "messianic people" the Spirit "dwells as in a temple." (art. 9) This "priestly community is brought into operation through the sacraments," and it is only after the sacraments of initiation followed by the sacraments of penance and anointing which all the baptized normally receive have been mentioned, that the constitution refers to two sacraments that not all the faithful receive, holy orders and marriage (art. 11). It is not, then, only that the Church is not conceived of primarily in hierarchical terms but the whole concept of clergy and laity is avoided in these first two thoroughly scriptural and patristic chapters that describe the fundamental nature of the Church, which does not primarily consist of clergy and laity (plus religious) but of all the baptized.

Now if we turn to the ecclesial communities and movements, we find exactly the same avoidance of the usual clerical way of looking at the Church. This is why to call them lay movements and communities, as they often are, is radically to misunderstand them. On the contrary, they are truly "ecclesial," as Pope John Paul II

[44] *Parochial and Plain Sermons*, 3: 224; 5: 41; 3: 270; 4: 170, 174, 171.

always insists in calling them. Faithful to the organic conception of the Church as described in *Lumen Gentium* and as understood by Newman, these movements of the Spirit are, in the words of Piero Coda, a theologian belonging to the Focolare movement, "constitutionally open (by virtue of their original charism) to all the vocations and to all the states of life present in the People of God." Coda calls the classification of them as "lay" mere "inertia of reflection."[45] In fact, the description reflects that very ecclesiology which perceives the Church in clerical-lay terms that the first two chapters of *Lumen Gentium* carefully avoided. The ecclesial movements and communities are "ecclesial" or movements of the Church precisely because they share the same ecclesiology of organic wholeness. They consist of bishops, priests, religious, and lay people, as well as those who are so committed to the charism of the particular movement or community that they are quasi-religious in their acceptance of the religious state, albeit without formal vows.[46]

Ratzinger is certain that this new phenomenon in the life of the Church represents the fourth great charismatic movement of the Spirit in the history of the Church, the others being the monastic and then the mendicant movements, followed by the rise of the Jesuits and all the other active religious orders, including the surge of missionary orders and congregations in the nineteenth century, particularly of women. The fact that the ecclesial movements and communities embody the ecclesiology of the first two chapters of *Lumen Gentium* is not surprising. For, as Ratzinger points out, "apostolic movements appear in ever new forms in history —

[45] *Movements in the Church*, 95.

[46] For a fuller discussion, see Ian Ker, *The New Movements: A Theological Introduction* (London: Catholic Truth Society, 2001), reprinted in a slightly abridged version under the title "New Movements and Communities in the Life of the Church," *Louvain Studies* 27 (2002) 69-95.

necessarily so, because they are the Holy Spirit's answer to the ever changing situations in which the Church lives."[47] The charism of Ignatius appeared providentially at the time of the Council of Trent. The letter of Councils needs the Spirit. The new ecclesial movements and communities have not arisen as a humanly planned response to the Second Vatican Council's renewed understanding of the nature of the Church, but they surely do represent the response of the Holy Spirit. And, as we have seen, Newman not only had the same understanding of the Church, but he himself inspired and led what was called a movement, and then joined himself to the charism of the Oratory of St Philip, which in its original form seems so extraordinarily contemporary today. But perhaps that is not so surprising when one considers how Philip also, like Newman and the Council, wanted to return to a more primitive and scriptural Catholicism, such as the new movements and communities themselves manifest. Free of the clericalism that Newman so deplored in the nineteenth-century Church, they are also free of the "laicism" which threatens the Church today and which Newman would no less have deplored. The truth is that both clericalism and "laicism" feel threatened by charisms, and that alone is an important reason for the Church never to lose sight of its charismatic dimension.

[47] *Movements in the Church*, 46.

NOTES ON CONTRIBUTORS

Colin Barr is Assistant Professor of History at Ave Maria University. His research focuses on the political and ecclesiastical history of Britain, Ireland, and the British Empire in the nineteenth century. He is the author of *Paul Cullen, John Henry Newman, and the Catholic University of Ireland, 1845-65* (2003).

Michael J. Buckley S.J. is Augustin Cardinal Bea Professor of Theology in the Religious Studies Department of Santa Clara University, California. He is the author *At the Origins of Modern Atheism* (1987), *The Catholic University as Promise and Project* (1998), and *Denying and Disclosing God: The Ambiguous Progress of Modern Atheism* (2000).

Brian E. Daley, S.J. is Catherine F. Huisking Professor of Theology in the Department of Theology of the University of Notre Dame. He is the author of *The Hope of the Early Church*, (1991, *On The Dormition of Mary: Early Patristic Homilies*, (1997), and *Gregory of Nazianzus* (2006).

Paul J. Griffiths is the Warren Professor of Catholic Theology at the Divinity School of Duke University. He is the author of *Problems of Religious Diversity* (2001),*Lying: An Augustinian Theology of Duplicity* (2004) and *Intellectual Appetite: A Theological Grammar* (2008), and co-editor of *Reason and the Reasons of Faith* (2005).

Keith Hanley is Professor of English Literature and Director of the Ruskin Centre at the Faculty of Arts and Social Sciences of Lancaster University. He is the author of *John Ruskin's Northern Tours 1837-1838: Travelling North* (2007) and *Wordsworth: A Poet's History* (2001) and co-editor of *Ruskin's Struggle for Coherence* (2006) and *Nineteenth Century Worlds: Global Formations Past and Present* (2008).

Ian Ker is Senior Research Fellow in Theology at St. Benet's Hall, Oxford. His books include *John Henry Newman: A Biography* (1988). *Newman the Theologian: A Reader* (1990), *The Achievement of John Henry Newman* (1990), *Newman on Being a Christian* (1990), *Newman and the Fullness of Christianity* (1993), *Healing the Wound of Humanity: the Spirituality of*

John Henry Newman (1993), and *The Catholic Revival in English Literature, 1845-1961* (2003) and the co-editor of the *Cambridge Companion to John Henry Newman* (2008).

Terrence Merrigan is Professor of Systematic Theology at the Catholic University of Leuven. He is the author of *Clear Heads and Holy Hearts: Tthe Religious and Theological Ideal of John Henry Newman* (1991) and co-editor of *Newman and the Word* (2000), *Newman and Faith* (2004), and *Godhead Here in Hiding: Incarnation and the History of Human Suffering* (2008) and the *Cambridge Companion to John Henry Newman* (2008).

John Milbank is Professor in Religion, Politics and Ethics at the Department of Theology and Religious Studies of the University of Nottingham. He is the author of *Being Reconciled: Ontology and Pardon* (2003), *The Suspended Middle: Henri de Lubac and the Debate Concerning the Supernatural* (2005), and the co-editor of *Theology and the Political: The New Debate* (2005).

INDEX OF NAMES

INDEX OF SUBJECTS

PRINTED ON PERMANENT PAPER • IMPRIME SUR PAPIER PERMANENT • GEDRUKT OP DUURZAAM PAPIER - ISO 9706

N.V. PEETERS S.A., WAROTSTRAAT 50, B-3020 HERENT